Investing For Dummies
2nd Edition

Basic Investment Choices

All your money decisions involve making up your mind as to where to put your hard-earned cash. Thousands of choices exist but you can cut that number down to just five basic investment opportunities:

- **Cash.** Many ways of investing your cash are available, including building society deposit accounts, online cash accounts, telephone banks, and postal accounts. With all these options, you swap a higher interest rate for the flexibility that comes with a very low interest-paying account.

- **Property.** The property you live in is probably your biggest financial project – assuming that you don't rent it from someone. Property beyond your home can also be a worthwhile investment.

- **Bonds.** A stock-market-quoted bond is basically an IOU issued by governments or companies. Bond issuers promise to pay a fixed income on stated dates and to repay the amount on the bond certificate in full on a fixed day in the future. In other words, you pay the government, say, £100, and the Treasury promises to give you £5 a year for the next five years and your £100 back in five years' time.

- **Shares.** Shares are what they say they are – a small part of a bigger picture. Buying shares (also known as equities) gives you partial ownership of a company. You can own as little as one share, and if that's the case and the company has issued one million shares, you have a one-millionth stake in that enterprise.

- **Alternatives.** This investment area covers a rag-bag of bits and pieces. For some people, alternative investments concentrate on items you can physically hold, such as works of art, fine wines, vintage cars, antiques, and stamp collections. But for an increasing number of people, the term means hedge funds, which are about as esoteric as investment gets. Put simply, you hand over your money to managers who, by hook or by crook, hope to increase it. And there is also a growing interest in commodities – natural resources ranging from wheat to copper. These are traded on specialist exchanges.

What to Look at When Selecting a Stockbroker

You may need to do some shopping around to find a stockbroker who's right for you.

Areas to research include:

- **Size of portfolio.** Make sure that your personal wealth is well within the broker's parameters. If the broker wants a minimum £25,000, then having £25,001 isn't much help because you could easily fall below the line if markets turn against you. Ask what happens if your fortune shrinks either through bad decisions or because you choose to spend some of your money.

- **Level of service.** Consider the experience of your contact or account executive, as well as whether e-mail alerts and regular newsletters or other forms of stock recommendation will be sent out. Find out whether the broker offers a portfolio based on unit trusts, investment trusts, or exchange traded funds.

- **Costs.** This shouldn't be your first consideration, but it's essential all the same. Excessive costs can wipe out gains from a clever investment strategy. Very excessive costs can turn good decisions into instant losses.

- **Protection from churning.** Unscrupulous brokers try to earn more from your investments by over-frequent buying and selling. You could agree to a limit on their trading activity.

For Dummies: Bestselling Book Series for Beginners

Investing For Dummies,®
2nd Edition

Cheat Sheet

What Fund Managers Can Do for You

Fund management companies will perform a number of useful tasks if you're a hands-off investor:

- They carry out all the purchase and sales dealing with stockbrokers, taking advantage of economies of scale.
- They deal with all the paperwork associated with dividends.
- They take care of taxation within the portfolio.
- They offer access to a diversified portfolio for a small sum of money.
- In some cases, they make asset allocation choices, such as moving from shares to bonds.
- They provide you with the comfort factor of being able to blame someone else if your investments head nowhere.

Sound Tips for the Cautious Investor

If you think the time is right, you may want to try one or some of the following:

- **A tracker fund.** This type of fund follows a stock market index such as the FTSE 100 (the Footsie) up and down. This option is a good idea if you want to be in shares but have no idea which ones to buy or which fund manager to back.
- **A no-lose fund.** You put your money in a special fund, usually for five years. At the end of the specified time, you either get your money back without any deduction or, if the index has risen, your original money enhanced by the percentage rise.
- **A bond fund.** Your money goes into fixed-interest securities tied either to governments or companies.
- **A distribution fund.** This type of fund focuses on a mix of lower-risk shares, bonds, cash, and property.

Knowing Your Bonds from Your Shares

Lots of investors mention shares and bonds in the same breath, but there are plenty of differences, including:

- Shares are permanent. Bonds usually have a fixed life, which is shown on the paperwork you get.
- Shares pay dividends. Bonds pay interest.
- Shares give holders a say in the company proportional to their holding. Bondholders, in most circumstances, have no ownership or annual meeting voting rights.
- Share prices can be very volatile. Bond prices vary less from day to day.
- Share prices depend on profits. Bondholders have to worry more about credit risk.

Investing
FOR
DUMMIES®
2ND EDITION

Investing

FOR

DUMMIES®

2ND EDITION

by Tony Levene

John Wiley & Sons, Ltd

Investing For Dummies,® **2nd Edition**

Published by
John Wiley & Sons, Ltd
The Atrium
Southern Gate
Chichester
West Sussex
PO19 8SQ
England

E-mail (for orders and customer service enquires): cs-books@wiley.co.uk

Visit our Home Page on www.wiley.com

For general information on our other products and services, please contact our Customer Care Department within the U.S. at 800-762-2974, outside the U.S. at 317-572-3993, or fax 317-572-4002.

For technical support, please visit www.wiley.com/techsupport.

Wiley also publishes its books in a variety of electronic formats. Some content that appears in print may not be available in electronic books.

British Library Cataloguing in Publication Data: A catalogue record for this book is available from the British Library

ISBN: 978-0-470-99280-7

Printed and bound in Great Britain by TJ International Ltd, Padstow, Cornwall

10 9 8 7 6 5 4 3 2

WILEY

About the Author

Tony Levene is a member of *The Guardian* Money team where he writes on issues ranging from investment to consumer rights. He has been a financial journalist for over 30 years, after spending a year or so teaching French beforehand. Over his career, he has worked for newspapers including *The Sunday Times*, *Sunday Express*, *Daily Express, The Sun, Daily Star*, and *Sunday Mirror*. He has also published eight previous books on investment and financial issues. He lives in London with his wife Claudia, 'grown up' children Zoë and Oliver, and cats Plato, Pandora, and Pascal.

Dedication

This book is dedicated to Claudia, for her patience during the book's gestation; to Oliver for persuading me to write it; and to Zoë for her suggestions and approval of my initial chapter. I would also like to thank my brother Stuart for giving me sanctuary away from phones and other distractions whilst I wrote much of it.

Author's Acknowledgements

I would like to thank Jason Dunne, Daniel Mersey, and Steve Edwards at Wiley for their patience and help during the various stages of this book. And an especial thank you to Sandra Lynn Blackthorn (Sandy), for all her work in turning my manuscript from a book about investment into *Investing For Dummies*. I am also grateful for the forebearance of my *Guardian* colleagues every time I mentioned 'the book'.

But most of all, I would like to acknowledge Peter Shearlock. Peter, whom I first met at school when we were both aged 11, was responsible for starting my career as an investment writer and has helped me invaluably along the way. He gave me my first lessons in the irrationality that often characterises financial markets and introduced me to 'City characters' ranging from spivs and chancers to the epitome of blue-blooded respectability. It is this variety that makes investing so fascinating. Thanks, Peter.

Publisher's Acknowledgements

We're proud of this book; please send us your comments through our Dummies online registration form located at www.dummies.com/register/.

Some of the people who helped bring this book to market include the following:

Acquisitions, Editorial, and Media Development

Project Editor: Steve Edwards

(Previous Edition: Daniel Mersey, Amie Tibble)

Content Editor: Nicole Burnett

Proofreader: Helen Heyes

Publisher: Jason Dunne

Executive Project Editor: Daniel Mersey

Cover Photos: © Getty Images/Peter Dazeley

Cartoons: Ed McLachlan

Composition Services

Project Coordinator: Erin Smith

Layout and Graphics: Stacie Brooks, Reuben W. Davis, Joyce Haughey, Stephanie D. Jumper

Indexer: Broccoli Information Management

Contents at a Glance

Table of Contents

Introduction

Many years ago, when I first started writing about investments and money, a City of London stockbroker took me out for a few drinks one lunchtime. He told me about a whiz-bang stock his firm was involved with. The company, Kitchen Queen, was in the fitted kitchens business. At the time, new kitchens were the most desirable home improvement, and the trend could only grow. He said I'd make a fortune if I invested.

I didn't have much money, but I put £100 into Kitchen Queen. A week or two later, my money was worth £110 and then £120. Then Kitchen Queen shares started to slide. Eventually, they were taken over by another firm and then another and then another. Luckily, I didn't need the money by that time, so I just sat back and watched.

Finally, about 20 years later, the company that used to be Kitchen Queen was bought out yet again by an American firm called Tyco. Tyco hit real problems in 2001, when it was found to have accounting irregularities, and the chief executive had to quit. But I still have the shares, now worth about £50, and, amazingly, Tyco sends me a cheque every three months for a dividend. It's usually the princely sum of 20 US cents or around 10p, less than a third of the cost of the stamp on the envelope.

I'm telling you about my lack of success with Kitchen Queen because *Investing For Dummies* is different from other books on investment. It gives you the facts up front and honestly. So you'll find no get-rich-quick recipe or magic formula here. Besides, even if there were one, I wouldn't be telling anyone about it, least of all in a book! I'd be operating it instead.

No one can predict which shares will do well and which will flop, although that doesn't seem to stop people from asking me for sure-fire tips at parties. What I seek to do with *Investing For Dummies* is provide a guide to help you make sensible decisions that suit your circumstances.

Investing involves more than reading the balance sheets that companies publish to show how the money comes in and out of their coffers. It involves more than understanding an economics textbook. Investing literally involves understanding a whole lot about human reactions to the ups and downs of money, plus (really important) understanding how you react. And it's fascinating because it's where all the drama of human life is to be found, because investment values represent nothing else than the combination of minds of all the people involved in investment markets.

Over the quarter of a century or so that I've been writing about money, I've continued to find investing a fascinating subject and endeavour, and I've become moderately more well off than I would've otherwise been. I hope that this book helps you become fascinated with investing too. And I also hope that by reading it, you'll be better off than you would've otherwise been.

About This Book

This book is designed to be read in several ways. It's a reference book, so you don't have to read the chapters in chronological order, from front to back. Of course you can read it cover to cover, like a novel, to gain appreciation for the huge variety of investment opportunities that are available. (If you approach the book this way, I suggest doing so with pen and paper at the ready so that you can note areas for further research on the Internet or from publications such as *The Financial Times*.) Or you can just pick a topic that interests you or go straight to a section that answers a particular question you have.

But my preferred way for you to read this book is to go through Part I and *then* pick up on the investments that concern or interest you. For example, after reading Part I, you may want to go straight to Part III to find out what collective investments are because, say, an advert about collective investments has caught your eye or a financial adviser has suggested one or two of them. Likewise, you may want to skip the chapter on buy to let properties because, say, being a do-it-yourself landlord is the last thought on your mind.

Regardless of how you approach reading this book, note that it's designed for dipping into reference-style, so you'll find some repetition. Doesn't matter. Some things can't be stated often enough!

Conventions Used in This Book

I've tried to avoid jargon as much as I can, but know that the investment world is full of it. Like all professions and occupations, finance and investment have their own insider language that's intended to mystify outsiders. When I do use the industry's language in the text, I *italicise* the term and define it for you in an easy-to-understand way.

Foolish Assumptions

While writing this book, I made some assumptions about you:

- ✔ You are either completely new to investing or have limited information about it, and you want someone to help you understand what investing is really about and what types of investments are available.
- ✔ You don't want to become an expert investor at this point in your life. You just want the basics – in informal, easy-to-understand language.
- ✔ You want to make up your *own* mind while using a guide through the investment jungle. You want enough pointers for you to risk only what you can afford to lose and for you to make a worthwhile return on your hard-earned cash.

How This Book Is Organised

This book has five major parts, or themes. Each part is divided into chapters relating to the theme, and each chapter is subdivided into individual sections relating to the chapter's topic. In addition, to help you pinpoint your specific area of interest, there's a detailed Table of Contents at the beginning of the book and a detailed Index at the end.

Part 1: Investment Basics

This is an essential part for understanding investing in general. I take you through what investment means, explain how to assess what you already have and the sort of returns you can expect, offer some insight on specific emotions that make investors tick, talk about the idea of risk and reward, and get you into the habit of reading the small print in investment situations. Most importantly, though, this part enables you to learn a lot about yourself and how you may face up to finance.

Part II: Shares and Bonds

In this part, you look at how financial markets operate and ways of analysing markets and companies. I explain what makes a market, examine the big companies and world markets, provide tips and titbits for when you begin investing in the stock market, cover what you need to know about stock-market-quoted companies, give you the scoop on investing in bonds, explain how to get pertinent information (because investment markets revolve around information), and tell you what you need to know in order to choose an adviser or stockbroker to best meet your individual needs.

Note that I do mention a few companies by name here, but those name drops aren't intended as a recommendation either to buy or to sell those securities. I usually mention specific companies to give examples or to provide some context. Note, too, that a lot of this part consists of investment fundamentals. You'll find some comment as well because you can't divorce one from the other. Investments don't live in a theoretical and factual vacuum.

Part III: Collective Investments

This part is where you find out about ready-made investment products. I talk about unit trusts, investment trusts, investment-linked insurance plans, and hedge funds, explaining what they really are and how they work – to help you decide whether investing in them is right for you. And I let you in on the fact that you can actually perform as well as the average fund manager or stock-broker by throwing a dart at a shares price page that's pinned to your wall.

Part IV: Property and Alternatives

Many people no longer want to confine investment to trading pieces of paper such as stocks and shares. Instead, they aim to buy and sell real things that they hope will go up in value. So this part covers investing in property, from a second home for renting out to tenants to big commercial buildings. In addition, this part covers alternative investments. I'm not talking about fashioned alternative investments, like art and vintage cars, but investments based on things like stock, commodity, and currency markets where you go nowhere near buying the shares, metals, or foreign exchange contracts on which they're based. Be warned up front, though, that these alternatives are *not* for the faint of heart. Risky, risky.

Part V: The Part of Tens

This part gives you a taste of *For Dummies* tradition. Every *For Dummies* book has this part, which always contains lists of tens. Here, I give you ten tips on how to find a good adviser and ten helpful hints to consider before investing that first penny.

Icons Used in This Book

I've highlighted some information in this book with icons:

This icon points out useful titbits or helpful advice on the topic at hand.

This icon highlights important information that you'll want to keep in mind, so don't forget this stuff!

This icon points out just that – a warning – so take heed. The investment world is full of sharks and other nasties, for example. I don't want you to lose your money to crummy schemes and criminals.

This icon highlights, well, technical stuff that you may want to skip right over. I've been sparing with this stuff because investment can be pretty technical anyway. (Note that even though you may want to skip this material on your first reading, and please feel free to, this info may be worthwhile coming back to later with your greater knowledge of the fundamentals.)

Where to Go from Here

This book is set up so you can dive in wherever you want. Feel free to go straight to Chapter 1 and start reading from the beginning to the end. Or look through the Table of Contents, find your area of interest, and flip right to that page. Or better yet, read Part I and *then* flip right to that page of interest. Your call.

Wherever you go from here, if you find a piece of advice or a warning that you think applies especially to you, copy it down and then fix it to the fridge with a magnet or pin it on a board.

And as you read through this book, either in part or in whole, why not practise some dry-run investing? Buying a dummy portfolio using pretend money is always a good way of getting familiar with investment without the worry of losing money.

Part I
Investment Basics

In this part . . .

The absolute basics. If that's what you need, then this part is where you'll find it.

Here, I tell you what the term *investment* really means and introduce you to five basic investment choices. In addition, I explain how to assess what you already have and the sort of returns you can expect. I get into a little bit of investor psychology, too, letting you know some specific emotions that make investors tick. I also talk about risk and reward – the benefits and drawbacks of various investment possibilities and ways to increase your odds of successful returns. And I discuss the great importance of reading the small print in all investment situations. A lot of info, yes. But it's presented in a friendly, easy-to-understand way, especially for beginner investors.

Chapter 1
First Steps on The Money Trail

In This Chapter

▶ Understanding basic investment philosophy

▶ Discovering your own money make-up

▶ Looking at what you may be investing already (whether you know it or not)

▶ Getting familiar with five basic investment choices

*T*his chapter explains the first steps you must take in your investing ventures. But take heed: In this chapter (and throughout the book, for that matter) you need to think deeply about some personal matters, to better understand yourself and know where you're going in life. In other words, you need to wear two hats – that of investor *and* philosopher. So be prepared for some tests that ask just what sort of person you are, what you want for yourself, and what you're prepared to do for it.

Understanding the facts and mechanics of investment decisions is just a start. Knowing how to apply them to your own circumstances, and to those of your family and other dependants, is what will make your strategy succeed.

What's Your Reason for Investing?

This section is very basic, comprised of just one simple investing test question: Why did you buy this book? Chances are, you probably did so for one of these three reasons:

✔ **You have no money but want to make some.** Most people fall into this category. You want to invest some money and accumulate funds but don't know where to start. How you go about it depends on how well you can discipline yourself. Take heart, though: Even the most confirmed shopaholic can build up a nestegg for later use.

✔ **You have some money, want it to make more, and currently make your own investment decisions**. You're the traditional investor who wants to make your personal wealth grow. You already make your own investment decisions and want to get better at it. How you go about it depends on who you are, how you made your money, and where you hope to be in 5, 10, or 20 years.

✔ **You have some money, want it to make more, and currently have others handle the investment process for you.** Maybe you have fund managers handle your investments so you can gain tax advantages or because your savings are lumped together with those of others in a pension or similar fund. Or maybe your life is just too busy or complicated for you to do the investing yourself. Regardless, you now want to understand how investing works so you can either take over your own investment decisions or monitor what fund managers are doing with your hard-earned cash. I'm not sure many people will pick up this book to check up on fund managers, but I could be wrong.

What's Your Personality Type with Money?

Some of us spend all we have each month (and then some). Others put away a bit in the bank or building society on a regular basis. And still others buy and sell stocks and shares, some going in for some very complex investments.

Test time: You need to decide whether you're a spender, a saver, or an investor. Doing so isn't as easy as it looks, though. Spenders can be savers or investors. Savers can be spenders and investors. And investors are generally also savers and must, at some stage, be spenders. But most people are predominantly one of the three types – spender, saver, or investor. Which category you think you fit into determines what you do from now on, how you react, and how you progress.

Spenders have fun

Spenders are generally people who live for the here and now. They may want more than they can have and end up borrowing money. For many spenders, accumulating cash for the future has no priority.

Here are ten attributes of spenders. If the majority of them apply to you, then, yep, you're a spender:

- ✔ You don't look forward to the end of the month.
- ✔ You love new things – the glossier the better.
- ✔ You have more than one credit card.
- ✔ You can't resist two-for-one offers.
- ✔ You buy unnecessary clothes.
- ✔ You're always first – and last – to buy a round of drinks.
- ✔ You believe in living a lot now.
- ✔ You see the future as a foreign land.
- ✔ You worry about money at times.
- ✔ You buy glossy magazines as much for the advertisements as the articles.

If you're in this category, your first priority is to recognise that investors can't always be spenders. Getting familiar with investing is a good way to accomplish this priority because it offers an alternative use of your cash.

Know that while on your way to becoming a saver or an investor, you can start with very small sums. You can become a saver with £1. And some stock market-based investment plans start at £20 a month, less than a large packet of crisps a day.

Savers have cash

Savers are people who want to keep their financial cake and eat small slices at a later date. Here are ten saver attributes. Tick those that apply to you, and if the majority do, then you're probably a saver:

- ✔ You have a surplus at the end of each month.
- ✔ You go to the supermarket with a shopping list.
- ✔ You don't have a credit card, or you pay it off in full each month.
- ✔ You're prepared to put off purchases.
- ✔ You'd rather buy second-hand than run up a debt.
- ✔ Your property is more important than your furniture.
- ✔ You look at the display windows at banks and building societies.
- ✔ You know what the current interest rates are.
- ✔ You believe in the saying *waste not, want not.*
- ✔ You've read *Frugal Living For Dummies* (published by Wiley).

'Hi, it's me, Spender. Can't I just use my credit card to finance an investment?'

You can't generally use a credit card to buy investment products over the phone, via the Internet, or in other circumstances where you can't send a cheque. Some of the reasons lie in the complexity of consumer credit legislation. Another factor is that financial companies only want you to invest what you can afford, although unauthorised offshore investment firms may try to sucker you into schemes by telling you to use your credit card.

But the most important reason you shouldn't borrow to invest or save is that doing so only makes financial sense if the return is going to be higher than the interest rate charged. Paying 22.9 per cent annual interest – and that's by no means the top credit card rate – is pointless unless you can be very sure that your investment will grow even faster and that your original capital will be safe. At the time of this writing (and for many years before), no such investments exist.

And note that even if you could borrow at 0 per cent annual interest, you'd still have to be sure of getting your money back with one of those rare investments that can't fall in order to be better off.

Saving is a stage you must reach before investing. You can be a saver as well as an investor, but you can't be an investor without first saving up some money to invest.

Investors build up future funds

Investors are people who are prepared to go the extra mile to try to ensure that their wealth goes the extra thousands, tens of thousands, or even more. Investors want control over their money but are ready to take a risk provided that they're in charge and know the odds. They want their money to work hard for them – as hard as they worked to get the money.

You don't need an MBA, a posh old school tie, or stacks of money. However, know that although you can sleepwalk into just saving your cash, you must be wide awake to be an investor.

As a pure saver, you really don't have to know what you're doing. You can just stash your cash under the bed, for example. As an investor, you *must* know what you're doing and have the self-discipline to follow your strategy, even if the strategy is doing nothing, buying and forgetting, or benign neglect.

So are you an investor? Check out these attributes to find out:

- You have spare cash.
- You have an emergency fund for the day the roof falls down or the car collapses.

✔ You want more than the bank or building society offers.

✔ You think about your money-making strategy and tactics.

✔ You can face up to bad days on investment markets without worry.

✔ You're ready to swap certitude for a bigger potential reward.

✔ You can afford to lock away your spare cash for five years at the very least.

✔ You understand what you're doing with your money.

✔ You're prepared to lose money occasionally.

✔ You're ready to invest your time into growing your fortune.

All of these attributes belong to an investor. So what's your bottom-line personality type when it comes to money?

✔ **You decided you're an investor.** Congratulations! You're ready to embark on the road to growing your money. It won't be easy. You may face stiff climbs, vertiginous falls, rocky surfaces, long deviations, and dead ends. But give it enough work and time, and I promise that investing will work out.

✔ **You didn't qualify as an investor.** You got as far as a saver and no further. Or you're really stuck as a spender. You're wishing you spent the price of this book on something else or stuck it in your savings account, where at current savings rates it will double in about 35 years. Well, don't regret your purchase or vow to send this book off for recycling or try to recoup some of the price by selling it in a car boot sale. Stick with it. The very fact that you bought this book shows you're ready to move on to investing when you're financially and psychologically ready.

And even if you decide you never want to buy a share, sell a bond, invest in a unit trust, or check on foreign exchange rates, this book is still for you. Why? Because you're almost certainly an investor already. (The following section tells you how, if your curiosity is piqued.)

Surprise! You've Probably Been Investing Already

Your financial fate already depends on the ups and downs of the stocks and shares markets. Few of us can escape this fact, and every day, the number of people who can ignore the investment world diminishes. You may be an unconscious investor or even an unwilling one, but there's no running away from it: You're already an investor.

Investing through your pension fund

The biggest amount of investment money you're likely to have is the value of your pension fund. And whether you pay into it yourself, rely on your employer, or build it up via a partnership with your employer, it all rides on investment markets.

Just to give you an idea of how much you may have, suppose that you earn £25,000 a year and put 10 per cent of your earnings each month into a pension fund that grows at a 7 per cent average per year. Here's what your fund will be worth over the course of 45 years (I've ignored tax relief on pension contributions, future wage rises, inflation, and fund and pension management charges to keep this example simple):

Number of years	Value of fund
5	£14,915
10	£36,059
15	£66,032
20	£108,525
25	£168,762
30	£254,157
35	£375,214
40	£546,827
45	£790,111

That's serious money!

Most people haven't a clue that they have the potential for anything like the preceding example over a lifetime. But even if you are aware of what you could achieve, I bet you didn't know that you have a good chance of taking some investment control over that sum. Even if you don't want to, at the very least you should be able to check up on what the pension fund managers are doing with your money. Understanding what other people are doing with your money can help you increase your own pension fund in good markets or prevent it from going down when the investment world turns sour. (There will inevitably be good and bad patches over a lifetime of pension savings.)

Note that your pension plan isn't the only area where you may be an unwitting stocks and shares investor. Endowment mortgages also revolve around stocks and shares.

Between a rock and a hard place

Northern Rock sounded, well, rock-solid. The branding people knew something about names that built confidence. All Northern Rock did was to take money from savers and lend it to people who wanted loans for homes – a recipe that worked for over a century without a hitch. The bank offered good interest rates to savers and, by early 2007, the shares were riding high at around £12. Business was booming and the company's directors were shiningly optimistic.

Savers with the bank and those owning shares in Northern Rock felt totally secure. They included many private investors who picked up their stake for nothing or for very little when the former building society turned into a stock market-listed bank in the late 1990s.

But – and there is always a but in these tales – the firm had abandoned the hard fault model of taking in from savers and lending out to home buyers. Instead, Northern Rock had entered the world of structured investment vehicles (SIVs) and collateralized debt obligations (CDOs). Now, don't ask me to explain what these are about. Firstly, you need hundreds of millions of pounds/dollars/euros to get involved. More importantly, not even those who claimed to understand really appreciated that they had created a house of financial cards that one unexpected breath could blow away.

Almost everyone in the home-lending game had some of these esoteric SIVs and CDOs, but Northern Rock had more than the others. The tiny ill wind, and one always comes along, was the failure of some poor people living in trailer parks in the United States to keep up with their loans.

Because all the SIVs, the CDOs, and all the other initials depended on each other, a few bad customers in Tennessee brought the Tyneside-based Northern Rock to its knees. The house of cards collapsed. Big banks in the United States lost billions.

Northern Rock savers queued all night outside of branches to rescue their money, the first run on a United Kingdom bank – where account holders so mistrust the bank that they demand their money back – for over 140 years. Shareholders saw their investments fall to under £1 a share. The government had to step in and organise a near £30billion rescue. If the government hadn't done this, other banks could then have tumbled, too.

But no one can say the shareholders were not warned. The share price had been slipping badly for some months before those queues outside the branches made television news headlines.

The moral of this story is the same as the one that applies to Equitable Life at the end of the 1990s. Back then, the pension savings of hundreds of thousands, who had trusted what was billed as a super-safe method of storing cash for retirement, went horribly wrong.

When it comes to your hard-earned money, never sleepwalk. Stay wide awake and figure out as much as you can about your saving and investing options. Check what the stock market says about shares rather than paying attention to the company's directors or public relations staff, who are paid to put a good gloss on a bad situation. Ask questions. Never put all your eggs in one basket. Remember that the absurdly highly paid City types have feet of clay (or worse) when their clever ideas run out of steam (as they always do). Research. And don't automatically go with the default options – even if everyone else says they are the best way forward. Here endeth the lesson!

Investing through a share in your firm's fortunes

Millions of people are potential investors in the company they work for. Most big stock-market-quoted companies, like British Airways or Wal-Mart's UK offshoot Asda, offer employees option plans that give workers the chance to acquire a stake in the firm. To acquire that stake, workers buy *shares*, also known as *equities*, which are explained in the section 'Get your share of shares' later in this chapter.

The original idea was that giving someone the chance to buy shares in the future at a price fixed in the past would help motivate staff members and make them put in more effort, but in reality the idea only works if all colleagues work *equally* hard. The original idea aside, the option plan is just a pay perk but one that can be valuable. A variety of schemes are available, but the most common one is linked to a savings account known as Save As You Earn (SAYE).

SAYE schemes have a monthly limit to encourage you to tread carefully, as it would be really daft to put your investment eggs in one basket. You don't want your savings to collapse if your employer goes bust or if you are made redundant.

In a SAYE scheme, you save from £5 to £250 a month in a special account that earns interest. When you start, you're given a price, called the *exercise price*, at which you can buy the firm's shares in the future. The account continues for three or five years (with an option to go to seven years). At the end, you can use the savings plus interest to buy shares in the firm at the pre-set price. If the price has risen, you make a profit, although you don't have to sell until you want to. But if the price has dropped, you can walk away from the whole deal with the cash you've saved in the account.

Some employee share option schemes aren't a perk. They're a danger. During the dotcom boom, for example, people were lured from well-paid, secure jobs into risky employment with the promise of share options but a substantially reduced salary. Most option plans involved locking in the employees for a number of years, and by the time they could take their options, the shares were virtually worthless, assuming that the company stayed in business. Putting all your eggs in one basket is always an error, so never tie your fortunes so closely to one company. No matter how attractive options sound, a wage packet bird in the hand is worth several options in the bush.

Five Basic Investment Choices

All your money decisions, outside of putting your family fortune on some nag running in the 3.30, simply involve making up your mind as to where to put your money. Literally tens of thousands of choices are available. At least a thousand choices are in most daily newspapers.

But you can cut that number down to just five possibilities by considering basic investment choices only. Get these right, or even just right more often than wrong, and you're well on the way to financial success:

- ✔ Cash
- ✔ Property
- ✔ Bonds
- ✔ Shares
- ✔ Alternatives

Here's a big investment secret: Most professional fund mangers – yes, those City of London types who pull in huge salaries for playing around with your pension, insurance, or other investment money – don't wake up each morning asking themselves which investments they should be buying or selling that day. Instead, they reduce the investment world to five big buckets that they call *asset allocation*, which simply means that they divide up investment money into five areas – cash, property, bonds, shares, and alternatives. They take your money and allocate a portion to shares, another portion to property, and so on. The fund managers, and the people who run large pension funds, know that if they get their asset allocation decisions right and do nothing else, they'll beat the averages.

Here's an example: Between December 1999 and March 2003, the UK stock market roughly halved in value. Some shares did better, some did worse, but only a tiny handful actually gained. Any fund manager who made the decision to take money out of the shares bucket and put it into the cash, bonds, or properties bucket did very well. Share prices then zoomed up again over the following four years, so anyone smart enough to buy shares in March 2003 would have doubled their money. While this was happening, cash, bonds, and to a lesser extent properties were bad places to be.

You can't go wrong with cash

Having cash under the mattress can be very comforting when everything is going wrong in your life. But keeping cash under the mattress, or anywhere else at home, isn't a good idea from a security point of view. Nor does it make sense for investors. Putting your cash in a bank protects it from thieves, fire risks, and perhaps the temptation to grab it and spend it in one shop.

You never earn much money just leaving your cash in the bank. Most bank account money is in current or cheque book accounts, which often pay just 0.1 per cent, an interest rate that, transformed into pounds and pence, gives you the princely sum of £1 for each £1,000 you have in the bank for a full year. And if you're a taxpayer, that £1 may be worth as little as 60p after HM Revenue and Customs take their slice. Ouch!

Better ways of investing your cash are available, including building society deposit accounts, online cash accounts, telephone banks, and postal accounts. With all these options, you swap a higher interest rate for some of the flexibility benefits that come with a very low interest-paying account.

The longer you're prepared to tie up your money, the better the rate of interest you'll receive. You can lock into fixed rates so you know exactly where you stand, but you must be prepared to hand over your money for a set period, usually one to three years, and throw away the money box key. Granted, some fixed-rate deals let you have your money back early, but only if you pay a big penalty.

Additional options include *cash unit trusts* (specialist funds which only invest in the safe cash vehicles only available to professional money managers) and cash options in pension and insurance funds. Know up-front that none of these options pays a fortune. Most do well if they approach the Bank of England base rate. And, unless you're a low earner or use an Individual Savings Account, whatever you earn will be cut back by income tax on the interest. But does this matter? No. The best you can really hope for from a cash account is that the interest equals the *rate of inflation* – that's the amount the price of things the average person buys goes up each year – after the tax charge on the *annual interest uplift*. If inflation is 4 per cent, then a 20 per cent taxpayer will need a 5 per cent headline rate to keep up with price rises – work it out and see! £100 invested at 5 per cent gives £5 less 20 per cent tax equals £4 or the 4 per cent needed!

The whole point of cash investing is to use it when you're uncertain or everything in your life looks awful. It's a security blanket you can retire to during periods when all else is confusion or contraction.

The cash unit trusts (only a tiny handful exist) and the cash options with pensions and insurance (most life companies offer these as a low- or no-cost switch option out of other funds) are intended to do nothing more than safeguard what you have. Don't disrespect this fact. Keeping a firm hold on what you have isn't just for fast-falling markets. It's a vital concept in the months ahead of retirement or any other time when you know you'll want cash and not risks. You lock in the gains made in the past and can go ahead and plan that big trip, your child's wedding, or the boat you want to buy. Cash is what you can spend, and expenditure is the endgame of investment.

Property is usually a solid foundation

The property you live in is probably your biggest financial project – assuming that you don't rent it from someone. Typical three-bedroom semis now change hands at £300,000 or more in many parts of the UK. And at the top end of the market, no one blinks an eye anymore at £2m homes.

But is property an investment? Yes, because you have to plan the money to pay for it, because cash going into your home is money not available for use elsewhere, and because you can make or lose a lot of money in property.

Property beyond your home can also be a worthwhile investment. Stock market managers run big funds like property because it rarely loses value, often gains more than inflation, and provides a rental income as well. Commercial property, such as office blocks, shopping centres, business parks, hotels, and factories, is usually rented out on terms ensuring not only that the rent comes in each month (unless the tenant actually goes bust) but also that the rent goes up (and never down) after each five years, when the amount is renegotiated.

Bricks and mortar are as solid an investment as you can find outside of cash, as long as the bricks and mortar are real. A fair number of property schemes take money from you for buildings that only exist on the architect's plan. This is known as off-plan purchasing. In most cases, these buildings eventually go up. Some don't, however, and these cases leave you nursing a loss as the developers gallop off into the sunset with your cash.

Besides building up value in your own home, you have three main routes to invest in property:

- ✔ **Buy to let.** You become a landlord by purchasing a property that you rent to others.

- ✔ **Buy into a property fund run by a professional fund manager.** You can do so through personal pension plans, some insurance-backed savings plans, and a handful of specialist unit trusts.

- ✔ **Buy shares in property companies.** This is the riskiest method but the only one that can provide above-average gains.

A number of firms have advertised high guaranteed returns from portfolios of low-cost properties that, they say, are then rented out to housing association and council tenants in receipt of social security payments. Don't fall for this one. There can be no guarantees, and some of the companies offering this deal have already been shut down by the Department of Trade and Industry 'in the public interest'.

Bonds are others' borrowings

A stock-market-quoted *bond* is basically an IOU issued by governments or companies. There are loads of other sorts of bonds around including Premium Bonds, which give you the chance to win £1m each month at no risk. But here we're talking bonds from governments and firms, which go up and down on stock exchanges.

Bond issuers promise to pay a fixed income on stated dates and to repay the amount on the bond certificate in full on a fixed day in the future. In other words, you pay the government, say, £100, and the Treasury promises to give you £5 a year for the next five years *and* your £100 back in five years' time.

Sounds simple, right? Well, it's not at all. Bonds are complex creatures with many traps for the unwary. (We devote a big slice of this book to the ups and downs of bond investment.) But if you reckon price rises will be kept to a minimum and interest rates will stay where they are or go down, then bonds are a good bet if you need regular income.

Bonds are becoming more common as well. The reason is partly because many investors have been taken with the relative safety and steadiness of bonds compared with shares and the relatively higher income they offer compared with cash. (Everything in investing is relative to something else, by the way.) But the reason is also because the people running big pension funds need the security and regular payments so they can afford to pay cheques each month to the retired people who depend on them.

The easiest way to buy into bonds is through one of the hundred or so specialist unit trusts. But don't take the headline income rate they quote as set in stone. It can go up or down, and there are no guarantees or promises. Some even cheat by hiding costs away. Always remember that the capital you originally invest in the bond fund isn't safe, either. It can go down or up along with investment trends and the skills of the manager.

Get your share of shares

Shares make up the biggest part of most portfolios. They can grow faster than rival investment types and produce more. They're probably your best chance of turning a little into a lot.

Shares are what they say they are – a small part of a bigger picture. Buying shares (also known as *equities*) gives you partial ownership of a company. You can own as little as one share, and if that's the case and the company has issued one million shares, you have a one-millionth stake in that enterprise.

You can't chip off that one-millionth portion and walk away with it. What you get is one-millionth of the profits and a one-millionth say in the future of the company. But you won't have a one-millionth share of clearing up the mess if the firm goes bust. You can never lose more than you put in.

Ownership rights are becoming more important and more valued. Put a lot of small stakes together and companies start to notice you, especially if you have a media-attractive project such as protesting against excessive pay for fat-cat executives who fail to deliver anything to shareholders and then collect big bucks when they're sacked.

Most shares are bought because owners hope that they'll produce more over the long term than with cash, property, or bonds. They generally have done just this, although there are no guarantees. Shares are your best chance for capital gains and the top choice if you want a portfolio to produce a rising income. But take heed: They can also be an easy way to lose your money.

 Want to know the most dangerous sentence in investment? 'It will be different this time.' That sentence is trotted out whenever share prices rise rapidly and brighter investors start to question how long it can continue. That sentence was a regular mantra from 1998–2000 when dotcom shares were booming like nothing ever before, except, of course, for the previous market insanity and the bubble before that. Thing is, it never is different. Anything that is promised as a one-way bet is bound to run out of steam some time, whether you're looking at property prices, the price of wheat, or shares in African economies. Share prices, and the values of every other single investment in this book, go up with greed and down with fear. As long as these human emotions exist, 'It will be different this time' will be the same nonsense as the last occasion it was trotted out. Expect to hear this phrase many times during your investment life!

Alternatives are a hodgepodge to consider

This investment area covers a rag-bag of bits and pieces. For some people, alternative investments concentrate on items you can physically hold, such as works of art, fine wines, vintage cars, antiques, and stamp collections. But for an increasing number of people, the term means hedge funds, which are about as esoteric as investment gets. Put simply, you hand over your money to managers who, by hook or by crook, hope to increase it.

In most cases, don't even ask how those types of managers hope to gain cash for you. They won't tell you. Or they won't be informative, instead just coming up with some meaningless jargon phrase. And don't even ask what will happen if they fail. They don't like to talk about this possibility, even though you could easily lose all the money you have with them.

So is there a plus side? Yes. Hedge funds are the only realistic way you can make money out of shares when prices are falling all over the place.

In the section 'Surprise! You've Probably Been Investing Already', I explain in detail that, well, you've probably been investing already – without knowing about it. On that same line of thinking, you may also unknowingly have some of your wealth riding on hedge funds. Hedge funds make their main pitch to really big investment and pension funds, as well as to private investors with lots of spare money. Chances are that a hedge fund or hedge fund type of tactic is in your pension plan.

You can't invest directly in a hedge fund unless you're really rich. Some funds work on an invitation-only basis, so you wait until you're asked! But you can sometimes put your money into a fund of hedge funds. This is a special vehicle that buys, holds, and sells hedge funds and they are sometimes offered to the general public – or at least those who can afford the minimum £7,000 they usually require.

One new alternative is the wonderful world of commodities where you can bet on the price of anything from potatoes to potassium, from sugar to silver. Commodity investment looks like soaring into fashion. Some people will make a lot; others will lose their shirt. But no one can foretell who, when, and where. That's the fascination of investment.

Chapter 2

Checking Your Personal Life Before You Invest

Investment truth #1: It's easier to lose money than to make it.

Investment truth #2: More domestic breakups and rows are caused by money, or rather the lack of it, than anything else.

Investment truth #3: You'll be a better investor if you've secured your home base – getting a roof over your head whose costs are sustainable is the vital first move. Buying is usually better than renting, so a mortgage is the number one investment.

Investment truth #4: Paper profits have no more value than the piece of paper they are written on. What your investments are worth on paper is just a bit of paper. Until you turn that investment into cash, it won't put a roof over your head, put food on your table, or provide an income for a household if something happens to the breadwinner.

Investment truth #5: Borrowing money to buy investments can be a fast route to the bankruptcy court.

*F*eel down and low after reading that? Wondering why Chapter 2 doesn't launch straight into how to analyse stock futures and double your money in minutes? Or how to be a day trader and clean up?

There's nothing new under the sun

At the end of the 1990s, I was able, day by day, to watch the stock market bubbling up fast from my vantage point at *The Guardian* newspaper. And every time share prices advanced to new highs, I used to ask myself just how long it would last.

The further share values went up, the more I asked myself that same question. But I was told over and over again that we were in a 'new paradigm' in which the whole financial structure was changing. Amazingly, the further and faster share prices advanced, the more I was informed by highly paid people in very influential positions in world-famous investment banks that I was witnessing the ushering in of a new financial age.

First in the US and then in the UK, people gave up secure, well-paid jobs that earned the respect of family, friends, and neighbours to spend all day trading shares in front of a computer screen. (They couldn't do so before, because the technology didn't exist.) Others, including some I knew well, quit similarly good jobs to take up Internet posts that came with huge salaries and even bigger stock option packages. Their option shares needed only to double before they'd be able to retire at a young age with a million or two. Being that these shares had already tripled and quadrupled, a mere 100 per cent uplift would be nothing.

'Why don't you join us? Your job's toast. You'll never make real money', they taunted me.

And when I asked the day traders what they'd do if the share price rises halted or even went into reverse, and how they'd explain it to their nearest and dearest, they looked at me as if I'd just got off a spaceship from Mars.

'That's impossible,' they said. 'So we don't even think it.' They were, after all, backed by all those highly paid investment bankers, and the New Year's bonuses at one firm alone were greater than the wealth of the 40 poorest countries in the world.

Well, in the end, my gut feeling was right, my traditional job was still secure, and the dotcom jobs were toast. I just wonder what happened to all the mortgages and credit card bills of those day traders, as well as all their personal and family relationships. The truth is, I don't know. But I do know that the day traders have long ceased writing those Sunday newspaper columns where they reported how much money they made.

The morals of all this? Don't chase fads. Never assume there is a quick or easy route to riches. And never give up the day job!

You've every right to be depressed and puzzled. But it's a good thing you are. Investment knowledge has as much to do with *when not to do something, when to hold on to what you have, and when to hold back and let the next person pick up the problem* as it has to do with plunging into financial markets.

And that's what this chapter is about. Before you invest, you need to consider all the above truths. You need to take a close look at yourself, and those around you. You should be aware that there are no easy routes in finance. But more importantly, everything revolves around you and your family – not what need the assorted advisers and hucksters have to push commission-earning opportunities at you.

Assessing Your Personal Wealth

Before you start investing, take a long cool look at your personal wealth. Draw up a balance sheet (an example is shown in Figure 2–1) so you can check how much comes in each month from work, interest payments, dividends, or pensions. Then look at where the money goes.

Repeat this exercise over three to six months so that low-spending months are balanced out by months where you had to lay out a lot of money. Also take into consideration months where earnings are boosted by a big, one-time bonus or overtime. Compare those boosted-earnings months with regular-earnings months.

An essential first step before investing is knowing what your incomings and outgoings are (how much money is coming in and going out). This knowledge will help you focus on your goal of increasing your wealth. And what if your outgoings leave nothing left over? Well, you know you should consider holding back from active investment at this time. But you can still use this time to look, learn, and get a real feel of money markets.

Figure 2–1:
Use a balance sheet like this one to keep track of how much money comes in each month and where it all goes.

Income	£
Your earnings (after all deductions)	
Your partner's earnings (after all deductions)	
Interest on savings	
Dividends from investments	
Other sources of income	
Total	
Outgoings	
Mortgage / rent	
Supermarket bills	
Children's school fees	
Public transport	
Car – petrol, insurance, tax	
Meals in restaurants	
Snacks – sandwiches, coffee	
Pension	
Life insurance	
Newspapers, magazines	
Gym membership	
Cinema, theatre, video hire	
Sports	
Hobbies	
Interest on credit cards / loans	
Rainy day fund savings	
Total	

Savings quickly mount up thanks to compound interest

Pennies really can turn into pounds and pounds into thousands. And they can grow even faster thanks to *compound interest,* which is interest on interest.

Suppose, for example, that you manage to save £10 a week and put it in the bank. That's more than £40 a month and £520 a year. These sums can start you on an investment habit.

Here's how much various weekly savings would be worth after five years with a very modest 2.5

per cent interest paid each year – some are more generous, adding interest more often.

- ✔ £10 a week: £2,733
- ✔ £15 a week: £4,099
- ✔ £20 a week: £5,466
- ✔ £30 a week: £8,199
- ✔ £40 a week: £10,932
- ✔ £50 a week: £13,665

Taking Care of Family Before Fortune

Investing involves taking chances. Serious investing, as opposed to taking a wild punt on a stock market move, will tie up your money for a good length of time. Assuming that you have some spare money (see the preceding section to find out whether you do), think about how investing it rather than spending it will affect your household.

Weigh up the happiness quotients for all concerned. For example, compare spending the money now on piano lessons with investing it for later use on college tuition fees.

What you do with your money should have a goal. Investment is intended for future consumption. It's not a game where you concentrate on ego-boosting by building up a big cash score. There are plenty of computer and arcade games for that.

Talk over investment strategies with adult members of your household. You'll feel all the better if you get them on your side. But if they aren't happy with your strategies and you can't convince them, then hold back.

If you have some spare cash but don't want to take chances with it or may be tempted to spend it – go for National Savings, now renamed National Savings & Investments. National Savings offers a number of products where you can put your money away for a set time, ranging from one to five years, and more flexible accounts are available as well. The rates aren't chart-topping, but you have the security of the UK Treasury and Exchequer backing your decision.

Studying How to Save without Sacrificing

Almost everyone can save some money without sacrificing too much lifestyle. Even small amounts each day can soon mount up. Here are some initial ideas – and how much you can save each week:

✔ Give up smoking. A person who smokes 20 cigarettes a day will save £50 a week.

✔ Buy milk at the supermarket instead of using home delivery. You'll save £5 a week.

✔ Take a sandwich from home instead of buying one at work. You'll save £5 to £7 a week.

✔ Go shopping with a list and stick to it. You'll save at least £10 a week – and probably avoid some fattening snacks as well.

✔ Ditch expensive cable or satellite TV stations you hardly ever watch. You'll save £3 to £10 a week.

✔ Put every £2 coin you receive into a box. When you have £50, put the money into a special bank or building society account.

✔ Buy a copy of *Frugal Living For Dummies* (published by Wiley). You'll save a fortune each week!

Think about your lifestyle and then make your own additions to the list, from saving on transportation to cutting out unnecessary mobile phone calls. The point is to see how you can create big savings with some discipline – the same style of discipline you'll need to be a winning investor.

Looking After Your Life and Health

None of us knows how much time we have left on this planet. The good news is that your chances of living longer have never been better. Most people nowadays are likely to live to around 75 to 80 years of age. The bad news? You can never forecast when you're going to be hit by a bus or succumb to a mystery virus.

So you should always make sure there is sufficient life insurance and cover against your succumbing to a serious illness or losing your livelihood that you can provide for your family.

Life insurance won't replace you, but it will replace your money-earning capacity.

Always shop around for all insurance. A recent table from *Moneyfacts* showed that a 40-year-old non-smoking man could buy a £100,000 policy covering the next 20 years for £10.55 a month from Marks & Spencer (yes, the high street store now sells life insurance as well.) But exactly the same plan from Bright Grey would cost £21.20 a month. As in fashion, you pay twice as much for the funky label compared with the best value brand.

Before buying life insurance cover, decide how much you need. One rule of thumb is four to five times your yearly take-home pay. But also look at any death or illness benefits that come with your job. There is no point in doubling up cover unnecessarily. And know that if you have no family commitments, then life cover is just a pricey luxury.

As well as buying life cover, you can purchase *critical illness policies* that pay out a lump sum if you have a serious illness, such as a heart attack or cancer, and survive for a month. Some policies also pay if you die during the policy period. The same huge range of prices exists, so never, ever go for the first quote you get.

Some policies, known as *permanent health insurance* or *income protection plans*, promise to pay a monthly sum until your normal retirement age if you can't work due to illness or injury. These policies can be expensive, especially for women because insurers think women are ill a lot more often than men.

Always look at all your family and personal circumstances before signing up for a policy. If you don't really need it, then don't buy it. The monthly premiums could be used to help build up an investment nestegg.

Paying into a Pension Plan

Your pension plan is an investment for your future but with tax relief in the here and now. This means that, if you're a basic-rate taxpayer, you pay £78 for each £100 that you get in investment going into the plan (£80 from April 2008) – a pretty good deal. Many personal pension plans, including *stakeholder plans* (these are pensions whose costs are limited by UK government rules – almost all employers have to offer one but they don't have to put any contribution into it for you) as well as some workplace-based top-up schemes, technically known as *Additional Voluntary Contributions* or *AVCs*, let you choose from a wide range of investment possibilities both initially and later on and also allow low- or no-cost switching between investment options in the plan.

Those with larger sums and a DIY (do it yourself) attitude to investment can opt for a SIPP (self-invested personal pension) where the holder gets to choose what goes in. You can start a SIPP with anything from £5,000, although £50,000 is a more normal minimum. However, on the downside, the costs can be high and if your strategy all goes wrong, you have only yourself to blame.

If you want to be a less-active pensions investor, look at a lifestyle plan, which most pensions companies now offer. This type of plan invests in riskier areas, such as shares, when you are younger and have time on your side. Later, as you approach retirement, the plan automatically moves you down the risk profile. One way is to switch 20 per cent of your fund into safer bonds starting ten years before you retire. Then five years before you want to stop work, the fund moves again, bit by bit, into a cash fund. You can always override a lifestyle plan if you want.

Taking Care of Property Before Profits

The roof over your head is probably your biggest monthly outlay. And it's also likely to be your biggest investment. So don't begrudge what you spend on it. In the long run, it should build up to a worthwhile asset. (At the very worst, it'll shelter you from the elements!)

Always look at what it would cost each month to rent the same property compared with buying it. Doing so is easier nowadays thanks to the buy to let boom, because you can find rented properties on most streets. If you're paying more in mortgage costs than in rent, the excess is your *opportunity cost* to make gains later if you sell up and move somewhere smaller or to a less-expensive area. This makes it an investment. On the other hand, if you're paying less in a mortgage than renting would cost, look at the savings as another area for potential investment cash.

Pay off home loans early

'Psst! Want an investment that pays up to 80 times as much as cash in some bank accounts but is absolutely safe and totally secure? And what about a 100 per cent guaranteed return that can be higher than financial watchdogs allow any investment company to use for forecasting future profits?'

Sounds like a snake-oil salesman scam, doesn't it? But if your first reaction is, 'You've got to be kidding', then you're wrong. Paying off mortgage loans with spare cash offers an unbeatable combination of high returns and super safety.

To see what I mean, take a look at the following mathematics. In this particular example, I've used interest-only figures for simplicity, although anyone with a repayment (capital and interest) loan will also make big gains. And, again for simplicity, I've assumed that the interest sums are calculated just once a year. That said, here's the scenario:

Your home is your castle

Homes have generally been a good medium- to long-term investment. They've beaten inflation over most periods and more than kept up with rising incomes in most parts of the country.

Some parts have seen spectacular gains. But even in the worst parts of the country, you would've been very unlucky to lose over the long run, even counting the big price falls of the early 1990s.

There's every chance that the future won't show such spectacular gains. But homes should continue to be a good investment and at the very least keep up with rising prices over a period. Putting whatever you can into a house purchase is probably the best thing you can do with your money.

Someone with a standard mortgage and with £100,000 outstanding at 6 per cent pays £60 a year, or £5 a month, in interest for each £1,000 borrowed. On the £100,000, that works out to £6,000 a year or £500 a month.

Now suppose that the homebuyer pays back £1,000. The new interest amount is £5,940 a year or £495 a month.

Compare the £60 a year saved with what the £1,000 would've earned in a bank or building society. The £1,000 could've earned as little as £1 at 0.10 per cent. And even at a much more generous 3 per cent, it would only make £30 – half the savings from mortgage repayment.

'But you've forgotten income tax on the savings interest,' you rightly say.

Ah, but the money you save by diverting cash to your mortgage account is tax-free. It must be grossed up (have the tax added back in) to give a fair contrast. Basic-rate taxpayers must earn the equivalent of 7.5 per cent from a normal investment to do as well. And top-rate taxpayers need a super-safe 10 per cent investment return from their cash to do as well.

Now where else can you find a 7.5 per cent a year guaranteed return, let alone a guaranteed 10 per cent a year? Nowhere.

After a payment is made, it reduces this year's interest as well as that for every single year until the mortgage is redeemed. If interest rates go up, you'll save even more. But if they fall, you'll keep on saving and be able to afford to pay down your mortgage even more.

Some flexible or bank-account-linked mortgages let you borrow back over-payments so you can have your cake of lower payments with the knowledge that you can still eat it later if you need to. Alternatively, you can re-mortgage to a new home loan to raise money from your property if you need it.

Check your home insurance coverage

You need insurance coverage both for the buildings of your property and the contents. Buildings insurance is compulsory with most mortgages. It should be enough to pay for the total clearing of the site and the rebuilding of your house from the foundation up.

 Take a look at the buildings or contents insurance that you can buy from your mortgage lender. The lender's insurance policies are likely to be more expensive than those of other companies, so shop around. And the bigger your home, the more you'll probably save from searching the market. Some insurers concentrate on more expensive houses, looking at them as better risks than smaller properties. The savings – £200 to £600 per year is possible – can form the basis for future investments.

Setting Up a Rainy-Day Fund

Before investing for the longer term, you need to set up your own personal emergency (or rainy day) fund for contingencies that you can imagine but couldn't pay for out of your purse or wallet. The fund should contain enough money to pay for events such as a sudden trip abroad if you have close family in distant lands, any domestic problem that wouldn't be covered by insurance, a major repair to a car over and above an insurance settlement, or a vet's bill not covered by insurance.

Here are some additional snippets from experience for you to keep in mind:

- ✔ Don't put your emergency-fund money in an account that offers a higher rate of interest in return for restricted access such as not being able to get hold of your money for five years. The problems and penalties associated with getting your cash on short notice outweigh any extra-earning advantages.
- ✔ An emergency cash reserve serves as reassurance so you can ride out investment bad times more easily.
- ✔ Monitor your potential emergency cash needs on a regular basis. They can shrink as well as expand.
- ✔ Know that you'll rarely be able to access investments in an emergency. You shouldn't be put in a position where you're forced to sell.
- ✔ Know that your credit card can be a temporary lifeline, giving you breathing space to reorganise longer-term investments when necessary.

Chapter 3

Recognising What Makes an Investor Tick

In This Chapter

▶ Understanding components of investor psychology

▶ Looking at the standoff between greed and fear

▶ Investing as a casino wheel or sensible strategy

▶ Investing routes for the cautious

*N*eedlework and carpentry are among the skills where you need a firm hand and a good eye as well as technical ability. You need technical ability in investing, too. But instead of the firm hand and the good eye, you need an understanding of investor psychology – how you tick and how the other investors who make up the market tick as well. This chapter looks at psychology – but don't worry, there are no huge tomes to read or big words to learn.

Good investors know all about the mechanics of buying and selling stocks and shares. They know which side of a balance sheet is good and which is bad. And they understand the relationship between interest rates, inflation, and what they end up earning on their investment cash.

Great investors do all that *and* something more, something far more vital. It doesn't involve learning how to interpret share earnings forecasts, how to understand credit risks, or how to evaluate the future of small companies. What it involves is far more basic – and far more essential.

This extra something is investor psychology, and it's what this chapter is all about. In this chapter, I tell you what investor psychology actually is and explain some specific emotions that make an investor tick. In addition, I explain that although gambling and investing share certain similar characteristics, they're actually very different ventures. And for those of you whose emotions range from cautious to scared stiff, I provide some starting-point investing advice.

Understanding Investor Psychology

Investor psychology comes in two parts – the psychology of the marketplace and the psychology of the individual. This section helps you understand each part.

The psychology of the marketplace

Both small and big investors used to direct research toward where companies were going, what their likely future earnings would be, and what shape their business would be in three to five years into the future. Investors still do this research. But a new dimension is appearing in stock market analysis, especially that coming from the United States. This new way of thinking recognises that even the brightest and best investors make mistakes and lose money when they should have made profits. Why? It could be because their judgement was clouded by the comfort of being with the crowd or by hating the idea of standing alone or by refusing to accept early enough that they made an error. In other words, they went for the comfort blanket of conformity.

You need to stand back from the crowd and its noise. Instead of following the herd, understand how it works so you will know where investment values are going and why. The winner thinks 'outside the box'.

The psychology of the individual

Knowing how you'll react to what goes on in investment markets is vital. As you read this book, you'll experience some very basic emotions, such as 'I am comfortable with this' or 'I wouldn't touch this investment with the proverbial bargepole' and a whole range in between.

Couple these emotions with setting your own investment goals. Depending on the sort of person you are, your goals could range from the reasoned ('I want to make my spare cash grow a little over the next five years') to the ridiculous ('I want to quit work in three years' time').

Working out where you are on the line that goes from a need for complete comfort and security to wild gambling will enable you to make more rational decisions, including probably the most important one – the decision that at times it's best to walk away. The psychological aspect of investing is what separates figuring out investing from figuring out plumbing or gardening.

The anatomy of some mad markets

'Every age has its peculiar folly; some scheme, project, or fantasy into which it plunges, spurred on by the love of gain, the necessity of excitement, or the mere force of imitation,' wrote Charles Mackay in 1841. What was true then is just as true now – or even truer given the speed that information and financial decisions cross the globe. So take a look at some of the irrational madnesses and greed that have convinced some very bright people into a bubble investment. And we all know about blowing bubbles from childhood – they are really attractive and they grow in front of your eyes. But they have no substance and burst at the first pinprick.

- **The Dutch tulip mania of the 1630s.** Dutch merchants noted how rare tulip bulbs were expensive. So they started to buy and sell them. And the more they bought, the higher the price went. Mostly, the buyers just held on and watched their paper fortunes soar to the extent that one bulb could be worth more than a solid middle-class house in Amsterdam. But when one or two tried to sell, the price collapsed. That brought in more sellers so the prices fell even faster. The economic ruin of the tulip mania in the Netherlands was so far-reaching that it pushed the Dutch out of 'New World' exploration, leaving it all to the English, French, Spanish, and Portuguese.

- **The South Sea Bubble in 1711.** Huge fortunes were made and lost betting on the shares of the South Sea Company, which had never traded and was never going to. Much of the trading took place in Exchange Alley, City of London, which still exists today. Other bubble companies at that time were set up to 'make a wheel of perpetual motion. At the height of the bubble, companies were set up 'for matters so secret that no one should talk about them'.

- **The UK railway mania in the 1840s.** Like so many technological ideas, railways were destined to change the way people lived in a very short time. They transformed travel and even changed the way wars were conducted. But changing lives is not the same as making profits to justify share prices. Companies were set up that had no hope of ever laying a rail, let alone running a train. And others simply overstated their earnings potential.

- **The US radio bubble in the 1920s.** Radio was the big change in the United States during the 1920s, and share prices of any firms connected with radio went higher and higher. The more share prices soared, the more investors jumped on board. As a result, the shares went up a lot more, and, inevitably, even more investors were suckered in. But eventually, there were no investors left with dollars to buy from people wanting out of their investment. In October 1929, the market in radio shares collapsed and took everything else with it. The US stock market didn't recover fully until after the Second World War.

By the way, radio shares boomed after the great Florida land bubble in the mid-1920s burst. Somehow speculators were led to believe by clever promoters that land was running out fast in the Sunshine State. There's still plenty of it.

- **The Japanese stock market boom of the 1980s.** Japan's stock market multiplied fourfold between 1984 and 1989. A combination of falling interest rates, rising property

(continued)

(continued)

values, a rising currency, and money rushing in from investors elsewhere looking for the fastest moving market all helped. At the height of the boom, Japanese phone company NTT was worth more than every company on the German stock market taken together; the Tokyo market was worth one and a half times the value of the rest of the world's shares excluding those in the United States; and the value of the land that the Canadian embassy occupied in Tokyo was worth more than all of Montreal's property. The bubble burst, although fairly slowly. Now the Japanese market has fallen around 80 per cent from its peak and has returned to the levels before the mania started.

✔ **The dotcom boom of 1999.** This is probably the best documented example of investor psychology going to extremes. Share promoters from the world's top investment banks convinced enough investors that they had found a new paradigm using the undoubted potential of the Internet. These million-dollars-a-month bankers told investors that basics such as assets, earnings, and profits were old economy. The same was said of anything connected with day-to-day reality, such as building firms, food manufacturers, and engineering firms. Internet-related stocks didn't need any of those things to succeed. As a result, the prices were propelled upward, helped by fund promoters in the US and UK who bought the shares. But reality intervened in early 2000. Dotcom became dotcon or dotbomb. Many shares joined the 90 per cent club, meaning their prices fell by that amount. Others made the 99 per cent club. And a lot went bust. (If you're interested, check out the Web site tulipmania.com, which foresaw the panic and chronicled the dotcom demise. And, bonus time, the site also provides a link to details about the first mania in this list – the Dutch tulip madness.)

Looking at the Emotions That Drive Investors

Two specific emotions often drive investors to make the decisions they do. These powerful emotions are greed and fear. Knowing the effects they can have on investors is a powerful tool.

Greed is the accelerator

Greed is what you want that goes beyond pure need. Granted, negative connotations are sometimes associated with greed, but consider these facts: Without the greed for more and better food, we'd still have the monotonous diet of medieval times. Without the greed for spices and other treasures, Columbus would've never set out for the East and landed in what became America. And without the greed to go faster, we'd all still be on horseback. But although greed powers civilisation, no two investors act identically.

Fear is the brake

People often ask me why share prices move so wildly during a very brief timescale when little, if anything, has changed in the underlying company. They also want to know why downward movements tend to be more violent than upward gains.

I reply that the stock market is like the first day of post-Christmas sales in posh department stores. If someone shouts, 'Designer frocks are reduced by another 75 per cent!', there's a big rush to the women's clothing floors. That's the greed factor in action. But note that not everyone joins the rush. Men, for example, just stand and stare.

But there's another factor to consider. If someone at that same posh department store shouts, 'Fire!', then *everyone* rushes for the exits. That's the fear factor in action. And it takes only one or two people to panic for even more people to panic, thus reducing the hope of an orderly evacuation. The result? It could take some time for that store's reputation as a safe environment to return.

Coming full circle here, the scenario is much the same with investment markets. And the point I want to stress is that fear is a stronger emotion than greed. When fear, justified or not, gains the upper hand, pandemonium can break out as investors rush for the exit and the safety of other investments.

So as an investor, how do you deal with the market pandemonium caused by fear – and with the prices that are falling all around you?

Well, first, know this fact up front: When a real stocks and shares panic is going on, don't even think about beating the professionals to the selling exit. Their training makes them faster and heavier than you. And they have a direct line to the stockbroking professionals who'll deal with their £10m selling order before they even pick up the phone or look at the screen for your £1,000 worth of business.

So if you can't beat the herd as it thunders to the exit, you need to develop other strategies for the inevitable bear markets. (Falling share prices are known, for reasons now lost in history, as *bear markets*. Investors who think prices will fall are *bearish*. The opposite, rising share prices, are called *bull markets*. Optimists are, of course, *bullish*.)

Here are some strategies to consider (check out Part II of this book for specific directions on buying and selling shares):

- ✔ Sit tight. If you don't need to sell, don't.
- ✔ Look at your investments and assess whether they're directly affected by whatever is behind the panic or whether they're just being pushed along by the market as a whole.

- ✔ Be counter-intuitive. Use the panic to buy selected investments at knock-down prices.

- ✔ Consider potential tax bills if you decide to sell. The UK's Capital Gains Tax can take up to 18 per cent of your profit.

- ✔ Use the bear market period to hone your research. Filing away all the negatives that come out during this time is valuable for future reference in a bull market, when all you hear is positive talk.

- ✔ Don't sit up all night worrying. It won't help!

And here are some tips to keep in mind during this tough time:

- ✔ Time is the healer. Share prices have always eventually recovered in major markets such as the US and UK.

- ✔ You're still earning dividends from your shares. They tend not to fall with downward stock price moves.

- ✔ If you fancied a share at £1, it could be better value at 75p, assuming that nothing else has changed.

- ✔ This year's big losers are often next year's major gainers.

Debunking the 'Stock Market as a Casino' Psychology

Stock market columns in newspapers often refer to investors as *punters* and talk about *having a fun flutter*. So it's not surprising that many people see the stock market as a giant casino, admittedly without the overblown decorations of the Monte Carlo model.

It's true that some comparisons can be made. For example, in the stock market casino, you pay your admission fee in the form of brokerage commission (the percentage you pay a stock broker for working for you) or upfront charges on an investment fund, and your fate is decided by the roll of a dividend increase (that's good news – it means you will get a bigger cheque for each share you own) or the cuts in an earnings warning (markets don't like companies that let you think they will do well and then change their minds).

In addition, some superficial comparisons can be made, not the least of which is that when you lose, all you have to say is that the fruit machines were coming up with lemons instead of plums.

Regardless of these types of comparisons, gambling and investing are very different ventures. This section sorts out the differences.

How things work in gambling

In gambling, you're totally dependent on some random acts. For example, in a roulette game, you have no control over the wheel and no way of knowing which number will turn up after the wheel stops spinning. All you can do is ration out your bets in such a way that you minimise your losses.

You may gain in the short term on a few lucky choices. But if you play long enough, you will lose, thanks to the zero on the wheel, because when it turns up, the house wins everything bet on black or red, on odd or even, and on individual numbers. Because zero turns up once in 37 times, it's equal to chipping away approximately 3 per cent of all the money bet. And wheels that contain a double zero, well, they double that tax.

Now consider for a minute another gambling game – the fruit machine. In theory, the fruit machine is a zero sum game. It can only pay out what's been put in. But even the most optimistic gambler knows that those machines are made to repay only about 80 per cent of what's put in, so the casino company is bound to win.

How things work in investing

Investing is different from gambling. You aren't totally dependent on random events like the drawing of a card or the spinning of a wheel. You know beforehand many (although not all) facts about where you're placing your money. Your skill comes from evaluating these facts and then allowing a percentage for the unknown.

Equally important, time is on your side. You aren't forced into an instant appraisal. No one is (or at least shouldn't be) hassling you to make a decision on what to do with your money. And the game isn't over when the fruit machine shudders to a halt or the roulette wheel stops spinning or the cards are finally put face up. Stocks and shares have very long lives – most have no set expiry date. As an investor, you always live to fight another day unless your investment goes bust.

But most important of all, investment is not a zero sum game. New money comes into the market all the time. New investors put in fresh cash, and in addition, either knowingly or from pension fund deductions, the companies into which you buy also put fresh money into the equation through dividend payments on shares and interest on bonds.

Trading too much can backfire!

One of the wonders of investing is that the fundamentals driving those involved – a mix of greed and fear – never, ever change. So although the following case comes from a 1998 study by US researchers Brad Barber and Terrance Odean, the story is as relevant today as it ever was.

The researchers showed how many investors earn poor returns because they overtrade with too many buy-and-sell decisions. And they make matters worse because they tend to go for smaller companies that are more volatile.

Barber and Odean looked at the trading records of 60,000 small investors in the US. They found that these individuals managed to beat the averages of all share prices and indexes such as the UK's FTSE 100 (the Footsie) or the US Standard & Poor's 500 by 0.6 per cent per year. Not a lot, no, but it builds up to big sums over a lifetime of investing.

So far, so good.

Now for the bad news. Because these investors tended to buy and sell often, and because the gap between the price at which you buy a share and that at which the share is sold to you is wider in small-company stocks than big-company stocks, the average investor paid more than 2.4 per cent of his or her money into trading costs.

So the original 0.6 per cent gain turned into a 1.8 per cent per year loss.

What's worse, the most enthusiastic traders lost 5.6 per cent in costs, so they underperformed the averages by 5 per cent per year.

Note that this study was completed before the dotcom boom. But during the dotcom boom, many small shareholders bought and sold several times a day, often encouraged by online broker tariffs that encouraged frequent dealings. This activity would've worsened the figures. And had this research been carried out in the UK, the figures would've looked worse too. All share purchases in the UK attract a 0.5 per cent stamp duty tax.

For some investors, overtrading occurred because buying and selling shares had become a hobby and those investors had become addicted. Psychologists say that over-activity is a way some people control their environment. But sadly, this psychological requirement some people have (and it's close to compulsive gambling) runs counter to the need for good money discipline.

The moral? Don't overdo share buying. Doing it occasionally is inexpensive, but it can eat into profits if you let it control you.

Most investors just look at the share price but ignore the dividends – the half-yearly (sometimes four times a year) payments where companies divide out part of their profits for the benefit of shareholders. That's a big mistake. Money is money wherever it comes from. All those small amounts add up to big cash over time. Always remember that a dividend bird in the hand is worth a lot more than *maybe money* in the bush.

Two dangers investors share with gamblers

Even though gambling and investing are two different ventures, there are two dangers investors sometimes share with casino-frequenters.

The gambler's fallacy

The *gambler's fallacy* is that the past can affect the present and the future. Say, for example, that you have a two-pound coin fresh from the mint. You toss it once. It lands heads up. What will the next throw bring? You really have no idea. So you toss the coin again, and it lands heads up again. How will it land next time? You're not too sure, but you think it might land tails up. After all, it's landed heads up twice and the coin is perfect. But it doesn't. And with each successive head, you get more desperate and your belief grows that it should go to tails.

Suppose, also, that you're betting on these coin tosses. With each loss, you double up your original stake in an increasingly desperate attempt to make your fortune. After ten losses in a row, your original £10 bet has now become £20,480. That's the gambler's fallacy in action – and the negative result it can bring.

You can see the gambler's fallacy in investments. So-called experts quoted in newspapers say the market is going up (or down). On what do they base their assertion. Often it is no more than the direction last month has to repeat itself this month; or that it's time the market changed direction. Distrust this – it's no different from the coin-tosser hoping for tails after a run of heads or the coin-tosser who believes that a run of heads will result in another head.

The gambler's fallacy is also present when so-called stock market historians attempt to call the market by reference to the number of months since an event took place. History tells you about the past. And it suggests that all empires eventually crumble. But could anyone have used the timing of the Roman Empire to predict how long the British Empire would last?

Overconfidence

Overconfidence leads you not so much to magnify possible gains but to minimise the effect of losses. 'It can't happen to me' is the way people express this kind of overconfidence. But, oh yes, it can.

Overconfidence can also cause you to keep increasing your investment stakes to recoup previous losses. Doing so is really easy if you trade electronically via the Internet. Just a few clicks, and you've committed yourself to a deal.

Combine the gambler's fallacy with overconfidence, and you could move into short-term investment tactics such as spread bets and options and be asked to pay out more than you've invested.

Sound Tips for the Cautious Investor

It's only natural to have doubts as you consider investments. Having doubts is actually a good thing. Otherwise, you'd run into the overconfidence trap (see the 'Overconfidence' section earlier in this chapter).

So if you're not quite sure about whether to invest, why not invest *part* of the cash you have and keep the rest for later when you gain more experience?

Or maybe look for a lower-risk alternative. For example, instead of making investment choices yourself, look for a low-cost collective fund such as an investment or unit trust. Dealing with one diversified fund is easier than attempting to build your own portfolio.

If you think the time is right for venturing outside of cash, you may want to try one or some of the following. (All these options are examined in later chapters of this book, and I spell out the advantages and drawbacks of each one. This list provides a starting point for your research.)

- **A tracker fund.** This type of fund follows a stock market index such as the FTSE 100 (the Footsie) up and down. This option is a good idea if you want to be in shares but have no idea which ones to buy or which fund manager to back.

- **A no-lose fund.** You put your money in a special fund, usually for five years. At the end of the specified time, you either get your money back without any deduction or, if the index has risen, your original money enhanced by the percentage rise.

- **A bond fund.** Your money goes into fixed-interest securities tied either to governments or companies.

- **A distribution fund.** This type of fund focuses on a mix of lower-risk shares, bonds, cash, and property.

For those of you who are seriously scared, your motto should be safety first. Here are a few suggestions:

- If the thought of losing any of your money gives you the heebie-jeebies, then don't invest in anything that could cause you grief or sleepless nights. It's as simple as that. There's no point in worrying yourself sick.

- Don't just go for the deal your bank or building society offers. Instead, shop around for the best deal using Internet listings or a magazine such as *Moneyfacts*.

- You can invest up to £3,600 a year into a mini-cash Individual Savings Account from April 2008. That way, you won't pay tax on your interest.

Chapter 4

Squaring Risks with Returns

● ●

In This Chapter

▶ Working out risk and reward theory in practice

▶ Deciding the level of gains you want

▶ Calculating what you could get

▶ Knowing about the advantages of diversification

▶ Keeping an eye on how time works for you

● ●

*W*hen we walk down the street or drive a car, we're aware of risks. We know, for example, that we might risk life and limb crossing a road when the Red Man symbol is displayed. And we know that our safety (not to mention driver's licence) is threatened if we drive 60mph in a 30mph zone.

Granted, if we run helter-skelter down the street or drive recklessly down the road, ignoring everyone and every rule, we might arrive more quickly at our destination. But the faster we go and the more corners we cut, the greater the chance of losing everything. So we generally take simple precautions to avoid risks. That way, we make some progress through life.

But what if we never took risks at all and, instead, wrapped ourselves in cotton wool? If we only walked on perfectly kept, deserted fields and drove on empty roads at exactly 20mph? We'd simply not get anywhere, and our lives would be boringly empty. We'd make no progress through life. We'd be taking the risk of missing out on something interesting and perhaps profitable.

The same can be said about investing. Investment risk is no different from the risks of daily life. There are steady-as-you-go investments that give a moderate rate of return with perhaps the occasional loss (after all, even the most careful driver can have a bad experience). There are hell-for-leather investments that can offer massive returns or huge losses. And there's the investment equivalent of surrounding yourself with layers of cotton wool – where nothing will happen at all.

In this chapter, you examine investment risks – specifically, the benefits and drawbacks of various investment possibilities and ways to increase your odds of successful returns.

Examining Two Investing Principles You Should Never Forget

Here are a couple of clichés that sound banal but should be carved in mirror writing on every investor's forehead, so she or he can read them first thing each morning when facing the wash basin:

- There's no gain without pain. This means that in your daily life, you have to move out of the couch potato position to achieve.

- You have to speculate to accumulate. If you don't take some chances with your money, you'll never get anywhere.

Financial markets – indeed, all of capitalism – work on these two principles.

Here's an example to help you see the importance of these two philosophies. Suppose that you're running a company and need £10m to expand your firm into a new product. You could borrow the money from the bank knowing that you'll pay 10 per cent interest a year whether the new venture works or not. If the new venture fails, you still have to pay the bank its £10m plus interest even if it means selling the rest of the business. But if your business goes on to be a winner, the bank still only gets its £10m plus interest while your fortune soars.

Alternatively, you could raise the cash through an issue of new shares, where the advantages for you are no fixed-interest costs and, if the project is a flop, your investors suffer rather than you. They could lose all their money. That's the risk they run. But if the venture is a success, the shareholders receive dividends from you and see the value of their stake rise due to everyone demanding a share of the action. You shared the risk with others, so now they get a slice of the reward.

Now suppose that no one had taken any risks. You decided not to expand into the new product. The bank manager vetoed all loans. And the share buyers sat on their hands and kept their money under their beds. There'd be no pain – no one would lose – but there'd also be no gain for you, the bank, the investors, or the wider economy.

Granted, all these potential participants could've argued that they'd taken a risk-free stance with their cash. But had they? No. They'd taken the very severe risk of missing out on something positive. They didn't speculate. They didn't accumulate.

Absolute safety means little or no reward

The most secure place to keep your money is in a low-interest guaranteed account from the government's National Savings & Investments department. In certain circumstances, this is a good place for some of your money. But unless you have very good reasons to deposit your money there, you risk losing out on potentially better investments.

Putting your money in such an account also presents a second danger. When you protect a piece of china in cotton wool and bubble wrap, you expect it still to be there years later, but money is different. Its buying value erodes each year due to rising prices. You'll go backward in real terms if all you do is put all your money in the safest possible home. And the longer you look at investing your money, the truer that becomes.

Suppose that two people coming back from the Second World War in 1945 each had £100 to invest. One person invested the money in a basket of shares, each with an uncertain future, and the other person put the money in super-safe UK government stocks. Both investors told their family and friends that they'd re-invest all the dividends and interest they received.

By the end of 2006, the investor who took the safe route had a fund worth £4,322 according to figures from Barclays Capital. But when inflation is taken into the calculation, the £100 is only worth £156. And it took until 1996 before that original £100 regained its value in terms of what it would buy on the day it was invested. You could only have bought half as much again as you might have done in 1945 – not much gain for over 60 years.

The shares investor did far better. Although some of the original investments failed, more did well. Despite the pain of a roller-coaster ride at times, the investment showed big gains. On paper, the £100 became £125,243 (almost twice as much as four years previously). Rising prices and recent falling stock markets took their toll, but speculating did produce an accumulation. Adjusted for the cost of living, that original £100 became £4,531, so this investor multiplied what the money could buy by some 45 times.

Determining the Return You Want from Your Money

The starting point of any risk-reward assessment is to determine the return you want from your money. The harder you want your money to work, the more risks you need to take.

You may want your money just to maintain its buying power – to keep up with inflation. Or you may want to see it grow in real terms by a relatively small amount – just enough to keep ahead. Or you may want some aggressive growth to fund a pet project. Suppose, for example, that you have a 10-year-old child who's been given a £10,000 lump sum by an adoring relation who had one proviso: The money must be spent on university education when the child reaches 18.

The most basic education costs £10,000. But most will need more – especially if they wish to study for a post-graduate qualification. So what rate of return over the eight years would you need to produce the result you want? Inflation, which erodes your target figure in real spending terms, investment fees, and taxation have been ignored here to simplify the figures:

£10,000: 0%

£12,000: 2.31%

£14,000: 4.3%

£16,000: 6.05%

£18,000: 7.62%

£20,000: 9.05%

£25,000: 12.14%

£30,000: 14.72%

£35,000: 16.95%

£40,000: 18.92%

The higher figures are more than what you're likely to earn on your money unless:

✔ You're prepared to take big risks, including losing your original capital,

or

✔ Inflation returns with a vengeance so you appear to obtain substantial gains even if they don't translate into real spending power at the shops.

To show you how your money could grow, I want to give you recalculated figures using the official rates for salespeople from the Financial Services Authority (FSA). The FSA first instituted these rates, which are adjusted from time to time, to prevent unscrupulous salesfolk from coming up with the first growth rate they could think of and then multiplying that by their phone number (and yours as well if they really fancied earning extra commission that day). The current rates are 7 per cent for untaxed investments such as pension plans and Individual Savings Accounts (ISAs), and 6 per cent for taxed investments such as unit trusts, life assurance savings bonds, and investment trust savings plans.

The FSA's official rates aren't what they seem. No one ever earns the full rate, so you can't just assume 6 per cent or 7 per cent as the likely targets. Instead, the quoted rates are cut back by costs and commissions so firms have to show actual returns adjusted for these expenses. That means you get less. Here's an example. The paperwork for a £100 investment would show £106 at the end of the year at 6 per cent. But a 1 per cent cost structure brings it down to £105.

So take a look at the recalculated figures to see how long it would take your £10,000 to grow assuming a 6 per cent annual return:

£10,000: No time

£12,000: 3 years and 1 month

£14,000: 5 years and 9 months

£16,000: 8 years and 1 month

£18,000: 10 years and 1 month

£20,000: 11 years and 10 months

£25,000: 15 years and 9 months

£30,000: 18 years and 10 months

£35,000: 21 years and 6 months

£40,000: 23 years and 9 months

Investments are for the medium to long term – from five years upward. So over this timeframe, what can you expect? The following sections tell you.

The likely return from shares

Anyone reading newspaper headlines or watching television news can be forgiven for believing that shares only go in one direction. Over the past decade or so, the stories of the dotcom boom shouted that 'prices can only go up'. Then when that bust, the stories changed to 'shares can only go down'. And when shares reached rock bottom in 2003 and started to rise again, all the media tales were optimism, happiness, and light.

This tells you two things about shares. Firstly, the media doesn't present a balanced view. Secondly, and more importantly, the media fails to understand that shares work because you have to take a long-term view.

Shares are volatile, but over the very long term, say the whole of the last century, a basket of typical equities has produced average annual gains of around 12 per cent before tax.

Using different start and finish dates can produce almost any other figure you care to think of. But however you cut it, the trend in share prices is upward provided that you're patient. No one would bother to take the inherent risks with shares if he or she didn't expect to make greater gains than with bonds, property, or cash over the longer term.

When the shares pay more than the savings

There's a fine balancing act between the capital value of a share and the dividend you get from that share – as the holders of what was then Abbey National found out a few years ago.

For a time, putting your money into Abbey National shares produced higher annual amounts than placing your cash in even one of the bank's top-paying savings accounts. Lots of newspaper columns told their readers to take their cash out of the savings accounts and buy the shares instead, as the annual cash from the dividends was more than half as much again as the yearly return from the savings account. This plan sounded like a no-brainer, even after taking the cost of buying shares into the equation.

It was a no-brainer, but not in the way the press pundits expected. A reason always exists why a dividend is very high – usually because it comes from a company riding for a fall. And fall Abbey National did. Shares more than halved as profits and prospects tumbled. With far lower earnings, Abbey National couldn't afford to reward its shareholders so royally. So all those investors who switched cash into the shares lost a large part of their money.

But Abbey National had to keep up rates for its savers or they would all have moved their cash to find more competitive accounts.

The upshot was that Abbey National shares fell so low that Spanish rival Banco Santander made a successful takeover bid for the bank.

For those who held their nerve and didn't panic, though, this story has a happier ending. Santander issued its own shares to replace those of Abbey National. Since then, Santander shares have seen gains.

The return from shares comes in two forms, although neither is guaranteed, let alone even promised:

- Dividends
- Capital gains

Dividends are the way companies have of returning part of the profits they make, or the reserves they've built up over good years, to the part-owners of the firm. That's you, the shareholder.

These are small amounts compared to your initial investment. But if rein-vested into more shares, they can boost your holding. A 3 per cent annual dividend after any tax reinvested would add around 40 per cent to your shareholding after 10 years.

The beauty of dividends is that you should get them whether share prices as a whole are going up or down. Dividends are regular, and a company cutting out or missing a payment is a very bad sign indeed. Oddly enough, missing dividend payments was the only thing Northern Rock didn't do as it fell from grace in 2007. Even when Northern Rock was in severe trouble, the bank maintained its ambition to pay shareholders their twice-yearly cheque. The dividend was only cancelled when it was pointed out that this dividend would have been paid from rescue money supplied by the Bank of England. This was further bad, but hardly unsurprising, news for shareholders. (Refer to Chapter 1 for more information.)

The second return from shares is that the capital goes up. Is this a sure thing? No. But should it happen? Yes.

Adding capital gains to the dividend produces the likely annual gain. A typical share offers a 3.7 per cent dividend. And a reasonably well-run company should be able to produce about 5 per cent a year growth on top of inflation, which is now around 2.5 per cent a year. Add all this up, and your shares should produce around 11 per cent a year.

What you get from a share depends on the exact price you paid. If you bought at the top of the market and the share subsequently halves in value before returning to the 10 to 11 per cent I suggest, it could take the best part of a decade before you're back on the growth track.

The likely return from bonds

Are you an avid reader of Victorian novels? If so, you know that the heroines always know the value of the hero's (or villain's) fortune by turning his lump sum wealth into so much per year. And the figure selected is always 5 per cent because this was the long-term return on investments the Victorians expected.

And how do heroines of Victorian novels always know this? Because in Victorian days, most money went into bonds. Those from the government were the safest. Those from railway companies and iron works were riskier. So although the Victorian novel heroine may not be able to recognise all that much of the world around her, she is at home with the finances on bonds.

Nothing much has changed now that inflation is once again moderate. As a result, her 5 per cent isn't a bad long-term guess for today. You'll get a little less if you head for the super-safety of UK government bonds, or *gilts* as they're known in the money trade. And you'll get a percentage point or two more if you aim for *corporate bonds*, bonds issued by commercial companies raising loans.

But how do you get the 8, 9, or 10 per cent on offer from some bonds and bond funds? Easy! You just aim at bonds – known as *junk bonds* – from firms that have a dodgy track record. In addition, the bonds of some countries have junk status because the country's underlying finances are a mess. Nations from Latin America or south-east Asia have often been guilty parties.

If you're willing to take the risk that they'll miss a payment or, worse, fail to give back your capital on time or at all, then you may be rewarded for your bravery by the potential doubling of your return over safe bonds. But although you may end up with more, you may equally get your financial head blown off in a crisis.

Investors who like to sleep at night should look at bonds paying out a maximum of 6.5 to 7 per cent. Bond fund purchasers should go no higher than 5.5 to 6 per cent. Why the gap? Because the fund carries an annual fee, typically 1 per cent, which must be paid out from somewhere! And it's usually from the income on the bond.

The likely return from property

According to the Nationwide Building Society, the average price of a modern property throughout the UK was around £184,000 in Autumn 2007. Fifteen years before, in 1992, the price of that same typical home stood at £51,630. Track back to 1983, and it was just under £26,000. And three decades or so ago in 1973, it was £9,800.

But for purposes of this discussion, leave aside what you might make from your own home because you have to live somewhere, don't always have much choice on where you live, and would be paying rent if you weren't buying. Instead, think in terms of commercial property.

Professionals invest in commercial property, such as factories, office blocks, and shopping centres. You can't go out and buy a business park unless you have tens of millions and the ability to manage your investment. But you can tap into commercial property through a number of funds.

What you get from a property investment comes from two sources. One source is the rent tenants pay you. You won't get this straight into your pocket, though. You'll have to find management costs, repairs, interest on borrowings, and tax.

The second source is the hoped-for gain in the underlying value of the buildings. Add the two together, and you get the full return.

Since 1971, the overall annual returns from property have only declined in four separate years according to figures from experts Investment Property Databank. One year was 1974, when a financial crisis occurred in the UK. The other three years were during the economic downturn at the start of the 1990s. In addition, during a handful of other years, property failed to keep up with inflation.

In present-day conditions, you can expect to earn around 7 to 9 per cent a year averaged over long periods. So you can expect more from property than from bonds but less than from shares. However, you don't need to repair a bond, have security guards for bonds, or worry about a bond going out of fashion. And properties come with more expenses.

Commercial property is different from domestic property. Figures for the two seldom go in tandem.

The likely return from a cash account

Don't expect too much from a cash account. In return for the security, you'll do well to get around 5.5 to 6 per cent from a bank or building society. You may get a lot less. You should only invest in cash for safety, never for the long term unless it is of paramount importance that you know exactly what you will have in the future to meet a known financial need such as a child's education.

Since 1971, cash has only been the best performing asset type during two years – 1974 and 1990. And both years, the financial system was in trouble. Cash was the worst place to put your money during at least 12 separate years. And over almost any long period, cash has been easily out-gunned by bonds and property, and it's been beaten out of sight by shares.

The building society or National Savings is the starting point for any calculation of whether a risk could be worthwhile. There's no point investing in a speculative enterprise if the best you can foresee is a fraction of a percentage point above the bank branch.

Leaving medium- to long-term money in a current bank account is a guaranteed loser. Rates can be as low as 0.1 per cent, and yes, that's before tax on this virtually invisible return at 20 per cent for most people and 40 per cent for the better off. Inflation means your money is worth less each year.

The government inflation target is 2.5 per cent, so your money needs to earn that much after tax to stay level. For a basic-rate taxpayer, that means a headline rate of around 3.2 per cent, and a top-rate taxpayer needs 4 per cent just to go nowhere. Shopping around and being prepared to accept restrictions on withdrawals should produce around 4 per cent.

What happened to the 10 per cent rates on bank and building society accounts of a decade or so ago? They disappeared along with high inflation. A 10 per cent rate when prices are rising at 12 per cent equals a guaranteed annual loss – even before taxation. At least a 4 per cent savings account when inflation is 2.5 per cent offers the chance of slight gains.

The likely return from other assets

Investors have seen spectacular returns from gold, diamonds, works of art, and even special shares offering guaranteed tickets at the centre court at Wimbledon for the All-England championships. Others have made big money out of racehorses, vintage wine, and stamp collections.

But all these ventures demand a whole lot of specialist knowledge combined with a whole load of luck. Fans of this sort of thing tend to flag up the good times and ignore the bad years.

Figures are fairly unreliable because you're always comparing apples with bananas. A painting by Pablo Picasso may double in value over a year, but that doesn't say anything about a Salvador Dali or even other works by Picasso.

Many illegal investment schemes have been offered in areas such as stamp collecting and fine wines. These schemes offer big gains for supposed small risk. The authorities have shut down some of these ventures but usually not before hapless investors have lost their savings.

Hedge fund returns are all over the place. Much depends on what the fund sets out to do. Some go for maximum returns. Others aim at protecting your money.

Increasing Your Chances of Successful Returns

Risk and reward, risk and regret can't be separated. You must take risks and put your head above the cash investment parapet if you want to win.

Now turn risk on its head and call it opportunity. It's really the same thing, but now you have a positive phrase. You can increase your chances of success by diversifying (not putting all your investment eggs into one basket) and being patient.

Plenty of factors affect your chances of success

Suppose that you acquire shares in ABC Bank and XYZ Insurance, perhaps as a result of free share handouts. Obviously, you have to work out whether the opportunities in each company are worthwhile. And that's something you look at in detail in Part II.

But for now, you need to consider the bigger picture altogether. No company is an island, and none lives in a vacuum. Plenty more factors can enhance your opportunities or increase your chances of making a mistake:

- **Currencies.** Foreign exchange markets can have an impact on your investment. They have a habit of moving in slow trend lines, although they jump about at the umpteenth decimal place all the time. Each day, even each minute, exchange rates can go either way by very small amounts. There are no investment straight lines!

- **Interest rates.** You may invest in a brilliant company, but if interest rates go up, it will be less attractive because the cash it needs from the bank for expansion will cost it more. Rising interest rates are bad news for almost everyone other than holders of cash.

- **Stock markets.** When share prices are generally booming, even badly run companies do reasonably well. And when share prices are falling, the best organised firms with the greatest prospects tend to lose out.

- **Inflation.** Nope. Not car tyre pressure but rising prices. Inflation can be good for some sectors, such as retailers, because it takes the pressure off, meaning they don't have to run perpetual sales and price cuts.

- **The economy.** You can't really beat it. If it looks good, everything shines; when it turns down, only a handful of assets manage to hold their heads up.

Diversification is your best friend

Diversification is putting your eggs in many baskets. So if you trip up and choose a poor investment, you still have some capital left to help your finances recover.

Understanding the multi-layered approach that professionals use

Professional investors consider what the fund they manage is supposed to achieve. If the fund's main role is to provide a regular pension income for those whose retirement needs it has to meet, the fund goes in the main for safer assets, such as bonds, property, and cash. But if the fund advertises itself as a route into, say, higher risk Far Eastern share markets, it must be restricted to these investments, although the fund may have a small percentage in cash to give it the flexibility to move around stock markets.

Those running a fund with a wide remit, such as a life-insurance-with-profits fund (the basis of many retirement and endowment plans as well as the cornerstone of investment bonds sold to older people), work out their asset allocation as percentages of the whole fund between the main asset classes, including shares, bonds, cash, and property.

Within each of those asset areas, they then buy a wide range of investment assets. The idea is not to be caught out if one area catches a cold. Within property, for example, a fund manager may buy some office blocks, shopping centres, and industrial premises. Within shares, a well-diversified fund manager may have holdings in the UK, the US, mainland Europe, and the Far East.

Wide-remit managers then further subdivide. Say, for example, that a fund manager has holdings in the UK, the US, mainland Europe, and the Far East. Regarding the fund focusing on UK shares, the fund manager may decide to have a percentage in different stock market company sectors, such as bank stocks and engineering companies.

Only after looking at all those various things do fund managers look at individual shares, deciding to hold pharmaceutical company A rather than B.

Note that those running narrowly focused funds may not bother with sectors. And they concentrate even less on wider factors. But they still diversify so that they don't have too much riding on one fund. They know that companies and share prices can fall apart very quickly. (Examples include Polly Peck in the late 1980s, Marconi in the 1990s, and perhaps most spectacularly because of its public profile, Northern Rock in 2007.)

Concentrating too much on one or two investments is a mistake. Another mistake is not looking at all your wealth. If your pension fund is riding on UK shares, then you should consider other points in your own investment strategy for money under your direct control.

Spreading your money in practice

Suppose that someone gave you £1,000 in 1971. In addition, assume that you managed to avoid the temptation to spend it all (it's big money, as, after adjusting for inflation, you would need at least £10,000 now to have the same spending power) and invested it instead. And, to simplify matters, say that you had a choice of just four investments – cash at the building society, UK government bonds, a commercial property portfolio, and the UK stock market. The results would have been widely different depending on how you had invested that money. Our timeframe is well over the span of a generation, so plenty of ups and downs have occurred. They are all well documented by Barclays Bank offshoot Barclays Capital in its excellent annual number-crunching exercise, whose figures we mostly use here.

If you had put all your money into one area and left all the income and capital gains to grow back in your fund, your £1,000 would've been £15,750 in the building society by the end of 2006 – sounds pretty good, but that figure is before the taxman has taken his substantial slice. Putting your money into government bonds would've given you a more respectable £37,250. Property would've fared even better – around £53,000, or more in hotspots such as central London. And despite the up and down nature of shares, an equity portfolio would be valued at £111,000, again not counting tax.

Now had you been really cautious and divided your money into four equal parts for our four asset classes, you'd still have a considerable £54,250, or more than five times the amount you would've needed to keep up with inflation. Most of the gains would have come from shares.

But what if you had been a real speculator, believing that you knew the best of the four each January 1 for the following 12 months? If you had perfect foresight, your £1,000 would've grown to over £2million. Yippee!

And, finally, what if you had got it wrong each time, picking the following year's disaster zone? You would have around £500 – just around a half of what you started with. What would've bought a new car in 1971 was just about enough for a medium-priced bike by 2007!

By the way, as you're assessing all the preceding figures, keep in mind that all those figures ignore tax and the cost of moving money from one asset to another. These factors would've lessened all these returns.

Over that timeframe, cash was the best asset in only 2 years and the worst in 12; the government stock portfolio was a superstar in 5 years and the worst in 8; property was the best 11 times and the worst 6; shares were the best in 17 separate years but the worst in 8.

Note that the great outperformance in shares wasn't gradual. It came in fits and starts. During 8 of the 36 years, the index made 25 per cent or more in gains in a 12-month period. But bad years were really bad – down as much as 50 per cent in the very worst 12-month period. And if you scratch those figures more closely, you find that the big gains in equities were concentrated on just a relatively low number of days in that period. If you missed them because you were moving in and out of the market, you might have fared little better than with your money in the safe and solid building society.

Patience is your pal

To be a good investor, you need to have a good strategy and good diversification, but to be a savvy investor, you also need patience and time. Your investments may need years to mature. There may be more days when your investments go nowhere or down than when they rise. But when they do increase, it can be by substantial amounts over a short time.

Your own time horizons determine the risks you can afford to take. Investment is not a short-term punt on financial markets. It requires at least five years, preferably longer. Short-termism can also increase your costs and your tax bill.

Chapter 5

Being Aware of the Small Print

- -

In This Chapter

▶ Knowing that shares can go down as well as up

▶ Knowing that bonds can go bust

▶ Understanding that super strategies can turn into sand

▶ Being aware that property investments can crumble

▶ Avoiding the tax freedom trap

▶ Putting a stop to scamsters

- -

So you've taken a long, hard look at how ready you are to take the risks inherent in investing. You know that you have to take chances and step, a little or a lot, into the financial unknown. And you know that if you weren't prepared to take a risk, you'd stand no chance of beating the bank or the building society. And now you've made up your mind to invest rather than merely save. (If you *haven't* taken a long, hard look at these things, then you really, really need to. Look through Chapter 1 to make sure that you're even ready to invest and check out Chapter 4, which is all about investment risk.)

Congratulations on making an informed decision. Now you have just one hurdle to cross before you're ready to look at the nitty-gritty of investing. That one hurdle is getting into the habit of reading the small print in investment situations before looking at the headlines. You're in the right place because this chapter tells you all about those nasties.

'Um, Where Do I Actually Find the Small Print?'

Small print exists in virtually all investment situations. You'll find the small print in places like the bottoms of adverts and way down through official documentation. Small print is virtually invisible for a purpose. It has to comply with the law (which never defines how small is small) but does not draw attention to itself.

At times, you won't always understand what you read. When that happens, ask the person you're buying from. If the reply is still incomprehensible, then shred the deal. Plenty of other opportunities are out there with words that make sense.

Know that if small print exists, you'll be deemed to have read and understood it, even if it's located on page 199 of a document and written in language only the lawyer who wrote it could possibly follow. The Financial Ombudsman Service (the last port of call before court for complaints about financial products) won't look kindly on you if you complain that you lost your money through not reading the small print.

And know that even if you're buying and selling shares for yourself without professional advice, you'll probably have to sign a piece of paper accepting all responsibility for your own actions. Buying without a broker or adviser giving specific advice is called *execution only* dealing. Expect to see phrases such as 'You are responsible for selecting the stocks and shares, and you take full responsibility for the outcome of your investments and your actions.'

Shares Can Go Down As Well As Up

Seems simple enough: Shares can go up and down. Yet that information took many people by surprise from 2000 onward because they'd been lulled into a false sense of security by the silver-tongued investment sellers who convinced customers (and possibly even themselves) that share prices would go on rising forever. 'Treat any price reverse as a reason to buy more,' they said.

But you need to be prepared for the value of your shares to go down, and the small print in investment documents addresses this very issue. The wording is often something like this: *The value of your investment and the income you receive from it can go up or down, and there is no guarantee you will get your full investment back.*

The small-print people could've added that there's no guarantee you'll get anything back at all. But otherwise, this information is clear and means what it says. So take it to heart.

Of course, shares can go up, too! Anyone who bailed out when shares had more or less halved in value from their 2000 peak to their floor three years later missed out on the big rises that took many share prices back to where they were before, if not higher. But don't treat this paragraph as an excuse to plunge in regardless. Some shares and some investment funds bought in late 1999 were worthless by 2003. Others, in unfashionable areas such as tobacco and mining, did really well.

Even the best companies' share values go backward when shares are falling all around. Sometimes the top companies suffer unduly. When share purchasers want out quickly, they sell the good stuff first because the rubbish is harder to shift. (Think of which properties in your area would be easiest and quickest to sell if the owners needed to raise cash.)

Besides being prepared for the value of your shares to go down, be aware of the following truisms about past performance:

> ✔ **Past performance isn't necessarily a guide to future performance.** The Financial Services Authority (FSA) says that there's no relationship between the future and the past. All too many funds like to sell their wares on the basis of past performance, and they show this in the most flattering light (surprise, surprise!). Investment companies not surprisingly disagree with the FSA as they spend a fortune advertising their past successes, hoping customers accept that the future will be the same. Academic research supports the FSA line, with some experts reckoning that the past of a fund has no more relevance to the future than using past winning lottery numbers as a guide to winning the next draw.
>
> Three degrees of falsehood exist: lies, damned lies, and investment statistics from companies trying to sell you something.
>
> ✔ **Past performance may not necessarily be repeated.** Even if an investment remains successful, it's not likely to be successful in the same way as before. The investment may do better or worse. In any case, it all depends on which time period you use for the comparison.

You also need to know that if you buy individual shares rather than collective investment funds, you normally only receive specific warnings if you buy during the initial public offering (or flotation) period or other time when new shares are covered by an official prospectus. Keep in mind that any forecast of future business is based on assumptions that the directors of the company consider reasonable from their point of view. They want your money, so they put the most optimistic spin on the future.

The specific warnings from the company, which you'll find in prospectuses or other cash-raising documents, may be worded something like this:

> ✔ *The price you get for your shares should you wish to sell may be influenced by a large number of factors, some specific to the company and some extraneous.* This type of small print covers almost everything.
>
> ✔ *Competitors may arise and make large investments to enter the market this company is focusing upon.* Little can be protected by patents.

✔ *The directors and their connected interests will be interested in 55% of the share capital and be in a position to control the outcome of certain matters requiring a shareholder vote.* Forget shareholder democracy and voting at annual general meetings where it's one share, one vote on any issues raised. Your views will always be outvoted if the board and their mates have more than half the shares – unless you can persuade any of them to change their minds.

✔ *The company may require further funding to achieve profitability.* In the future, you and other shareholders may be asked to put your hand into your pocket again or risk the company flopping from a lack of cash.

The Best Bonds Can Go Bust

Fixed interest securities, or bonds, can fail to pay their regular promised income or the final repayment of the original capital, a scenario called *default*. You need to be aware that the higher the payout, the greater the chance of a default. Here are some bond warnings which you will find in bond fund literature, and sometimes in the legal material that accompanies a bond issue. You won't find anything about these risks if you simply buy a bond through a stockbroker.

✔ *This fund invests in higher yielding bonds (non-investment grade).* The risk of default is higher with non-investment grade bonds (also known as junk because they could go bust or fail to pay out on time) than with investment grade bonds (they're the ones from really respectable governments and top companies). But what you can't know is how much higher this risk will be.

✔ *Higher yielding bonds may have increased capital erosion than lower yielding bonds.* This small print means that your chances of losing serious money are greater with higher yielding bonds.

✔ *The level of income on offer could indicate a likely loss of some of your capital.* Some bonds offer a high income now but with the certainty of capital loss later on. This may not matter to pension funds, but it could be bad news for your tax bill because you have to pay income tax on the income you get but can't claim anything back if you make a loss when you sell the bond or it comes to the end of its life.

Great Ideas Don't Last Forever

The investment world is full of bright ideas that once worked but no longer do. You need to know that you won't necessarily receive any specific warning about this fact, so you need to be aware of it all on your own. Not to worry. That's what I'm here for. A couple of examples will help you understand what this concept is all about.

One now-defunct investment firm came up with a bright idea. It had a list of 30 big company shares, and it looked at which shares offered the highest dividend payments for a $1,000 stake. The firm decided to hold for one year whichever three shares fitted this recipe on January 1 each year. Then, 12 months later, the firm would repeat the whole exercise. At that time, the firm would sell shares that had moved out of the target area and buy whatever new high-dividend payers suited its formula.

The firm then stretched its initial idea so investors would get five shares that most fitted the profile and then shrunk the concept to just one share a year.

Moving the goalposts like this usually suggests desperation on the part of the concept's promoters. They move the goalposts so you hopefully don't notice that their scheme isn't making money. Surprise, surprise. High ones, threes, fives, and probably any other number they might've come up with all failed.

Another brainwave was the January effect. Someone noticed that shares went up in January, so an idea was born: Buy the day or so after Christmas Day.

Problem was, once the idea got around, it ceased to work. Clever share-buyers decided to anticipate the January effect by purchasing equities *before* Christmas. Then another group decided to pre-empt those clever sharebuyers by putting in orders at the end of November. Give this practice a few more years, and it would've got back to January!

Any investment scheme that depends on back-testing (using the past to suggest good performance in the future) to prove its worth is suspect. Once an idea is known to more than a tiny handful, it ceases to work.

Property Investments Can Crumble

Whether you read it or ignore it, there is a lot of small print around bonds and shares. But when it comes to property, hey, you're out there on your own. There is scant documentation for you to consider, even for those with the sharpest eyesight.

So here are the warnings property purveyors would have put in, if they had been obliged to do so.

✔ *No one might want to live here.* The danger here is when a new project doesn't attract any tenants or doesn't attract tenants of the quality and deep pockets expected.

✔ *No one might want this property in the future.* Properties can fall out of fashion. I can't be the only person to live near a 1930s shopping area that once hosted top retail names but now is a mix of low-rent takeaways, even lower-rent charity shops, and zero-rent boarded-up premises.

A good property fund or property company whose shares you've bought will work all this out and so come up with a value for the building or rent for the tenant that better reflects reality. Low rent is better than no rent; £5,000 per year rent on a property without bank debts that cost £5,000 to build decades ago is a lot better than £10,000 rent on a new building in hock to the banks that cost £100,000 to build.

Plenty of property opportunities aren't so well managed or require you to put all your bricks onto one site without diversifying your risk. Some are attached to tax-saving opportunities such as Enterprise Zone allowances (a UK government scheme to re-generate downtrodden neighbourhoods by attracting new money via tax concessions). These sound very clever but aren't so bright if you're locked into an investment for years in a zone that enterprise continues to pass by.

Tax-Free Can Be a Dead Loss

I hate paying taxes. You hate paying taxes. Anyone who can legally cut their tax bill generally tries to do so.

The government has a number of legitimate tax-saving schemes, primarily pensions but also Individual Savings Accounts (ISAs), which are intended to encourage people on modest incomes to put money away for the future. Also available are a number of more obscure schemes involving everything from high-tech start-up companies to conifer plantations. The rationale for some of these schemes has been lost in the mists of antiquity.

'Tax-free investment' or 'Pay no tax with this plan' are such powerful draws that they're featured as huge headlines in a large number of investment ads. The obvious idea is to grab your attention. But there's hidden subtext you need to know about.

Some investment product firms use tax benefits as a 'feel the width, never mind the quality' approach. These sellers hope that you'll be so impressed by the chance to get one over on the taxman that you won't look too closely at what they're really pushing. So be very aware of the following:

✔ Product providers and sellers use phrases such as 'government-approved tax savings' to imply that the scheme has state approval or that it's as solid as the Bank of England. But in reality, the tax benefits are a few pennies a week while the risk is still there. If your investment falls, you won't get any government handout.

✔ The advertised tax benefits may only apply to a minority. Sometimes, they may be positively harmful to others. For example, non-taxpayers can actually lose out on some deals because they can't claim anything back. HM Revenue & Customs (a.k.a. the taxman) reckons that if you pay no tax, you can't get a refund.

✔ Many tax deals come with a deadline. Product providers know that no one wants to miss out on a bargain. They hope you'll buy in a last-minute rush and, again, not look too critically at what's on offer.

If you're tempted by saving tax (and who isn't), consider the following facts: Basic-rate taxpayers now gain nothing from tax freedom on the dividends on equity ISAs. Higher-rate taxpayers may save a few pence a week for each £1,000 on equity dividend payments. Bond ISAs are a better deal taxwise, with basic-rate taxpayers typically saving £12 a year (25p a week) for each £1,000 invested.

Stock market ISAs also give you freedom from capital gains tax (CGT), which may be worth something if your holdings and potential profits are large enough to warrant it. *Capital gains tax,* which is designed to get the government a slice of your investment success, can grab up to 18 per cent of any gain you make. However, everyone has an annual CGT exemption (£9,200 for the 2007–8 tax year and the exemption generally rises each year), which can be used. CGT only applies when you sell, so it's less useful if you adopt a long-term buy-and-hold strategy involving mainstream shares or well-diversified funds.

The worth of any ISAs held on your death count toward the value of your estate and any Inheritance Tax bill. So if HM Revenue & Customs doesn't grab your money while you're living, it will collect from your estate when you die. Great thought, that.

As an investor, you must calculate whether the tax saving on offer is sufficient to attract you into a deal that you'd otherwise let pass you by. It'd take a big tax freedom cushion to protect you against falls in your money. The tax relief is not the cake or even the icing on top of it. It's just the decorative finishing touch.

Foreign Scam Operations Are Bigger (And Trickier) Than Ever

All previous sections of this chapter paint a grey picture, meaning they warn you that promises of top investments can actually prove to be average or just plain mediocre investments. But this section paints a flat-out black picture, meaning it warns you of scamster investments that guarantee you'll lose every single penny. You may even lose more if you're persuaded to run up a big credit card bill in an attempt to get your money back. You won't. You'll just be even poorer. But despite the fact that many are run by organised crime, the mob just loves the veneer of respectability so some of these scams come complete with their own warnings. So just like the more legitimate investment plans, they can say you should have read the small print.

Beware the boiler rooms

With a particular type of scamster, you're dealing with organised crime that makes the bad guys in *The Godfather* films look like amateurs. This crime was perfected in Toronto nearly 30 years ago. Three decades on, it's bigger.

The scam can start with a simple letter. It may say that you're an investor in a company, which it names, and that you might like to receive a special research report on that firm, compiled by investment experts. Or the letter may be more general, simply offering a regular investment newsletter compiled by experts. The report or newsletter is, of course, free.

Those who reply are required to give details, including phone numbers. The company's return address is often in the UK, although that means nothing because it's just a mailbox. A UK phone number is equally meaningless because diverting calls to somewhere way beyond UK legal protection is easy. In addition, the company isn't regulated under UK investor protection laws.

Watch out for a dodge in which a foreign scam firm gets a regulated UK firm to supposedly authorise it. A loophole in UK law allows legitimate firms to 'approve an advertisement for marketing purposes'. So all the UK firm is really doing is saying it agrees the advert details are correct. These usually only run as far as having a name, phone number, and possibly address with the briefest description of what the firm purports to do. This authorisation means nothing. It gives no compensation rights. It guarantees nothing. It is a sham.

An alternative is an e-mail approach, where you're offered a free report on a currency or stock market, always supposedly compiled by expert analysts. A third approach the scamsters use is to send millions of junk e-mails (they're usually sent from Asia or Eastern Europe) lauding the prospects of a company you've never heard of. The scamsters try to cover themselves by revealing that the e-mail senders were paid a sum such as $30,000 for their work.

However they do it, they now have your interest. Often, they leave you alone for some weeks to receive your newsletter. You may notice that 75 per cent of the four-page letter is devoted to mainstream shares and economics. But the back page gives lavish praise to the money-making opportunities in a share you've never heard off, usually with a high-tech or scientific bent. They use all this stuff for the next stage of suckering victims from their cash.

Now here's the really dangerous bit unless you're prepared: They (invariably men) phone you. The firms, known as *boiler rooms*, may state that they're based somewhere like Beijing, Barcelona, Belgrade, Mexico City, or Mali. It doesn't matter. Wherever they claim to be and wherever they really are (rarely the same place as they claim), it's outside the UK jurisdiction.

Now for the sting. The caller may make some pretence at discussing your investment needs, but he's really trying to probe how much you can be taken for. The representative tells you that you could be in a great investment that could double your money in 30 to 60 days or make ten times as much by this time next year. It's a straight appeal to greed, and it works as these firms continue to proliferate.

Scamster representatives may use hard sell tactics to persuade you to buy the shares, commodities, currencies, precious stones, or works of art they're touting. The FSA is aware of *experienced* investors who've been pressured into buying things from these representatives, which shows just how persuasive these salespeople can be. If the representative sells you a commodity or currency deal, he may ring you back shortly with news of your winnings. The purpose is purely to persuade you that the firm is safe and that you can make really easy money. Don't bother asking for your winnings, however. You'll never get them. They'll suggest you re-invest. If you insist on your money, they'll ignore you and as you won't be able to find them, they'll pocket your cash. But if their appeal to your greed works and you want more, the scamsters will just 'trade' your cash until they have it all.

Alternatively, the representative sells shares in a tiny company, usually one with a miracle cure or technological wonder. Invariably, the shares are bought by the boiler room at their true worth – usually one-tenth of a US cent – and sold to you at $1 each. They're *restricted shares*, too, meaning that you can't sell them without the company's permission (never forthcoming) until a year has passed, by which time the company will have disappeared, assuming, of course, that a real company was there in the first place. (Check out the nearby sidebar for information about the types of names given to these companies.)

After buying the shares, you generally experience delays and difficulties obtaining your share certificates. The shares turn out not to be the great deal you were promised. When you try to sell the shares, you're usually told to wait a few weeks because really important news is about to emerge, which will transform the price. This is just another delaying tactic.

But even if you do appear to have sold the shares, you nearly always have difficulty obtaining the proceeds or are put under a lot of pressure to buy other shares from the same boiler room with the money, so you never get to see the cash. Or you may be contacted by an organisation with another name that offers to get the money back provided that you pay an upfront fee.

Knowing the types of names given to scamster companies

Often, the names of the firms that scamster representatives claim to work for sound just like real firms. Genuine organisations such as Barclays Bank or Norwich Union have found totally unauthorised versions of their names emerging all over the unregulated world of finance. Or the organisation's title is a collection of commonplace words, such as first, international, financial, capital, consultants, asset managers, capital markets, or bank.

Most of the firms now boast Web sites, although, strangely, they rarely emerge on search engines such as Google. However, if you express any interest, the scamsters give you the Web site address. All the sites are very similar and offer little detail of what the firms do, who they are, and where are located. Most try to give themselves a sheen of respectability by offering links to legitimate Web sites from information providers such as Bloomberg or the *Wall Street Journal*.

How to deal with boiler room operatives

Boiler room operatives don't worry about their phone bill. Spending £50 on calls is immaterial if they can convince you to part with £10,000. The longer they talk to you, the more persuasive they get. So just tell them that they're crooks and hang up. Don't worry about their feelings. They haven't got any.

There is absolutely no reason for any overseas organisation to call you in this way other than to scam you from your money. I've been writing about and tracking boiler rooms for more than 20 years, and I've yet to find an honest organisation with this approach. I won't. Ever. Why? There isn't one.

You have no protection whatsoever when dealing with boiler rooms. After you part with your money, you've lost it just as if your wallet or purse was stolen on the street, except the amounts involved are far greater than anyone carries around with them. And there is no theft insurance comeback. There's sadly little point complaining to the UK authorities. They can do nothing for you whatsoever. All you might get is the doubtful good glow from knowing that your experience might warn others.

Part II
Shares and Bonds

'I ignored the rumours about the recession
sweeping the city, and now I am.'

In this part . . .

Are you interested in how financial markets operate and in figuring out ways to analyse markets and companies? If so, this part is for you. I explain what you need to know about how stock markets work.

I cover in detail what shares and bonds are, how to invest in them, and the perks you get when owning them. I take you on a tour of world markets and examine the UK stock market up close. I tell you where the stock market entry routes are and provide tips you can use when you're ready to invest. I explain that being a successful share investor involves looking at numbers from stock-market-quoted companies and help you understand what those numbers mean. I explain how important information-gathering is and tell you how to build your own information bank. And I list all the factors you need to know when you choose an adviser or stockbroker, ensuring they best meet your individual needs.

Chapter 6

Comprehending How Stock Markets Work

All financial strategies, including those to keep all your money in cash or property, are based on what happens on stock markets – they are the big drivers of the world's economies. But stock markets can appear to be places of great mystery – even more so nowadays because most don't really have a physical presence at all.

This chapter unravels the mysteries of the stock market. I explain what shares and bonds are and tell you the perks you get (and don't get) when buying them. I spell out the reasons for the ups and downs of the market and offer tips for predicting market moves. And I describe the basic mechanics of the stock market so you can better understand those newspaper columns you read every day.

Looking at the Evolution of the Stock Market

For centuries, markets existed where items were bought and sold. Many of them, such as cattle and other livestock markets, were open to public scrutiny. They didn't require membership or passing exams. All people had to do was walk in with some money, and they'd walk out with an animal. If they knew what they were doing, the deal worked. If not, they ended up with the famous pig in a poke – not a good idea.

Financial markets started off in the same way, often in City of London coffee houses. But sometime in the 19th century, they became specialised. As life became more sophisticated and more companies were set up that needed to raise money from investors, it was soon obvious that share dealing had to be centralised (helped by inventions such as the railway and telegraph).

Once that happened, share dealing became focused on a small number of professionals. They did what all professionals do and set up systems to ensure that they kept the work for themselves at the terms they considered suitable. Stockbrokers formed partnerships and controlled the work through the stock exchange, which they collectively owned.

Life carried on like this until the mid-1980s, when the City found itself in the midst of a huge change in working methods. Out went the cosy arrangements of the past and sleepy stockbrokers who worked from 10 to 4 with three hours for lunch. In came big banks, big money, professionalism, long hours, and a sandwich lunch at your desk, if you were lucky.

In addition, out went the old stock exchange, where the public could watch goings on from a viewing gallery. Now, there's no actual place such as the stock exchange or a stock market. Everything's traded electronically. All you get to see in a stockbroker's office is an ocean of trading screens covered in a tidal wave of numbers.

But the fundamentals of what makes markets tick haven't changed. And another thing hasn't changed: Rising shares are shown on screens in blue; falls are in red. These colours are just as they were in the old days when prices were displayed using coloured chalks.

Understanding Shares

A *share* is literally that – a share, or part, of a company. And if you own shares, you have a stake in the fortunes of the firm involved and a say in its control, in proportion to the number of shares you hold.

British Telecom, for example, had 1,261,000 UK shareholders in March 2007. All bar 7,000 had fewer than 10,000 shares. Between them, the small shareholders who made up the majority held one billion shares out of the 8.6 billion shares in issue. The 7,000 big shareholders held the other 7.6 billion shares. Not many companies have as many shareholders, but many big firms count their shares in hundreds of millions, if not billions, and can have tens of thousands of shareholders.

Companies can raise money from banks and other lenders, and most do so. But share capital is what makes most companies tick financially because shares have big advantages: After the share is issued and paid for by the initial investor, that money permanently belongs to the company. The company never has to repay the money and has no obligation to pay for it in terms of dishing out regular payments such as a dividend. And no interest is charged. Of course, it's a good idea for companies to dish out dividends twice a year, but they don't have to.

All limited companies (a legal term meaning the liability of the company is limited to its resources, which leaves shareholders not having to find extra cash if the company hits problems) have shares. But only a few companies have shares that are traded on stock markets. They're generally the biggest companies, however, so what happens to their share price day to day is important.

All companies traded on stock markets in the UK are *public limited companies* (PLCs). But not all PLCs are traded on markets. Some PLCs are really tiny companies trying to look big and tough.

How companies get to the stock market

The process of bringing a company to the stock market is more complicated and vastly more costly than bringing a cow to a cattle market. The process involves lawyers, accountants, investment bankers, and public relations specialists. They all take big fees, often adding up to tens of millions of pounds in a big company, because they need to feed their expensive salary habits.

The process of bringing a company to the stock market is known as a *flotation* or an *initial public offering* (IPO). The IPO label, imported from the United States, is now the more popular way to describe a firm's arrival on the stock market list. The IPO is accompanied by a ferocious amount of documentation known as a *prospectus*. It gives you the following:

- ✔ Details about the company, including its past and its prospects for the future (including profit forecasts).
- ✔ A full balance sheet.
- ✔ The past records of directors and senior managers (including any disasters they've been involved with).
- ✔ Pay packages for the top people and details of any deals between directors and the company.
- ✔ The advisers, such as brokers, banks, accountants, and lawyers, used by the firm. The quality of these advisers is important. If some or all of them are small or not generally known, or have a past poor reputation, the IPO could be criticised.

Large companies generally bring their business to the stock market through a public offering, so anyone can apply.

Smaller firms often use a device called a *placing*, where they offer large parcels of shares to selected stockbrokers and investment banks who then distribute them to clients. This method has the disadvantage of locking out other investors but the plus point of a lower cost.

In addition, big companies that have a listing on a foreign market can obtain a London stock exchange quote through what's called an *introduction*. An introduction is just a formality. It doesn't require new shares to be issued or much formal documentation.

Note that companies list on other markets when they want to extend their shareholder base because some investors are limited to buying securities traded in their own countries or don't want the inconvenience of dealing with overseas-based equities. After the IPO period is over, the shares are traded in the normal way.

Ways to buy shares

Buying shares through an IPO is usually a good deal. One reason is that they're cheaper, because there are no brokerage fees or stamp duty to pay. In addition, companies like to bring their shares to market at a little less than the amount their advisers consider fair value. They want the headlines to say 'first day big share price advance' because an early gain grabs investor attention. They don't want stories that warn 'overpriced shares going down'.

An IPO should also signal a particularly good time for the company. It would fail completely if the prospectus were riddled with profits warnings.

Regardless, an IPO is no guarantee of long-term success. And watch also for directors and other large shareholders using a flotation to unload millions of shares for cash. If they had faith in the company, they'd want to hold on to as many shares as possible.

Sometimes, huge numbers can benefit from an IPO. Back in the late 1980s, the Abbey National was a building society owned by its members. But at that time, it decided to become a stock-market-quoted company. It gave each of its qualifying members a set number of shares in return for giving up their membership rights. These people received 100 shares worth £1.30 each. The company also sold additional shares at the same price to these investors. These shares are now part of Banco Santander, the Spanish bank which subsequently bought Abbey. Other companies often sell large numbers of shares to big investing institutions such as insurance companies.

Companies can issue more shares later on, offering them to all shareholders through a *rights issue*, which gives every shareholder the right (but not the obligation) to buy shares in a fixed ratio to their present holding, usually a lower price, or discount, to the then stock market value. So if a company launches a one for four issue, someone with 400 shares can buy up to 100. Firms can also issue shares to pay for companies they acquire, so those firms' former owners acquire equity in the new company instead of a cash payment.

The shares most people buy and sell, though, are properly called *ordinary shares*. Some companies have an additional type, known as a *preference share*. Note that ordinary shares are often called *equities*, but they have nothing to do with the UK actors' union Equity! In the United States, shares are usually referred to as *stock* or *common stock*, but the principle behind them is the same.

REMEMBER

Companies may offer other investment possibilities, such as bonds or loan stocks, but ordinary shares, or equities, are the most frequently traded. They're also potentially the most profitable and, also, the most at risk.

Equity holders only receive a dividend after other classes of investors, such as bondholders, have been paid. And they're last in line for a payment if the company goes bust. They usually get nothing in that event. But equity holders are the legal owners of the company. They get all the earnings of a successful firm after obligatory payments to loan stock and bondholders. Equity holders take the lion's share of the risks. They get the lion's share of the rewards.

The perks you get when buying ordinary shares

Each ordinary share counts equally. So each one is worth the same amount when it comes to the value quoted in a newspaper or on a screen. (This discussion ignores the higher cost per share of buying and selling a small amount.) The amount of dividend paid per share is equal.

And there's parity in voting rights. Companies are democratic, but instead of one person getting one vote, one share gets one vote. Shareholders can (but aren't obliged to) vote at annual general meetings (usually called AGMs) for items ranging from directors' jobs to approving the annual report and accounts. They may also vote at extraordinary general meetings, often held when the company acquires another company in a takeover or issues a substantial number of new shares.

You can attend both annual and extraordinary meetings no matter how many or how few shares you own, but you're under no obligation to do so. Most shareholders don't attend. That's actually a good thing because it'd almost always be impossible to find a venue large enough.

Attendance, however, gives you the right to quiz the directors in public. No matter how unpopular or controversial your views may be to the directors, you have a legal right to be at the meetings. The company can't refuse to admit registered shareholders. You can even sign a form to send someone (known as a *proxy*) in your place.

The ability to buy just one share and have the same rights to speak at annual meetings as investment companies who own millions is good news for environmentalists, consumer activists, those with a political point to make, or anyone looking for publicity for their cause.

If you unite with other shareholders, you can propose a resolution for a meeting, such as unseating a director and putting in someone of your preference. In some circumstances, shareholders or groups of shareholders with 10 per cent or more of the shares can force an extraordinary general meeting on a company.

AGMs also offer a good opportunity for you to protest about poorly performing directors. Besides giving you the chance to ask questions, directors have to offer themselves for re-election from time to time, so investors can vote against them. Many bigger shareholders, such as investment firms, are now flexing their muscles as well to show that they're serious about their roles as company owners. In the past, if they bothered to do so at all, it was behind the scenes with nods and winks.

Holding one share also gives you the right to an annual report and accounts. Many bigger companies save money by sending out an abridged version that leaves out most of the complicated numbers but often leaves in the pictures of directors smiling or showing off their new corporate helicopter! Know that you have a legal right to the complete version, which must be supplied to all shareholders who ask for one. Serious shareholders should always insist on the full version.

Understanding Bonds

Lots of financial bits and pieces are called bonds. Most come from life insurance companies. Some from the sometimes febrile minds of the ever-inventive people who work in marketing departments. Others are Premium Bonds, a once a month National Savings & Investment flutter. The word *bond* even sounds reliable. The reason is because of all that old stock market stuff about 'my word being my bond'. But this book doesn't focus on those bits and pieces called bonds. Instead, this book covers *bonds* that are loans made to a company or government that can be traded on stock markets.

Governments have raised money from citizens and others through loans called *bonds* for centuries. Now companies increasingly get cash by issuing bonds instead of, or as well as, shares.

A bond promises a regular and fixed interest payment and repayment of the original amount on a set future date. Between the date the bond is acquired and that of its final repayment, the bond's price goes up and down according to circumstances.

Owners of company-issued bonds, usually known as *corporate bonds*, must be paid before equity holders if the company is in a sticky financial situation. If the firm goes bust, bondholders will probably lose their money, however.

Chapter 10 deals exclusively with bonds, when you're ready for detailed information on the subject. For purposes of this discussion, I just want to point out the perks you *don't* get when buying bonds:

- Bondholders don't get the right to attend annual general or extraordinary general meetings (although most companies don't object) unless the meetings are labelled as specific meetings for bondholders.

- Bondholders can't legally put questions to directors, although nothing stops them from acquiring one share to do so.

- Bondholders don't receive an annual report as a matter of right.

- Bondholders can't apply for more shares if the company launches a rights issue.

- Bondholders generally have no rights when another company tries to acquire the firm via a takeover bid.

- Bondholders don't receive larger payments when the company does well.

Getting Familiar with the Ups and Downs of the Market

Every day, many newspapers carry hundreds, and often thousands, of share and bond prices. The Internet offers access to tens of thousands more, often changing prices not just once a day like print publications but either as the changes happen or with a 15-minute delay. Online investors who are prepared to wait a quarter of an hour often receive a no-cost service instead of paying a subscription.

Prices go up and down most days, if not most hours. Shares of the biggest companies with the greatest number of shareholders are the ones whose prices move the most frequently. These shares are called *liquid* because prices flow easily with buying and selling orders.

A digression into potato prices

Shares are just like anything else where a free, unfettered market reacts to supply and demand. Consider potatoes, for example. If the supply of potatoes falls due to a bad harvest or transport problems, the price goes up. But it doesn't go up forever.

After a time, new sources of potatoes may come on the market because the price has risen to a level where it's worthwhile for foreign firms to ship potatoes to the UK because it's now more profitable than selling the potatoes locally. When share markets rise strongly, companies launch new share issues to soak up the demand.

Alternatively, instead of supply rising, demand may fall. Some potato eaters may get fed up paying high prices and move to rice, pasta, polenta, couscous, or bread. When share prices get too high, investors switch to other shares, bonds, property, or cash.

The opposite happens when potato prices fall after a bumper harvest. Then foreign farmers decide it's not worthwhile sending produce here. But that scenario doesn't last forever, either. Those eating other starch forms, such as rice and pasta, may decide to switch back to potatoes, so demand increases again.

Smaller-company shares are less liquid or often illiquid. Dealing is less frequent, but when it happens, the effect is far more pronounced.

Why do prices move? It's the most frequent question investors pose. And it's the most difficult to answer. And even when the answer is obvious, such as a price rise due to the company announcing a juicy new contract or a price fall due to the company losing a juicy old contract, it's not so obvious why the price has changed by the percentage it has.

Not to worry. This section helps you sort out the reasons for market ups and downs.

Why do prices rise and fall?

A market truism is that prices rise because there are more buyers than sellers. Don't take that literally, though, because sometimes there are a few large buyers and thousands of small sellers. But if the number of shares being bid for by buyers exceeds the number being offered for sale by holders who want out, the price rises.

This stuff is basic supply and demand economics (see the nearby sidebar 'A digression into potato prices' for an example using, well, potatoes). If the demand from buyers is high, the price rises to persuade more holders to sell. This situation continues until buyers believe that the price has risen far enough or, as happens often in markets, too high.

Keep in mind, though, that supply and demand trends in stock markets are far from those neat supply and demand graphs you see in economic textbooks. Prices often tend to overshoot in one way or another.

The law of supply and demand, or the balance of buyers and sellers, is always there. What investors must do is calculate the plus and minus factors for any equity or bond.

Looking at specific and systemic risks

A share price is an amalgamation of many factors – some applying to the company you buy into and others applying to the stock market in relation to the general economy at the time. Factors that apply to the company itself are called *specific risks*. Factors that apply to the stock market itself (and thus to all shares) are known as *systemic risks* or *market risks*.

Don't forget that a risk can be good or bad. It's just something unknown to add into the share price equation.

A share in Real Ale Breweries PLC, for example, (not a real company, but one that I've made up) carries specific positive risks, such as a hot summer pushing up sales, beer becoming fashionable, more pubs and shops stocking the brewery's products, or someone discovering that a pint of beer a day is good for your health. The brewery also carries specific negative risks, such as the directors running off with the takings, health warnings on beer, new taxes on alcohol, and drinkers switching to wine.

Systemic risks are different from specific risks. When prices are generally rising and every evening TV news bulletin ends with an increase in the FTSE 100 (the Footsie) share index, almost all shares go up by some amount – even those with just mediocre prospects. And when prices fall, almost all shares go down.

You can never totally isolate the systemic risks from the specific. But if you buy individual shares, or subscribe to a fund that does so for you, the underlying quality or rubbish status of an equity usually works through eventually. A top-class company may fall in a collapsing market but less steeply than others. And when the recovery finally comes, it will gain more quickly and more strongly.

Much share analysis is concerned with relative values rather than absolute gains or losses. A share or fund that falls 10 per cent when the index or average of all funds loses 30 per cent is considered a success even though you still lost money. Likewise, a share or fund that goes up 10 per cent when the index or average gains 30 per cent is considered a flop despite your profits!

Looking at factors that can make share prices rise

Here's a checklist of factors that can cause a share price to rise. Use this list every time you think about buying into an equity to see how many factors apply.

Nothing ever happens in isolation, so never fixate on one point alone when considering whether to buy an equity!

- ✔ The company has a major new contract.
- ✔ The company has a big new product.
- ✔ Prices for what the company does are going up fast.
- ✔ The company has a new dynamic director.
- ✔ The company is expected to make record profits – more than previously forecasted.
- ✔ The company looks more lowly rated compared with expectations than rival companies.
- ✔ The company earns a lot of money from importing, and foreign currencies have fallen in value against the pound.
- ✔ The company earns a lot of money from overseas operations, and the pound has fallen against the principal currencies it does business in.
- ✔ The company has a lot of bank borrowings, and interest rates have fallen.
- ✔ The stock market overall looks like rising, and this share usually goes up faster than average shares in the market as a whole.
- ✔ Investors in the company believe that a takeover bid is likely for the company whose shares they own.
- ✔ The company is about to win a major legal battle.
- ✔ The company intends to raise its dividend by more than the average.
- ✔ The company has plans to cost-cut by shutting down unprofitable parts of the business and sacking superfluous staff.

Looking at factors that can make share prices fall

Many of the factors that cause prices to fall are the reverse of those that make prices rise. Other factors apply only to falling markets. And the last one in the following checklist has a special perversity of its own:

- ✔ Bad publicity is expected. For example, the company is responsible for an environmental disaster, or the accountants have been caught falsifying figures.
- ✔ The stock market is in a bad mood, and this share usually falls faster and further than the average.

- ✔ Figures show that trading is bad in the company's main business area.

- ✔ New government legislation will add to costs or force the company to operate in a different way.

- ✔ The company has launched a takeover bid, which could turn into a battle involving an auction that could get out of control.

- ✔ The company, to raise money, is issuing millions of new shares at less than the present price.

- ✔ The company's product range has been criticised as out of date or technologically inept.

- ✔ The company's credit rating falls with international bond assessment agencies.

- ✔ The company issues a profits warning.

- ✔ The company says that the dividend will be cut or not paid at all.

- ✔ There's an absence of news, and/or investors perceive the company as boring or forget all about it and thus divert their investment money to rival firms.

Can anyone predict these moves?

Billions of pounds a year are spent on share market analysis. Highly paid people look at every nook and cranny of bigger companies, consider the economic wider picture, and look at any other factors they consider relevant. And that's *before* fund managers enter the scene. (*Fund managers* are professionals who buy and sell shares on behalf of clients and big financial institutions. They focus their efforts on pension funds and unit trusts so they have their take on what they think is going on.)

Some market analysts get it right more often than they get it wrong, but many have less than a 50 per cent success record. This outcome sounds like they don't earn their money, and to be truthful, some don't deserve what they get. The difficulty all analysts face is that what moves markets is the sense of surprise – happenings either good or bad that haven't yet been factored into the equation.

Stock market operators are remarkably good at reacting to news. If something happens, the share price often changes in seconds. But after something happens and the market adjusts either up or down, it's too late. After news is revealed, these facts are referred to as 'in the market' or 'in the price' (both phrases mean much the same), and the share value has changed to take account of it.

You gotta admit, this insider trading scheme was clever!

One stock market operator, no longer in business, came up with an amazing way of circumventing the law. Here's the story:

He always found out pieces of price-sensitive information from an inside source at an investment bank. He knew that once the information was made public, the share price would go up by about 20 per cent, giving him a good profit if he bought beforehand. But he also realised that the Financial Services Authority, the UK investor watchdog, looks at all unusual share price moves and examines dealings that had occurred around that time. He was also aware that he had previously been a suspect.

His solution was neat. He had an accomplice set up a small shares magazine, called something like *Shares Secrets*. He printed a few thousand copies and sent all but a few to people who had never dealt on the stock market. The recipients were usually old-age pensioners living on state benefits. The operator and his friends received the few other copies.

When the inevitable inquiries were launched, he could always, hand on heart, say that he had read the information in *Shares Secrets*, or whatever it was really called. And the publisher could always, hand on heart, show that he had sent out many copies.

Take a look at the checklists of factors that can cause prices to rise and fall – located a little earlier in this chapter. At any one time, some or all of those factors are the subject of comment or a news release. It's only when these factors change for the better or the worse that prices will move – going nowhere or coming in exactly as predicted will leave a share price static.

However, this isn't as boring as it sounds. Behind the scenes, pressures build up and abate on all the checklist points. One way to predict market moves is to have enough information sources so you can spot a trend before others do and especially before the company has to reveal it.

What smart investors do

To predict market moves, smart investors can look for new products, scour the trade press and Internet sites to find details of potential new contracts, or, on the negative side, try to spot early signs of consumer discontent.

One way to spot changes before they're officially announced is to get inside information from someone working for the company, a practice known as *insider trading*. It's illegal as soon as an investor tries to profit from it. The illegality applies whether the investor works for the company or simply knows a source of factual material.

The authorities have rarely been successful in prosecuting insider trading. The reason, in part, is due to the way insider traders hide their tracks through offshore companies in exotic locations where there's little, if any, regulation. But the reason is also due to the difficulty of proving something in a market where so much rumour and tittle-tattle exist, ranging from the totally accurate to the downright and intentionally misleading. The nearby sidebar 'You gotta admit, this insider trading scheme was clever!' tells how one operator got around the authorities.

'But I don't have time to do all the stuff professionals do!'

You have a number of disadvantages compared with professional investors, including an almost certain lack of time and resources. Unless you give up your day job (definitely not advised!) or are retired (then only invest money in shares you can afford to go without!), you won't be able to spend hours on end looking at share movements and company announcements. And if you can afford the battery of screens the professionals use, then you're too advanced and too wealthy to need this book.

You also won't have access to a battery of brokers trying to sell you their services by offering research into markets and individual shares. Nor will you be able to call on in-house analysts and economists.

But don't worry. There's no evidence that all that material actually helps professional investors with the right calls. Instead, all that material acts as a prop and an excuse when things go wrong, as they inevitably will.

As a private investor, you *do* have a number of advantages. These days, with the availability of the Internet, any investor can know what's happening with a given share or market almost as soon as the professionals with their batteries of screens. Online services offer information for free with a 15-minute delay or instantaneously for a fee. And with online dealing, you can respond almost as quickly.

Don't feel disadvantaged if your reaction time is slower than the professionals. They're paid to deal quickly and often, and if they don't move shares around all the time, their bosses start to question whether they're worth their big pay cheques and bonuses. And when they deal, they're probably only buying or selling a small amount of their total holding in a company, whereas you're likely to be selling all you hold. There's also no one, other than yourself and your responsibilities, overshadowing what you do.

You also have the advantage of distance. You can look at shares and the companies behind them in a different way than professional investors. You're able to take a more reasoned and rounded view, away from stock market gossip, you're not part of the herd of professionals all heading the same way for fear of being out on a limb, and you don't have to respond instantly to anything.

You can't definitively predict market moves. But neither can the professionals. You have the advantage, though, of being able to set your own investment agenda.

Understanding the Mechanics of the Stock Market

Most small investors stand well back from the day to day, hour to hour, and minute to minute goings on in the stock market. They do just as well if not better following this course. But short-term movements can sometimes add up to a long-term trend, and understanding basic UK stock market mechanics will help you make sense of those newspaper columns where daily ups and downs are discussed.

Most markets are made up of four levels: the producers and the product, the middleman, the retailer, and the consumer. In the vegetable market, for example, the producer is the farmer; the middleman is the wholesaler at one of the big central markets, such as New Covent Garden in London; the retailers are greengrocers or supermarkets; and the consumer is you.

Stocks and shares are no different. The product is the tiny part of the company represented by each share, the middleman is the market maker, the retailer is the stockbroker, and the ultimate consumer is you.

The pivot in markets is the middleman, and the stock market middleman is the *market maker*, a market professional who assesses second by second the weight of buy and sell pressures and adjusts prices accordingly. This activity determines what the brokers charge you or give you when you sell – adjusted, of course, for their fees.

Market makers always try to find a price level where both buyers and sellers are satisfied at any one moment. This practice is called *balancing the book*. If there are more buyers than sellers, market makers are short of stock. They don't have the shares to satisfy demand. So they increase their prices to bring out sellers so they can achieve balance.

Equally, when there are more sellers than buyers, market makers are long of stock. Prices are marked down to entice new buyers. Market makers are no different from vegetable wholesalers who mark up prices when demand is high and mark down prices when buyers are scarce.

Buyers pay more than sellers receive. The gap between the bid (or the buying or asking) price and the offer (or selling) price is called *the spread*. The bigger the company and the more often its shares are traded, the narrower this spread is. A major company such as Vodafone or Lloyds TSB may only have 1p or 2p or so between the bid and offer prices. But smaller companies can have larger amounts. Note that the prices shown in newspapers are mid-prices – halfway between the bid and offer.

It's always vital to know just how much a share would have to rise for you to get your money back. The price you see in a newspaper is not the price you pay. You have stamp duty and commission. And on top of that there is the 'spread' or 'touch', which is how the market makers earn their living. The way it works is that your share has to rise more in percentage terms if it is priced in pennies than if it is priced in pounds.

Market makers make their spread (or *touch*) in pence or part of a penny, not in a percentage. A very lowly priced share could have a spread of one penny, but that would be a very large percentage. A share that the newspaper quotes at 5p could have a 1p spread. You'd then pay 5.5p to buy it but get 4.5p if you sell it. The price would have to go up 1p to a mid 6p (or 20 per cent more) before you could get out at the 5.5p you originally paid; that's because a mid 6p implies you will get 5.5p when you sell (you would have to pay 6.5p if you were buying). A big company share priced at 500p with a 2p spread would only need a 0.4 per cent uplift before you were back to the starting point. You would pay 502p for each share so when it goes up 4p to a mid 504p, you would be able to get out at 502p (the mid price less the spread that goes to market makers).These figures ignore broker fees and stamp duty, which make the real increase needed to get back to square one even larger.

Market makers have to quote prices in the bigger companies. There are often several market makers, so the competition between them should narrow the spreads. That means less for market makers, but it's good news for investors.

How big money moves big money

Around 80 per cent of the value of the London stock market is owned by big investors such as pension funds, insurance companies, unit trusts, and investment trusts. They don't really own it, of course, because they're merely working for the real owners – you and me and millions of others who have entrusted savings to them.

Nevertheless, they act as though it's their money, and they're the people whose influence moves share prices most readily. They have more effect on big companies because they trade shares in these major corporations more often. Many smaller companies may have their share register dominated by the firm's directors and private investors.

The *Financial Times* prints a daily list of trading volume in large company shares. This list gives figures for the amount of shares changing hands on any day. The figure, in thousands, must be divided by two because each share will have been traded twice – once as a buy and once as a sell. Every fully quoted share can be traded every day, but volume can vary from zero (rarely) to hundreds of millions.

High volume (jargon for 'lots of trading') in a share often occurs just after a statement from the company. But if you can't see an obvious reason why shares in a company are heavily traded, make some more enquiries, especially if the price changes substantially. Look through newspaper market reports and scour Internet sites. They won't always give you the reason, but high volume should always alert investors in those shares. It could be good news if prices are higher on high volume but bad news if the opposite!

Smaller companies whose shares aren't actively traded may not always have a market maker. Instead, shares are bought and sold through *matched bargains* posted on an electronic bulletin board. Think in terms of the Wanted and For Sale columns in your local newspaper. If you want to buy 500 shares in TeenyWeeny PLC, your broker posts your requirement on the bulletin board and the price you're willing to pay. Eventually, someone posts a sell order at a price that's suitable, and if it's for 500 shares or more, the deal is done. Matched bargains can sometimes take days or even weeks.

You may have previously heard the term *market movers*. Don't confuse market movers with market makers. A market mover is anyone with enough influence to shift investor thinking. Market movers include certain newspaper columns, big fund managers, major stockbroking houses, economists, and analysts. And there are legendary individuals, such as George Soros and Warren Buffet. Watch to see how prices change after a comment from any particular source to see who is just hot air and who can really influence share values.

Knowing How Companies Leave the Market

Companies disappear from the stock market lists for all sorts of reasons. Some (hopefully not many!) go bust. A second group of companies get taken over, but investors can end up with shares in the firm that bought their company. For example, the Abbey National shareholders I mentioned earlier on in this chapter now have a stake in Banco Santander, the Spanish bank which took it over, instead.

But many others *go private*. Going private and hence dodging the scrutiny of regular stock market reporting used to be the preserve of small companies. Now very large companies including Boots, the high street chemist, and BAA, which runs most of the big UK airports, have been taken off the stock market by *private equity* companies.

You can't get involved in this as private equity is very private indeed. With private equity, a handful of banks and entrepreneurs get together, buy out the shareholders, and run the company as their personal property. They hope to get a lot more money out than they put in by using clever strategies known as *financial engineering*.

For a company's shareholders, this means an exit from that company accompanied by a cheque. That cheque should be greater in value than it would have been if they'd been sold on the stockmarket before people knew about the private equity bid.

Now the shareholders have to decide what to do with their money! So, they could be heading back to this book's basics.

Chapter 7

Taking the Top-Down View of Investing

. . . .

In This Chapter

▶ Thinking of foreign investments as a huge pool of opportunity

▶ Examining stock markets worldwide

▶ Looking closely at the UK stock market

▶ Looking at which shares march to the market rhythm and which ones go their own way

. . . .

*B*ack in the early 1990s, there was a popular idea known as *chaos theory*. It was supposed to make sense of the seemingly random patterns of the world in all sorts of areas, from finance to the weather. After a brief flurry of popularity and big book sales, chaos theory returned to the academics who invented it. But one quite poetic image remains for me: Butterflies flap, hurricanes happen.

In other words, a butterfly flapping its wings over Beijing can cause a storm over Buenos Aires. The idea is that a small and unexpected movement in one place can have a slightly larger knock-on effect somewhere else. Take this on a few times more, with each move growing in size and significance, and you eventually get to something dramatic. Which leads to the purpose of this chapter.

There are two styles of investing. One is called *top down*, and it says that you start with the big events, the big companies, and the world view. Top down is like looking for the hurricane over Buenos Aires. The other is called *bottom up*, and it says that you should construct your investment portfolio starting with companies you like, irrespective of the wider context. Bottom up is like looking for the butterfly flapping its wings over Beijing.

For investors, chaos theory has taught the lesson that the trees make up the woods – that everything small counts toward the whole. But it has also suggested that nothing happens in isolation. What occurs in one country has an effect elsewhere. So even if you never invest outside the UK, you still need to be aware of what goes on elsewhere. While one market suffers, another may prosper. Money is mobile. That's why this chapter focuses on the top-down view, examining the big companies and the world markets.

The Current Lack of Foreign Investing

All the world's a stock market, and men and women are merely investors on it. That's twisting the words of William Shakespeare until they scream and spit, but over my lifetime writing about investments, the focus has changed from the purely parochial to the truly global.

When I started out writing about investments back in the 1970s, there was something really complicated called the *dollar premium*, which meant investors had to bid for foreign exchange money, and it was nearly always dollars because no one had heard of any market outside the UK other than the New York Stock Exchange. They paid over the odds for each investment dollar and then paid it back when the shares were sold. So on top of everything else, investors had to second-guess the ups and downs of the dollar premium market. Ouch, that was really complicated and only for the 100 per cent professionals.

The result? No one bothered to buy shares or anything else outside the UK. Granted, a few foreign companies got around the issue by listing on the London stock market, but they were the exception. Now the good news. All this is history and no one has to bother about it any more.

In the early 1980s, the dollar premium was abolished, and everyone was free to invest wherever they wanted. But did they? Not really. UK investors weren't alone in their insularity, however. Share buyers in the United States were even more reluctant to put their toes in foreign waters. As for those in continental Europe, they didn't buy shares at all, preferring to stick to bonds and cash.

Now fast-forward a couple of decades. Are investors any better nowadays at looking overseas? Yes, they've made some progress but not a lot. There are very few overseas shares held directly by UK investors. The shares owned are either worldwide brands, such as Coca-Cola or Microsoft, or shares in foreign companies that have taken over UK concerns, such as AMP, the Australian insurer that acquired and then sold small UK life company London Life.

Look for a minute at the UK in context. UK investors are a bit better at holding foreign shares through funds such as unit or investment trusts. Around 20 per cent of all unit trust holdings are invested outside the UK. Investment trusts fare better. Most have always had a non-UK bias, so around half the total value of the trusts is invested outside the UK.

Yikes! Investing styles in opposition

Although I think that the best investing approach for most people is to take the top-down view, both the top-down and bottom-up styles of investing have benefits and advantages. Take a look at the following key points in favour of each investing style:

✔ Top down triumphs in times of stability and economic prosperity. When everything is progressing smoothly, investors are more willing to treat all shares and all equity markets in a similar way.

✔ Bottom up triumphs when life is uncertain. Picking winners in troubled times means you have to look at individual circumstances.

✔ Top down triumphs because it is less effort. You're only looking at markets and not the thousands of stocks that make them up.

✔ Bottom up triumphs because there will always be winners and losers. The smart investor hopes there are more of the former!

✔ Top down triumphs because you can concentrate on the big picture and go for the 'best in class'. You think getting into oil stocks is a good idea? Then just put all your money on the best-rated oil firm.

✔ Bottom up triumphs because going for the micro view means you can look through nooks and crannies and come up with tiny firms that will grow.

And just for reference, try guessing how much of the world's total stock market value can be attributed to UK companies. Is it maybe 20, 30, 40, 50, or 60 per cent? Nope. The exact figure varies over time because of the ups and downs of share prices and moves in foreign currency rates, but even roughly, it's nowhere near any of those numbers.

The ball park number for the percentage of the world stock market attributed to UK shares is around 6 per cent. Even that's an exaggeration. Some foreign companies such as SABMiller, a worldwide brewery firm, and Anglo American, a South African mining firm, are listed on the London Stock Exchange even though they have few if any operations in the UK. The London quote gets them attention and respectability. It may also help these firms gain investors who'd otherwise not be allowed to buy their shares if they were quoted on their home stock exchange. There are a great deal of individual opportunities out there so you need to take a world view when investing. Information is easier than ever. With the Internet, you can find stuff out about a firm based in Buenos Aires just as easily as one in Birmingham.

Here are a couple of helpful titbits for you:

✔ Where a company is quoted is important. Investors look at factors such as the currency used on the exchange where the shares are listed. They also notice the ease of buying and selling and the reliability of additional services, such as share registration and custody. It's no good buying a share if you can't sell it easily the next day (or even the next minute) or, worse, if you find that ownership is hard to prove.

✔ Where a company is listed is also vital because of the increasing trend to buy index-tracking funds. These tracker funds buy all the shares listed on an index, such as the FTSE 100 (the Footsie) or the American Standard & Poor's 500, in their correct proportions so if a share makes up 5 per cent of the index, the fund will hold 5 per cent. If the index has a number of companies not really dependent on the host country's economy, working out what's really happening can be harder. (You can have a look at index trackers in detail when we take a closer look at unit trusts.)

A Tour of World Markets

More than 60 countries have stock markets considered serious enough to buy and sell shares in by international investors. They range from the United States; through smaller countries with long stock market histories, such as New Zealand and Finland; to nations whose stock exchanges have recently emerged, such as Slovakia and Jordan. The number of these stock markets is increasing all the time. Who'd have thought about investing in Zimbabwe, Botswana, or Ecuador a few years ago? Mind you, I'm not recommending you do so, at least not without a lot of specialist advice first!

Like football teams, stock markets can be divided into divisions. This section works through them – from the Manchester Uniteds and Arsenals right down to the Peterborough Uniteds and Chesterfields of the stock market.

Note that in the top-down world, the usual starting point for information is the national share price index. It can be dominated by one or two very large companies or one or two industries. So in this section, I also provide the names of various share price indexes that cover the shares of each nation.

The premier league

The premier league is comprised of countries that have the most powerful and influential stock markets in the world. The premier league members are the United States, the United Kingdom, Japan, France, and Germany.

The United States

The United States has the biggest stock market by miles and miles. It's the powerhouse of the world's economy and has the widest range of companies listed on it. Investors can't ignore it. It's simply too important.

The two biggie markets: The New York Stock Exchange and NASDAQ

The New York Stock Exchange (NYSE) is the top share-trading venue. In 2000, its 3,000 or so companies were worth $16 trillion. That's 16 followed by 12 zeros. Three years later, the value of the NYSE had fallen to $13 trillion. At the end of 2007, the exchange was worth about $22trillion (although the fall in the value of the dollar against the pound and the euro meant that this statistic was not quite so impressive this side of the Atlantic).

The New York Stock Exchange is situated on Wall Street, hence the whole US stock market is often referred to as *Wall Street*. This market is a traditional stock exchange where dealers do business with each other on a trading floor with figures flashing up on big screens. It's pure Hollywood.

Not all US company stocks are listed on the New York Stock Exchange. Smaller regional exchanges exist for areas such as the Pacific and the Midwest. But the most important exchange outside the NYSE is NASDAQ, which stands for National Association of Securities Dealers Automated Quotes.

NASDAQ has always been more welcoming to smaller companies with big ambitions. Listing on NASDAQ is easier than on the NYSE. It is home to such stocks as those of online retailer Amazon and coffee shop Starbucks, although technology dominates. Microsoft, Apple, and Intel are all listed on it. NASDAQ is mainly for the high-tech market, and trading is screen-based via electronics. There's no physical building for this exchange other than an administrative site, just thousands of dealers linked by computers.

At the height of the tech market boom in early 2000, NASDAQ's nearly 5,000 companies were worth $5 trillion, making it the second biggest market in the world at the time. But many of its companies had ambitions greater than their ability to deliver. By the time the tech bubble had truly evaporated in 2003, NASDAQ's total value had fallen by some three-quarters .Since then, NASDAQ has made a big recovery with new companies with good prospects replacing the bust flushes.

Note that in addition to the companies being traded on the NYSE and NASDAQ, thousands of companies are traded on the Pink Sheets (old fashioned share dealers used to use pink paper for the shares of these firms so the idea caught on in publications and Web sites). Pink Sheet companies are usually very tiny. Some of these have never made anything, let alone a profit. Very little regulation is involved. Even if a dealer says the companies are 'pre-NASDAQ listings', you should avoid them unless you want to take a total gamble.

The two biggie indexes: The Dow Jones Industrial Average and Standard & Poor's 500

The most quoted US share index is the Dow Jones Industrial. It's been around since 1896 and consists of the share prices of 30 big companies on the New York Stock Exchange. They're chosen not just because they are big but more importantly to represent a wide swathe of American industry and commerce. Companies rarely leave the Dow Jones as it is not purely size based. And although it is probably the most widely quoted index in the world, it is not one that fund managers try to follow as an indicator of whether they are beating the averages or not.

You're probably familiar with most of the companies. The list includes American Express, Boeing, Citigroup, Coca-Cola, Dupont, Exxon, General Motors, Hewlett-Packard, IBM, McDonald's, Microsoft, Procter & Gamble, Wal-Mart, and Walt Disney. The Dow Jones Industrial is made up of mainly *old economy* (meaning companies that were around before Internet technology burst on the scene) as well as some newer tech-based companies.

If you buy packaged portfolios of shares, such as investment or unit trusts, another index is quoted – the Standard & Poor's 500 (S&P 500).The S&P 500 lists 500 major NYSE-quoted companies. Between them, these firms account for around 80 per cent of the NYSE's total value. Because of its bigger number of companies (compared with just 30 in the Dow Jones) and the way it's calculated, the S&P 500 is considered a better indicator of the strength of shareholder and corporate America.

Fund managers need to have an index to measure their achievements against, called a *benchmark*. Most US funds, or funds with a substantial US component, are measured against the S&P 500 because of its wide range of companies.

The UK

The UK stock market is one of the world's most important stock markets, so it's included in the premier league. It's also (obviously) an integral player in this book, so rather than provide a brief overview of the UK stock market here, I provide intricate details about it in a big section later in this chapter. So just divert thine eyes to the section 'The UK Stock Market: Up Close and Personal' when you're ready for the whole scoop.

Japan

OK, so lots of investment commentators have written off Japan as an economic basket case that needs a whole load of US-style financial strategies. Well, it's true that Japan has seen better stock market days. In the late 1980s, the value of the shares quoted in Tokyo were worth one and a half times the value of all those quoted everywhere else outside the United States.

At the height of the Japanese stock market bubble in late 1989, the Nikkei 225 index (the most widely quoted measure of the health or otherwise of the Tokyo market) peaked just short of 40,000 points. Now it is a fraction of that. But, and here's something those knocking Japan rarely tell you, despite all this, it is still a huge economy with a massive stock market.

The Japanese stock market is the most vivid illustration that not everything that goes up and then down recovers to its previous glory days. It may do so one day, but no one is taking bets on that now.

You may, however, think that Japan is worthwhile at its present levels because you are starting out without the baggage of the past. Even if you do, here's another word of warning: Japanese shares can be very complicated. They feature a device known as the *cross-holding*. Here's a simple version of how it works: Company A holds a 20 per cent stake in Company B, which in turn holds 20 per cent in Company A. So Company A's value depends to an extent on Company B. But Company B also depends on Company A.

And, again, that's the simple version! The reality is far more complicated. For example, Company A may have a stake in Company B, which buys into Company C and so on. Then, just to add more fun, a holding company such as an investment bank may also buy stakes in each of the companies. Then there are the offshoots of the quoted companies, called subsidiaries. These can sometimes have such complicated share structures that more than one major quoted company has a stake in them. To make matters even worse, some of these firms are backed by banks which could go bust, pulling the total structure down. The whole thing is a nightmare. It's little wonder few UK investors ever buy shares in Japan.

France and Germany

The main share index covering France is the CAC 40 of 40 leading companies. Shares are traded on the Paris Bourse.

The share index to follow for Germany is the DAX. It has a good mix of industrial companies and financial firms. The main German stock market is in Frankfurt.

Note that both the French and German markets and those in ten other European countries, including Belgium, Finland, Italy, Portugal, the Netherlands, and Spain, are part of the euro zone. All their shares are listed in euros. More and more companies based in the euro zone have businesses and activities that cross traditional national boundaries. European companies are trying to make their shares look more 'Anglo-Saxon' after the model of America and the UK. This means they are cutting back on 'cross-holdings' where banks, insurance companies, and some industrial concerns hold shares in each other.

A number of European indexes are available, such as the Dow Jones Eurostoxx 50, the FTSEurofirst 100, the MSCI EMU, and the S&P Euro. All these indexes cover big companies. The firms are all registered in one or another of the euro countries but have activities that go far beyond.

The championship league

Hot on the heels of the premier league in terms of stock-market power and influence is the championship league of stock markets. Its members are

- ✔ **Australia.** Best known for its mining stocks but also for breweries, such as Fosters, and a number of big banks and insurance companies. The main index is the S&P All Ordinaries. It is well regulated.

- ✔ **Canada.** A mix of natural resources shares and more general stocks based on the Toronto stock exchange. Its principal index is the S&P TSX Composite. Canada also has smaller, regional exchanges where the quality of shares traded can vary from hopeful to hopeless to downright dangerous.

- ✔ **Italy.** Now in the mainstream but once regarded as a difficult market to deal in. The market is centred in Milan, and an emphasis is on banks, car makers, electronics, and luxury goods. The main index is the Banca Commerciale.

- ✔ **Netherlands.** Heavy on industrial firms and financial companies. One of the best-run exchanges, the Amsterdam market features shares such as Shell and Unilever. The main index is the AEX.

- ✔ **Spain.** Two decades ago, the Madrid market was a little-used facility. Now Spanish stocks are mainstream with companies ranging from mining to banks to department stores. The main index is the Madrid Stock Exchange Index. But there is also a second index called the IBEX35. It suffered from severe overheating in 2006–7 as the Spanish building boom came to an end.

- ✔ **Switzerland.** The folk of Zurich, the financial centre of Switzerland, know a thing or two about making money. And despite its relatively small size as a country, Switzerland is home to many of the biggest companies in the world, such as Novartis, Nestlé, Roche, and insurance company Swiss Re. You don't need to know much about Switzerland to invest in Swiss companies. The main index is the SMI (Swiss Market Index).

League one and league two – a.k.a. the third and fourth divisions

League one (that's the third division) of stock markets consists of stable but smaller countries, including Austria, Belgium, Denmark, Finland, Greece, Iceland, Ireland, Luxembourg, New Zealand, Norway, Portugal, Singapore, and Sweden. These countries have perfectly good economies and good prospects, but don't have enough big companies to satisfy big-league share buyers.

League two (or the fourth division if you're not football-inclined) consists of markets that are moving up in world investor estimation. The countries include Bulgaria, the Czech Republic, Hungary, Hong Kong, Israel, Mexico, South Korea, Taiwan, and Turkey.

Some markets have big question marks hanging over them. These markets make up the fifth division of stock markets, and the division's members include Argentina, Chile, Colombia, Egypt, Indonesia, Jordan, Malaysia, Mexico, Pakistan, Philippines, Thailand, Venezuela, and Zimbabwe. Don't treat this list as either complete or set in stone, though. Markets have a way of going in and out of investor fashion depending on the political risk assessments of the countries. Chile is generally seen as stable, Mexico has had ups and downs, while by 2007, astronomic inflation and an unstable political situation means that Zimbabwe is a market where only the bravest (or the most outrageous gamblers) would buy. Investors don't want to put money into countries that could fall to a revolution. But those who do may win later. The scariest markets can both make and lose the most money.

Note that plenty of stock markets are currently viewed as too small for big investors, but they may attract money later. These markets include Croatia, Cyprus, Estonia, Jamaica, Latvia, Lithuania, Morocco, Nigeria, Romania, and Sri Lanka. This is a list which can change at any moment. In fact, just like sports teams which go up and down the divisions, no position is ever fixed in perpetuity.

You can find out more information about the premier league and other stock markets in the *Financial Times*.

The Brics

You may have noticed that my list of countries as if they were football divisions in England missed out four very, very large countries – Brazil, China, India, and Russia. Rearrange that order and the initials become *Bric*. Now that sounds solid, just like a real brick.

Bric is not some sort of entertainment award. Instead, Bric is an investment buzzword standing for Brazil, Russia, India, and China. But just what do these four nations have in common? The link is that they are very big countries, they have some 45 per cent of the world's population, and all their economies are booming away. Brazil and Russia are also very rich in natural resources such as oil and metals. These four countries' economic growth has been reflected in some super stock market performance.

The idea is that as they grow their economies, more and more of their people can afford Western-style luxuries such as mobile phones, travel, entertainment, and expensive food. This should create a virtuous circle of yet more growth. But at the same time, they have a seemingly endless supply of lower-cost labour, so they can provide Europe and North America with goods and services at cheaper prices.

Risks obviously exist in all this. From time to time, these economies will overheat. And when that happens, investors will take fright and run. So Bric investors can't expect an easy ride.

A number of specialist investment funds exist that concentrate on the Bric nations. And many more funds put a part of their money into these countries.

The UK Stock Market: Up Close and Personal

Buyers of UK shares have approximately 3,000 companies to choose from. The value of the biggest 20 of these by *market capitalisation* is worth more than the rest put together. Market capitalisation (usually called *market cap*) is the figure you get by multiplying the number of shares a company has issued by the price of one share. A company with 100 million shares worth £3 each would have a market cap of £300m. The market cap is a widely quoted and used figure.

The FTSE 100 (the Footsie)

The UK stock market's main health measure is the FTSE 100 index, usually known as the *Footsie*. The Footsie is recalculated every second, so any up or down movement in prices from trading in any of its constituent stocks automatically changes the index for good or bad. Most no-cost Internet or teletext services quote the figure (as well as share prices of individual companies) with a 15-minute delay. Services that you pay for, including some services offered by stockbrokers as part of an overall package, offer the numbers in real time.

The Footsie contains the 100 biggest UK-quoted companies by market value. The list is revised once per quarter. Companies whose capitalisations have shrunk are replaced by those who've grown larger. There's a relegation zone and a list of companies who may be promoted from among the biggest just outside the Footsie. Arrangements are also in place for immediate substitute companies if an index member drops out either because of a takeover or, less often, from going bust.

Being in the top 100 brings prestige. It also ensures a lot of buying interest from fund managers. Some funds only buy Footsie stocks; others have to keep a substantial proportion of their investment money in the top company shares both because the rules of their fund say they have to and it would not make much sense for a mainstream fund to ignore all the most important companies.

The reverse, a fall in prestige, happens if a company drops out of the list. It's often sliding down the table anyway, and expulsion adds to the company's woes. There's nothing to stop a company from bouncing back to the list in the next set of ups and downs, of course. A few companies have behaved like yo-yos in this respect!

Investors who look regularly at market values can often work out the likely promotions and relegations ahead of the official announcement from the Footsie folks. You just look at the capitalisations and take it from there. The advantage? You're ahead of the game, beating those fund managers, such as those running index tracker funds who buy all the shares in an index in their correct proportions so their fund looks like a replica of the index, going up and down in line with the publicly available calculations. (Index tracker fund rules say that managers can only buy shares after a company is firmly in the index and must sell shares only after they've been properly thrown out.)

Is Footsie feeble?

The Footsie is quoted all day long on news programmes as a measure of the health of the UK stock market and, by extension, of the UK economy. It's not perfect, however. Whole sections of the UK economy are either not represented at all or underplayed, and some sectors are over-represented.

Table 7–1 lists the Footsie riders and runners at the end of 2007. Here's your chance to carry out some analysis. Look at the list and write in what each of these companies does. Some are household names; others are a lot more obscure. (You can find out what each company does from its Web site.) Then work out what's missing! You'll find some activities from the economy are not there at all, are only there a little, or are there too much.

Back in 2000 during the tech stock boom, the FTSE 100 index was biased (fund managers say *overweighted*) toward high-tech companies. Before that, the index was full of water, gas, and electricity shares. Go back a bit further, and financial companies ruled the roost. Now, in this latest list, you find lots of mining companies whose fortunes depend on the raw materials boom.

Table 7-1	The Footsie – end 2007 Style	
Rank	*Company*	*Market Value £ billion*
1	BP	112.0
2	HSBC Holdings	98.2
3	Vodafone	96.8
4	GlaxoSmithKline	71.1
5	Royal Dutch Shell	70.6

(continued)

Table 7-1 *(continued)*

Rank	Company	Market Value £ billion
6	Rio Tinto	56.2
7	Royal Bank of Scotland	45.9
8	Anglo American	43.5
9	British American Tobacco	38.1
10	Tesco	37.6
11	Barclays	37.2
12	BHP Billiton	35.7
13	BG Group	34.3
14	AstraZeneca	33.7
15	Xstrata	33.2
16	HBOS	29.8
17	Unilever	28.5
18	Diageo	28.4
19	Lloyds TSB	28.0
20	Standard Chartered	26.9
21	BT Group	23.0
22	National Grid	21.0
23	SABMiller	20.8
24	Reckitt Benckiser	20.6
25	Aviva	17.9
26	Imperial Tobacco	17.0
27	Prudential	16.8
28	BAE Systems	16.2
29	Scottish & Southern Energy	13.7
30	Centrica	13.4
31	Cadbury Schweppes	13.1
32	British Sky Broadcasting	11.0
33	Marks & Spencer	9.8

Rank	Company	Market Value £ billion
34	Rolls Royce	9.6
35	Man Group	9.5
36	Old Mutual	9.2
37	Wm Morrison Supermarkets	8.3
38	Legal & General	8.2
39	Imperial Chemical Industries	7.9
40	Reed Elsevier	7.8
41	Sainsbury	7.7
42	Reuters	7.6
43	Antofagasta	7.5
44	WPP Group	7.3
45	Scottish & Newcastle	7.1
46	Associated British Foods	7.0
47	International Power	7.0
48	Land Securities	7.0
49	Vedanta Resources	6.6
50	United Utilities	6.6
51	Shire	6.5
52	Kazakhmys	6.3
53	Compass	6.0
54	Pearson	6.0
55	Standard Life	5.7
56	British Energy	5.4
57	Smith & Nephew	5.2
58	Invesco	5.2
59	Lonmin	5.1
60	Resolution	4.8
61	Tullow Oil	4.8

(continued)

Table 7-1 *(continued)*

Rank	Company	Market Value £ billion
62	Royal & Sun Alliance	4.8
63	British Land	4.7
64	Cable & Wireless	4.6
65	Wolseley	4.6
66	-ICAP	4.5
67	Experian	4.3
68	3i Group	4.2
69	Smiths	4.1
70	Liberty International	4.1
71	British Airways	3.9
72	Johnson Matthey	3.7
73	Severn Trent	3.7
74	Kingfisher	3.6
75	Next	3.5
76	Carnival	3.5
77	Friends Provident	3.4
78	ITV	3.3
79	Carphone Warehouse	3.3
80	Yell	3.2
81	Rexam	3.1
82	Alliance & Leicester	3.1
83	Home Retail	3.0
84	Schroders	3.0
85	Hammerson	3.0
86	Sage	2.8
87	Intercontinental Hotels	2.7
88	Rentokil Initial	2.7
89	Enterprise Inns	2.7

Rank	Company	Market Value £ billion
90	Whitbread	2.6
91	Persimmon	2.4
92	Mitchells & Butlers	2.3
93	Taylor Wimpey	2.2
94	Punch Taverns	2.2
95	Tate & Lyle	2.1
96	Daily Mail & General Trust	2.0
97	DSG International	2.0
98	Barratt Developments	1.6
99	Schroders NV	0.8
100	Northern Rock	0.5

Footsie facts and figures

Here's a hodgepodge of Footsie information that you may find helpful (or at least interesting even if not helpful): It's all based on our table which comes from easy to find, publicly available information. Using the above as a model, it's not a bad idea to re-create an up-to-date version to get a good overview of the UK stock market.

- ✔ The total value of Footsie is around £1.5 trillion.

- ✔ The stocks from the top ten companies account for more than 40 per cent of the total value of the index. So a move in the price of any share in this leading part counts for far more than a change in the lower ranks. The top 20 listings are nearly two-thirds the value of the index.

- ✔ Oil companies and banks dominate the top ten companies. A bad day for the oil or banking sector means a bad day for the index. A good day for those areas brings loads of investor smiles as they perk up the index.

- ✔ Few companies with any engineering interests are on the list.

- ✔ A handful of house builders are on the list, reflecting the big residential property boom.

- ✔ Few companies in the top 20 are largely or totally UK-focused. Some, such as Anglo American and Rio Tinto, have few, if any, UK interests.

- ✔ Over the past few years, a number of well-known companies such as Abbey National, BAA (the airports company), and Boots have left the list because they have been either taken over by foreign companies or have become private, non-stock market companies.

Small can be beautiful

For many years, small companies as a group out-performed their bigger brothers. But although that outperformance was real enough on paper, investors had to be very lucky to capture it for themselves.

There were just a few front runners among the few thousand small companies. Their share prices doubled, tripled, or even sextupled in a year. But if investors' portfolios missed out on them, the investors received nothing very special. Investors made a fortune out of small companies only if they were lucky or very well informed.

Since the late 1990s, the small company outper-formance effect has been even harder to detect.

Big funds and major stockbrokers have been unwilling to research small companies. They argue that seriously researching one small com-pany can take as much, if not more, person power than looking at BP, Britain's biggest company at the time of this writing. It is not worth devoting loads of expensive research effort at a company worth £10 million at best, they argue.

If you invest in small companies, you'll find few mentions in newspapers or from online sources. But they are the life blood of tip sheets, newspa-per share advice columns, and a number of specialist services.

The FTSE 250 (the Mid Caps)

Mid Caps is stock market jargon for companies with a medium-sized market capitalisation. They're too small for the Footsie but too significant to be considered Tiddlers (see the following section for what Tiddlers are). Their measure is the FTSE 250, or the Mid Cap. As its name suggests, it is an index covering the next 250 shares after the Footsie. It contains many of the activities that are missing or under-represented in the Footsie, such as house building, entertainments, and engineering. A handful of specialist unit and investment trusts focus on this medium-sized company area.

Beyond the FTSE 250 (the Tiddlers)

The Tiddlers are the small companies beyond the largest 100 and the next 250 that appear in the Footsie and the Mid Cap lists. Approximately 2,000 of these small-quoted companies exist, and their combined market value is smaller than the biggest Footsie company on its own. Some are former large companies down on their luck; others are companies that came to the stock market on a wave of enthusiasm which quickly ran out of steam; and a third group consists of firms with a hoped-for glittering future.

Tiddler shares are unlikely to be traded on a regular basis. Sometimes, it takes days or even weeks for a buyer or seller to come forward, so just one purchase or disposal order can send prices shooting upward or spinning downward. But a number of specialist funds concentrate on small-company shares, arguing that small companies can outperform the big companies because the people running these concerns are nimble enough to come up with ideas that will turn out to be tomorrow's winners.

AIM (the Alternative Investment Market)

AIM, or the Alternative Investment Market, is a market regulated by the London Stock Exchange but with easier entry requirements and less demanding rules than the LSE demands. It's a bit like a golf club that lets in players with lower abilities – provided that they don't use the greens at weekends.

AIM quoted companies vary in stock market value from more than £200m to under £500,000. At the top end, they could easily graduate to the main market if they wanted to. Doing so would enable them to increase their attractions to big investment managers who often can't buy AIM stocks because their fund's rules put up a bar to their investing in shares which are not quoted on the London Stock Exchange itself.

At the bottom of the AIM list are companies worth less than a modest house in London. Most of these companies have shares whose values have plunged to 1p or even less. What these companies do is often unclear.

AIM shares vary immensely in quality. In general, they haven't performed well, although they did have a big spurt during the high-tech boom in 1999–2000.

Just because a stock is listed on AIM does not make it a good idea. Some really bad-quality companies have gone onto AIM – some designed to grab as much investor money as they could before disappearing into the blue yonder. A number have been sold by overseas *boiler rooms* (illegal offshore sales pushers) or by UK-based and UK-regulated *bucket shops*, which are like boiler rooms except that they have a veneer of respectability. No sure things exist in investing. Expect that investing in rubbish or companies with too-good-to-be-possibly-true stories, will lose you money.

Here are various AIM-related titbits to be aware of:

✔ AIM shares may be quoted every day in newspapers, but according to HM Revenue & Customs and its strange regulations, AIM shares are unquoted. The reason? So that they're given a special tax status. From April 2008, this status no longer matters for capital gains tax bills, but still counts as an advantage for some inheritance tax calculations.

✔ One advantage of AIM for people building up their own companies is that they don't have to sell many shares to outsiders to achieve an AIM listing. That way, they can keep control. Whether that's good for investors is another matter. A danger is that directors will continue to see the company as their own personal toy rather than run it in the best interests of all shareholders.

✔ AIM companies are unlikely to be researched, although some brokers send out material on companies in which they or their existing clients hold a major slice of the stock. This is hardly unbiased research!

✔ The gap between the quoted buying and selling prices from market makers can be huge in percentage terms, especially for very low-priced shares. (A market maker is a professional who assesses second by second the weight of buy and sell pressures and adjusts prices accordingly. This activity determines what the brokers charge you or give you when you sell – adjusted, of course, for their commission fees.) A company with a newspaper price of 2.5p per share may cost you 3p to buy, but you'll only get 2p if you sell. So your purchase may have to soar before you can sell for the price you paid in the first place. You're running fast to stand still.

PLUS Markets

PLUS Markets has replaced the old OFEX (or off-exchange) market as a way of trading companies that are either too small or too infrequently bought and sold to warrant a listing on the full market or on AIM.

PLUS was created to give investors more confidence than they had in the old OFEX. However, in the big scheme of things, the companies quoted on PLUS don't add up to a row of beans. Most investors, whether they are professionals controlling millions or someone with a few thousand, can go through their whole lives without any PLUS involvement. But you do need to know what PLUS is, as some brokers suggest shares quoted on it.

Over 200 smaller companies are currently on the *PLUS-quoted* market. These companies include long-established family-controlled breweries where few shares ever change hands, some football clubs, and new companies in technology.

For the love of penny shares

Small companies with a full quote, those on AIM, and those on PLUS often fall into the penny share category. Originally, a *penny share* was a share whose price was below one shilling in old money (that's 5p now) and so priced only in pence. With decimal currency, the term was first stretched to 10p or double figures and then to 50p. Many of the original penny shares were in speculative 'products of Empire', such as tea and rubber plantations in Malaya (now Malaysia) or gold mines in South Africa or Australia. Now they're just speculative.

Despite their very high risk, the penny share has a special place in share buying mythology.

UK investors love, for some unexplained reasons, to own a large number of lowly priced shares (as opposed to investors in the United States and most other places, where a high share price is prized). The UK dislike of heavy prices is so great that large companies often subdivide their shares once they reach £10. Somehow to UK investors, owning 1,000,000 shares worth 10p each is better than owning 1,000 shares worth £100 each.

The theory of the penny share is that even a small 1p rise is proportionately huge. A 1p gain on a 10p price is 10 per cent. On a £10 price, it's 0.1 per cent. The maths works in theory. But nothing else does in practice. For example, the opposite also applies! In addition, most penny stocks are from companies down on their luck, or where Lady Luck has yet to appear – and that's usually for a reason.

Some investors put money into these fallen stocks for no better reason than 'What was once up and then fell will always rise again' (or 'What has not yet risen will surely do so some day'). But while day follows night, no certainty exists that a stock market up will follow a down or a never-got-off-the-ground.

How Far Can You Rely on the Rhythms in a Market?

When share indexes rise or fall, which shares march to the market rhythm and which ones go their own way? This isn't just an academic question because investors need to know just how far they can rely on the overall good or bad feeling in a market.

No two individual shares and no two national stock markets remain in tandem forever. But plenty of evidence shows that the London market often takes a short-term cue from Wall Street. The direction the US market takes when it opens (usually 2.30 p.m. London time) can influence the direction shares take in the UK that day.

That's not surprising. Some of the biggest UK companies, such as BP and GlaxoSmithKline, have huge US interests and large US shareholdings. Equally, the US economy is so dominant in the world that its trading alone can have big effects on companies elsewhere, including firms that may not directly trade with the United States.

Japan is the one exception among the big markets. It had its own super bubble in the late 1980s, went down throughout the 1990s when most other stock markets were soaring, and only rejoined the general movement in the early 2000s. It kept on falling, but this time other markets were sliding dramatically as well. Since then, it has recovered along with other markets, but the main Japanese index is still less than half its value at the end of the 1980s.

To find markets that are truly out of step, you have to look to the smaller, emerging markets that cover countries moving out of low development to full participation in the capitalist world. So, a growing number of fund managers are showing an interest in Africa beyond the long-established South African market. This could be a case of investors creating the reasons for putting their money into a particular country after they've done it and then hoping others will follow on, pushing up prices, and giving them a profitable exit route! Or, it could be a case of some investors putting money in because they firmly believe that just as other parts of the world have come good in stock exchange terms, then it is now the turn of Africa. It's the old story of money chasing money around the globe. And Africa does offer that enticing mix of low-cost labour plus abundant raw materials.

Chapter 8

Investing in Markets

Do you ever look through those newspaper columns headed Recent Wills? I admit I do. And I bet I'm not alone.

One of the interests is seeing how much money the newly deceased but dearly beloved left behind and whether it all went to the local home for stray moggies. But the real fascination, for me at least, is trying to imagine how they made their money. A substantial number of people made theirs from shares, often doing little more than just buying mainstream equities when they could afford them and leaving them to grow. It was a policy of benign neglect.

Trading ten times a day (or ten times a month) is bad for your financial health. The typical share purchased by an individual must go up in price around 6 to 8 per cent before it can be sold for the money first paid for it.

This chapter provides some helpful tips and titbits as you begin investing in the stock market – so you can someday impress people – although it is to be hoped you can do this a long time before the curious read about it in Recent Wills. In this chapter, I show you the two routes into the market, explain the benefits of keeping an eye on the long-term trend, share a couple of industry secrets, focus you on some big-picture items to *always* keep in mind, and fill you in on the payments and perks you receive as a shareholder.

How easy making a million really is

American automobile manufacturer Henry Ford famously said that history is bunk. And I say that you can't ever rely on the past to prove the future in the investment world. But we can both be wrong sometimes.

If you have £25,000 now and are prepared to be patient, you can end up with £1m. All you have to do is invest in the UK stock market index, put all your dividends and other payments back into your fund, sit back, and wait. You don't have to be a stock market genius or even spend time looking at companies. All you have to do is buy a basket of shares in the constituent companies of a widely available share price index and let the power of equities do the rest. Or at least, that one lesson from stock market history. Now let's have a close look at the figures to back this.

Research from Barclays Capital shows how equities have the power to make you rich, provided that you're not tempted to spend your gains. Using the timeframe of 1919 to 1985, the researchers worked out how long it would take for £25,000 to become £1m. (They reduced the starting amount by inflation, based on prices at the end of 1999.) The researchers invested the starting £25,000 (or equivalent) into the FTSE All Share Index. This is a measure of the share prices of some 750 UK companies ranging from the massive to miniscule.

The researchers found that the quickest journey to millionaire status was 14 years – achieved by those who invested just after the First World War and also by those who were brave enough to put money in after the 1970s market crash.

For the majority of the investments, however, the magic million came in 20 years or less. In only seven instances (starting-point years), reaching the magic million took 25 or more years. The investments that took the longest to reach £1m included those that were started around the time of the 1929 market crash, which was followed by a huge economic slump; the Second World War; and the mid to late 1950s.

However you cut this one, you can see that getting big money over your lifetime is not impossible, but only if you re-invest the dividends rather than spending them.

Where the Stock Market Entry Routes Are

There are two routes into the stock market: You can either hold collective funds or buy shares in individual companies – or both.

With collective funds, money is taken from many small investors, pooled to give buying power, and then entrusted to a manager who decides what to buy and sell. Fund managers earn fees for this service. The main collective fund categories are investment and unit trusts.

The concerns you must consider with a collective fund are selecting the market and then choosing a good fund manager. You can own several funds and/or invest in a fund of funds that puts your cash into the funds its own managers choose. (Part III of this book looks at collective funds in detail, when you're ready for the full lowdown.)

The next stage is what I call *half and half* (although the exact proportions are up to you). This is where you mix 'n' match collectives with your individual shareholders. The advantage of having your own shares is that you are in control, and you don't have to pay yourself an annual fee for looking after them. Don't forget that while 1.5 per cent a year may not sound much, it adds up to a big sum over 10 to 20 years.

Alternatively, some opt for a pure do-it-yourself route, making all the decisions themselves and paying fund managers not a penny.

How the Trend Is Your Friend

A share may only seem to be a bit of paper (or a record in an electronic file if you've got rid of old-fashioned certificates for the joy of dematerialisation). But that bit of paper represents something very real. It shows that you own part, albeit a very small part, of a real live company. And as long as that company continues doing well, then so will you.

The likelihood, of course, is that you'll own more than one share, either directly through your own portfolio, so that you build up your diversification and spread your risk, or through a fund, such as a unit or an investment trust, where you pay someone else to do all the research, diversification, and risk spreading for you.

Now if your idea of a portfolio is a collection full of super-speculative penny stocks and no-hopers, you can skip the rest of this chapter. But the rest of you need to see how trends are your friends:

✔ What do you know about wages? They tend to go up.

✔ What do you know about prices? They tend to go up.

✔ What do you know about prosperity in general? It tends to go up.

Add all these things together, and you know that the profitability trend in companies in general should be upward over the long term. In turn, when profits rise, the payments from shares, known as dividends, should go up. And so should the share price.

Only a share can give you a direct interest in rising prosperity. Over the past 100 years, equities have given an annual return of nearly 10 per cent. Bonds have averaged just over 5 per cent, not far off half. The gap gets wider the longer you hold shares. This extra is called the *Equity Risk Premium*. It's what you get paid for taking a greater chance with your money.

Two Top Investment Trade Tricks

In this section, I let you in on two stock market secrets. The first one, which is about the benefits of the passive-investment path to profits, is actually just classified material, so it's really not super secret. But the second one, which is about the benefits of exchange traded funds, is top secret and for your eyes only, requiring the highest degree of confidentiality.

The passive versus active path to profits

One stock market secret is that the long-term investor can do quite well by buying all the shares in companies that appear in an index such as Footsie, the Eurostoxx, or the US's Standard & Poor's. Naturally, you'd do better if you could just spot the best 10 per cent. Try, though, and there's a big danger you'll get the worst 10 per cent!

You can't buy all the shares in an index yourself unless you're very wealthy and prepared to monitor your holdings constantly. You need a specialist fund to do this for you. Specialist fund types include index trackers and exchange traded funds.

Buying all the shares of companies in an index in their same proportions as the index compilers use, irrespective of what anyone may think about their individual prospects, is called *passive investment*. Footsie trackers are popular. A tracker is a fund that aims to replicate the ups and downs of an index (here the FTSE 100 or Footsie) by buying all the constituent shares. So if you look at the list of Footsie constituents in Table 7–1 of Chapter 7, you'll see that the biggest share at the end of 2007 was BP. So BP would be the biggest holding in a Footsie tracker fund. Ignoring Northern Rock, which was still in the index despite its problems because index constituents are only changed quarterly, Schroder (a firm of fund managers) was the smallest, so it would be the smallest holding in a tracker fund. BP's value was about 120 times as great as that of Schroder, so the BP holding would be around 120 times as great. If Schroder dropped out, the fund, or rather its managers or sometimes the automatic computer program controlling the fund, would have to sell it and replace it with whatever substituted for it in the index.

The opposite approach is called *active investment*, where you take a view on each company and only buy those that you think will do best. The problem is, as mentioned at the beginning of this section, you may end up buying the worst 10 per cent and losing a great deal of money!

Active versus passive investment is a very big debate. Most of the material published tends to come from those with prior positions and commercial interests on either side, so it tends to develop more heat than light. This dispute goes on whatever is happening to stock markets. Funds can only make money when the shares they invest in go up. So what happens when shares go down as they did from 2000 to 2003? Easy. The active versus passive argument turns on which side lost less money. And what happens when they reverse as they did from 2003 to 2007? That's easy too. The argument revolves on which approach made more.

The pros of the passive approach

Here are the benefits of the passive-investment approach:

- ✔ The only thinking you need to do is deciding which index to follow, when to buy, and ultimately when to sell.

- ✔ The computer works out which shares to buy and in what proportions.

- ✔ No index has ever gone down all the way to zero, so you'll never lose all your money. Bust and failing companies come out of indexes and are replaced by the shares of healthier firms.

- ✔ Following the ups and downs is easy. The index is published in newspapers and online.

- ✔ You're not wasting money on analysts and researchers, who often contradict each other. When some are saying sell and some are hollering buy, they can't all be right, can they?

- ✔ The charges are usually lower than other forms of investment. The typical tracker charges 0.3 to 0.5 per cent a year in management fees. Anything more is pure robbery because you're not getting any extra value. But active funds hit you for 1.5 per cent and sometimes more. All those yearly 0.5 to 1 per cent reductions in annual management charges plus lower entry costs add up to a big amount of money over 10 to 20 years.

- ✔ Over long periods, tracker funds usually come in at around the 35th to 40th percentile in fund performance tables. A percentile is a one-hundredth of the table, so in a table of 500 funds, each percentile would be five funds deep. A third of the way down would be the 33rd percentile; halfway is the 50th percentile. This means, trackers come somewhere just outside the top third in performance tables.

- ✔ You can use passivity for a *core and satellite* approach to investing. The passive fund is the core for your holdings, so you put 80 per cent or so of your money there. The satellites are your other holdings, where you back your hunches.

The pros of the active approach

Here are the benefits of the active-investment approach:

- ✔ You don't get landed with dud stocks. Index trackers have to keep failing shares heading to the knacker's yard until they're expelled from the index.

✔ You can buy into shares when they're still cheap or little known. The way indexes usually work is that companies are put on the list only when their value reaches a certain level, which may be too late for growth.

✔ You're not forced to change your portfolio just because an index compiler says to do so.

✔ You can pick defensive shares that will do better in falling markets and go for aggressive stocks in rising markets.

✔ You can buy shares in the proportion you want. You don't get landed with too many or too few in any particular company.

✔ You can avoid shares in dodgy or unethical industries, or if you really want to, you can opt instead for a basket of sin stocks, such as stocks from gambling, tobacco, and armaments companies.

✔ You can pick shares to suit the level of dividend income you want to generate.

✔ You don't waste money in tracking error. Tracking error comes from all the costs a fund hits its customers with and the expenses it has to lay out. It also comes from being unable to replicate each movement in the underlying shares at precisely the right moment.

✔ Some indexes, such as the Japanese Nikkei, are difficult to track.

The advantages of exchange traded funds

The usual route into the tracker concept is via a unit trust. And there are also a handful of investment trusts that track an index. But we talked about two secrets earlier on. So here's another stock market secret for you; the exchange traded fund or ETF. It's so hidden that most professional financial advisers don't know about them. Still, maybe they don't want to know. The commission earning possibilities are even less than with tracker funds.

Why look at ETFs? The problem is, both unit trusts and investment trusts have drawbacks as trackers. For example, most unit trusts only allow dealing once or, at most, twice a day and at times to suit the managers. So that's not much use if you spot a sudden buying chance. An index can move 3 per cent or more within a day. That's a lot of money if you get the wrong side of it.

In addition, investment trusts are continuously traded, but their share prices may not be the same as their underlying worth. They can trade at a discount (the underlying shares are worth more) or a premium (the shares are worth less than the sum you pay). If the discount or premium changes between the day of the purchase and the day of a future sale, you'll get more or less than the alteration in the underlying index. Believe me, discounts and premiums change all the time.

Both investment and unit trusts have a further disadvantage. Every time you buy into the fund, you have to pay stamp duty one way or another. (It's more hidden in a unit trust purchase, but it's there all the same.)

The answer to these difficulties is something called an *exchange traded fund (ETF)*. You buy this type of fund through a stockbroker just like any other share. But unlike other shares, an exchange traded fund doesn't give you a stake in a company. The ETF is a sort of artificial stock market creation, a piece of financial engineering from the guys who would be rocket scientists if they weren't so keen on money-making. Here the rocket science is called 'derivative trading'. And how this works would fill this book and a half, believe me (oh, and that's genuine understatement!).

But what it does is dead simple. The ETF does what it says on the tin. For example, the Footsie ETF would move up and down exactly in line with the Footsie index, second by second, tenth of a point by tenth of a point. It's always spot on. And you can get regular dividend payments just as with a normal tracker fund.

You can save money as well. Derivatives don't attract UK government stamp duty, which takes 0.5 per cent up front from your other shares investment money. Otherwise, charges are similar to those imposed at the low end of the unit trust trackers' fee range.

 You can use derivatives for all sorts of complicated strategies. The easiest is *shorting*, meaning that you can sell the ETF if you think the index is due to fall and then buy it back later at a lower price. The gap between the two is your profit (or loss).

ETFs are big business in the United States. When they get better known, they'll be big in the UK as well. Currently, you can buy into the Footsie, the Eurostoxx, and the Standard & Poor's 500 via UK-quoted ETFs. But things don't stop there. If you want, you can find an ETF to invest in international pharmaceutical companies, the price of wheat, or even one that finds shares in agricultural machinery firms. Where a demand exists, either real or foreseen, some investment bank or another comes up with an ETF.

ETFs are created by investment banks. Banks can go bust. The danger always exists, even though tiny, that the bank may not be able to meet its liabilities.

What to Consider When Buying Individual Shares

You need to know this fact up front: You can buy great shares that slump and equities in crummy companies that go up. In other words, stock markets are fickle creatures that have no permanent rules.

When you play or watch a game of football, you know that there are two halves and that each, ignoring injury time, should last for 45 minutes. You know what the object of the game is, and at the end, each team has a result, win, draw, or lose.

But stock markets are different. In particular, there are no fixed timeframes and no clear goals. Shares go on until a company ceases to exist. This could be tomorrow or in a hundred years' time. Quality will carry the day eventually, but no one knows when that *eventually* will be or even whether the company will change directions for the better or worse in the meantime.

What you have to do is look at the big-picture items, such as the economy or interest rates, that have the power to push the great to mediocrity (or worse) or the very average to a nice little earner. And you have to keep in mind that markets swing very easily between feast and famine.

Know the psychological impact of the economy

How do you feel when you get out of bed in the morning? Do you feel (Mondays not counted) confident of your job or your pension; that you can make ends meet; that you can cope with the credit card bills; and that the mortgage is not overwhelming?

Or do you worry about your job; fear for your pension payments; fret about being able to afford a holiday this year; know your credit card is ruining you; and have no idea how you're going to pay the mortgage this month?

The likelihood, of course, is that you're somewhere between the euphoria of the first description and the misery of the second. But wherever you are on the scale of being happy or sad about your money prospects, the reason is likely because of the economy. People who prosper in good times have problems when the economy turns sour, even though they continue to work as hard and budget in the same way.

Markets are driven by investor psychology. When most people are happy, they have the confidence to buy shares, so shares go up in value.

Know the power of interest rates

The most important single factor in the modern economy is the interest rate. In the UK, the base rate (which sets the tone for all other interest rates) is fixed at noon on the first Thursday of each month by the Bank of England. This base rate dictates the interest level at which banks and very large companies can borrow money. In turn, it gives the cue to banks, building societies, and loan companies in calculating the interest levels they charge to consumers for credit in stores, homebuyers for mortgages, and smaller firms for the finance their businesses need. Everyone else pays more than the base rate, of course.

Interest rates also set the tone for share prices because:

- **Most companies borrow.** Finance directors calculate that borrowing is fine if that cash can be used to produce a greater return than the interest bill. Suppose, for example, that a company borrows £1m at 5 per cent per year. So the company will pay £50,000 in interest. It uses the money to buy a machine or open a new outlet that produces £70,000 per year in profits. The company is now £20,000 per year better off. If interest rates fall to 3 per cent, the cost of the bank loan falls to £30,000, so now the company gets £40,000 per year in profits. But what if interest rates rise to 10 per cent? The company is now spending £100,000 per year on the money borrowed, which produces £70,000. So it's losing money at the rate of £30,000 per year. Higher interest rates mean higher costs of borrowing. If you pay more to borrow the same amount of money, your profits will drop – and vice versa if interest rates fall.

  Companies that borrow the most in relation to their size benefit the most from falling interest rates. This is called *gearing up*.

- **Most individuals borrow to buy pricey consumer goods.** Companies have to sell products or services either directly to consumers or to other concerns who provide items for stores and services that deal with the ultimate consumer. When interest rates fall, consumers have more money in their pockets (called *disposable income* by economists) because they don't need to spend as much on mortgages and credit card loan costs. If rates rise, shoppers have less scope to buy goods. So higher interest rates dissuade people from borrowing, so fewer goods are sold and companies make lower profits. This is all bad for shares.

- **Company payouts look better when interest rates fall.** Say that you bought a share for £1 that (ignoring tax) pays 5p a year in dividends. At the time you bought, a cash account paid 5 per cent, or 5p, for every £1. Now say that interest rates drop to 4 per cent. The dividend stays at 5 per cent, but the cash account rate falls to 4 per cent. Share dividends are now more attractive, so investors will buy the shares themselves, pushing up the price.

- **Falling interest rates mean the next time a company needs money, it won't have to pay the bank so much.** Therefore, it will be able to carry out its expansion, making the firm bigger and more valuable.

That said, interest rates are a blunt instrument, and they hit companies in different ways.

Here's a list of sectors that are bludgeoned the most by rising rates and that get top benefits from falling rates:

- **House builders.** They're usually big borrowers in comparison to their size. What they build is nearly always sold to consumers who need loans.

- **Retailers.** When rates rise, their customers have less cash because they're paying more for mortgages. Consumers are less likely to use credit cards. Most big purchases are nonessential and can be put off. But for how long? The new three-piece suite can nearly always wait; the new generation videocam is far from necessary; and the replacement for the clapped-out fridge can be put on hold for longer.

- **Fund managers and life insurance companies.** Firms that make their living out of the stock market hate rising interest rates, which scare people off equities. Customers put new money into savings accounts, so the fees these people get from investing other people's money fall.

- **Exporters.** Higher interest rates can often push up the value of your currency on foreign exchange markets. This is bad for exporters who get less when their foreign earnings are turned back into their home currency.

- **Banks.** Surprisingly perhaps, banks do badly when interest rates go up. They do charge more for loans, but not as many people want to borrow. Worse, banks can't hit customers with as big a gap (technically known as the *margin*) between what they give to savers and the amount they charge to borrowers.

And here are some stock market areas that should do better than average when rates are rising:

- **Food retailers.** We have to eat! In tough times, we still need a few shopping-therapy style treats, and these are more likely to be a bottle of wine or a box of chocolates than new clothes or the latest electronic goodies.

- **Discount shops.** Stores where nothing costs more than £1 or where you can buy a complete outfit with change from £50 are obvious winners in hard times.

- **Companies with cash.** Not all companies borrow. Some have big balances at the bank, so they profit if rates rise.

- **Tobacco companies and breweries.** People tend to smoke and drink more when they're miserable, whatever the health effects.

- **Importers.** Higher rates can mean a stronger currency so importers can buy their goods overseas with a smaller amount of their home currency.

Know the long-term trend

Ever heard that story in the Bible about seven good years followed by seven lean years? Thousands of years later, life hasn't changed that much, except now we call it the *economic cycle*. The good years are when interest rates are falling and people are happier. But interest rates can't keep falling forever, and one day they must go up, leading to a period of belt tightening.

Governments, investment banks, and big businesses spend a fortune trying to predict where the big economic wheel is, how fast it's going, and in what direction. They don't have a great deal of success. But here's a secret: Most of those earning a crust by giving forecasts of future economic conditions just follow the trend. If you follow what happened yesterday (or last week or last month) and repeat it today (this week or this month), you're statistically more likely to be right than wrong.

In any case, you don't have to follow the so-called experts' forecasts. You couldn't buy fully into their research and guesstimates even if you could afford to buy their material. It's not usually for sale because it's reserved for pension and other funds controlling billions, which give the researchers and their bosses huge volumes of business.

But don't worry. As the long-term manager of your own money, there are many ways you can do as well if not better than those highly paid City types.

The Payments and Perks of Owning Shares

Shareholding has its plus points including, in some cases, the chance to pick up a bargain when you go shopping or away for a break. These plus points can lighten the down moments and help your finances when the shares themselves are looking miserable.

Getting dividends

Most companies send you a twice-a-year share payment (occasionally four times a year), called a *dividend*. It's the various companies' way of saying thank you for your cash and loyalty in hanging in there through thick and thin.

The first dividend of the year is called the *interim payment*, and the second is called the *final payment*. Sometimes, though, the final dividend is called the *second interim*. The interim payment is usually announced with the six-monthly figures issued halfway through the firm's financial year, and the final dividend is usually announced with the *preliminary results*, or *prelims*, of the financial year, so called because they're revealed before the official annual report.

Shareholders get to vote on the amount that is to be paid out as a final dividend for the year at the annual general meeting, although the instances of investors turning down money can be counted on the fingers of one hand. This usually happens as a form of protest against either the company itself, an activity of that company, or some of the directors.

When a dividend is announced, the company sets a date on which it'll pay the dividend to those on the shareholder register at that time. Investors who buy from that date onward must wait until the next time (probably in six months or so) for their first payment.

Most companies send a dividend cheque, even for a small amount. You could even end up with a cheque worth less than the stamp on the envelope used to send it.

Most companies arrange for your dividend payment to be sent straight to your bank account. This arrangement has advantages for the company because it's cheaper than issuing cheques, and it has advantages for you because you get the money immediately instead of having to trust the post, deposit it in the bank, and wait for the cheque to clear. If they credit your cash automatically, they still send you a notice detailing the dividend payment and any tax deduction.

Another option, offered by many big companies and virtually all funds, is *automatic dividend reinvestment* (sometimes called DRIP, for Dividend Re-Investment Plan). Your money is used to buy new shares in the company at the price ruling on the day the dividend is announced. Of course, it's unlikely that your dividend payment will buy an exact number of shares, so usually some change will be carried over to the next dividend payment and then added to your dividend. Note that you must pay UK government stamp duty at 0.5 per cent on these purchases, but generally any stockbroker fees are minimal. This is a great way to build up a holding over time with little out-of-pocket financing needed! And you don't have to worry about brokerage fees or timing. Again, your paperwork will show the dividend your holding earned.

Re-investing dividends makes sense if you don't need to spend the money. Barclays Equity Gilt Study figures show that much of the advantage of shares is lost otherwise. An investor with £10,000 at the end of 1981 would have shares worth £102,867 a quarter of a century later at the end of 2006 (ignoring costs and tax). Putting the dividends back into shares would've turned that same £10,000 into £258,446. Even making allowances for tax and costs, re-investing dividends pays huge dividends.

And now for some bad news: You may have to pay more tax on your dividends. But you can't reclaim the amount the firm has already paid even if you don't pay tax yourself.

If you pay no tax or pay at the 10 per cent or, as most do, pay at the basic rate, you *probably* have no more tax to pay. Why probably? Your dividends could push you into the top-rate tax. This situation could apply to anyone earning the personal allowance and the full basic-rate tax band. The starting point for the top tax band changes every year in the budget, but if all your earnings including dividends and interest payments top the £40,000 mark then you will probably be a top taxpayer. You may also think that you're a basic-rate taxpayer and then get a big pay rise or bonus that takes you into the 40 per cent top level. Keeping all your dividend paperwork means you can fill in the HMRC tax self-assessment form properly.

Now about that document you receive with your dividend payment: It's very important, which is why many companies put an HMRC *KEEP THIS* label on it. This means what it says. HM Revenue & Customs rules say that you must keep dividend notice forms for 22 months after the end of the tax year in which you received the dividend payment, even if you don't have any tax to pay. If your dividend was paid in May 2008, the tax year ended on April 5, 2009. Your self-assessment tax return, essential if any dividend payment brings you into the top tax band or you're already there, must be sent by January 31, 2010. You must then keep all your returns until January 31, 2011 or longer if the tax inspector queries your assessment.

Chapter 9 looks at dividends in more detail, if you're interested. It explains what investors can understand from their payment levels, increases, and reductions. This stuff can be a good guide to future prospects.

Getting discounts and freebies

A number of companies do more than pay out dividends. They want their investors to share in the company in a more tangible way through share perks. These companies give private investors a discount on the group's goods or services. The discounts vary from money off a new house to a promotional goody bag handed out at the annual general meeting.

It's a win-win deal. Shareholders like perks because they get that little bit extra. Companies like perks because they get investors to sample the goods as well as create some extra, profitable business by offering items at a discount.

Table 8-1 lists some interesting perks offered by various companies.

Table 8-1   Perks Offered to Shareholders by Various Companies

Company	Perk and Minimum Shares Required
Aga Foodservice Group	1,000 shares
	10 per cent discount on purchases totalling £500 or more from Aga Shops
Associated British Foods	1 share
	Goodie bag at annual general meeting
Austin Reed Group	500 ordinary shares
	15 per cent discount at Austin Reed or Country Casuals
Beale	2,500 shares
	10 per cent discount (5 per cent on electrical products) on purchases of up to £5,000 worth of merchandise
Bellway	2,000 shares (held by a registered holder for a minimum of 12 months prior to reservation of the new home)
	Discount of £625 per £25,000 or pro rata on part thereof of the purchase price on new houses
Bloomsbury Publishing	250 shares
	35 per cent off the recommended retail price of Bloomsbury books
British Airways	1 share
	10 per cent discounts on some flights
CHE Hotel Group	1 share
	10 per cent discount on group hotels plus Argos points
Close Brothers Group	1 share
	Discounts on group ISAs
Dobbies Garden Centres	100 shares
	10 per cent discount

Company	*Perk and Minimum Shares Required*
Eurotunnel	1,000 shares held for at least three months
	30 per cent discount on standard long or short stay tickets for three return or six single car journeys per year
First Choice Holidays	500 ordinary shares
	A Shareholder Discount Line giving the best price plus £20 per adult on group holidays booked online provided each individual spends £250 or more
Fuller, Smith & Turner	1 share
	Discounts on group hotels and items for sale in the Brewery Store
Holidaybreak	200 ordinary shares
	10 per cent discounts on holidays
Inchcape	250 ordinary shares
	15 per cent discount on service, parts, and accessories and a £100 discount on any group new or used cars (excluding Ferrari and Maserati)
Irish Continental Group	100 shares
	Discounts on travel to Ireland for Internet bookings
Johnson Service Group	200 shares
	10 vouchers of £5 each for use against dry-cleaning orders
Jourdan	1,000 ordinary shares for a minimum of 6 months
	25 per cent discounts on Corby trouser presses and Suncrest fireplace surrounds and suites
Landround	1,000 ordinary shares
	Discounts on travel

(continued)

Table 8-1 *(continued)*

Company	*Perk and Minimum Shares Required*
Lookers	1,000 ordinary shares
	£100 discount on new cars
Millennium & Copthorne Hotels	1 share
	Vouchers for a 15 per cent discount on some accommodation, food, and beverages
Moss Bros	1 share
	20 per cent discount on full price merchandise
Mothercare	500 ordinary shares
	10 per cent discount on up to £500 worth of merchandise
Mulberry Group	500 ordinary shares
	20 per cent discount in company stores
N Brown Group	1 share
	20 per cent discount on purchases from the Group's mail order catalogues
Newbury Racecourse	100 shares
	Free entry to some race meetings
Next	500 ordinary shares
	One 25 per cent discount voucher
Park Group	1 share
	4 per cent discount on High Street Gift Vouchers
Persimmon	1,000 shares (held for at least 12 months)
	A 2 per cent discount on the price of a new property
Renishaw	1 share
	Travel discounts

Company	Perk and Minimum Shares Required
Shepherd Neame	100 ordinary shares
	Discounts on wine, beer, and brewery memorabilia
Signet Group	1 share
	10 per cent discount on goods from H Samuel, Ernest Jones, and Leslie Davis
Telecom Plus	2,500 shares
	Mobile phone discounts
TG21 Plc	1 share
	20 per cent discount on T range of audio, security, navigation, and multimedia systems
The Restaurant Group Plc	1 share
	25 per cent discount on meals for up to 10 people (subject to a £5 per person minimum: Garfunkel's, Chiquito, Frankie & Benny's, Blubeckers, and Edwinns
Thorntons	200 ordinary shares
	Discount vouchers
Trafficmaster	1 share
	10 per cent discount on group profits
Travis Perkins Plc	All existing shareholders (currently discontinued for new shareholders)
	Shareholder Privilege Card giving discounts
Unilever	1 share
	Goodie bag at Annual General Meeting
Whitbread Group	85 ordinary shares
	Discounts at group hotels
Wolverhampton & Dudley Breweries Plc	10 ordinary shares
	20 per cent discount on food and accommodation at Pathfinder pubs

Source: Hargreaves Lansdown

Perks are good; perks are fun. But don't let the perks tail wag the investor dog:

- ✔ Never buy a share just for the perks. They are extras.

- ✔ Companies are under no obligation to provide perks or continue with them.

- ✔ Some perks require just one share; others require a substantial number, which can be pricey or unbalance your portfolio.

- ✔ Perks can and do change from year to year. Some become more difficult to claim.

- ✔ Vouchers may have a limited life span.

- ✔ You may be able to negotiate as good if not better discounts on your own, especially at hotels.

- ✔ Some perks are restricted to shareholders who own the stock in their own name and not in a *nominee account* (an account that is run on your behalf by a stockbroker. The stockbroker is legally the account holder. Nominee accounts mean less paperwork for you but they can cost a regular fee, so you have to balance this against the convenience.)

- ✔ Some companies only offer goodie bags to shareholders who attend annual general meetings in person.

Chapter 9

Analysing Stock-Market-Quoted Companies

. . . .

. . . .

*B*eing a successful share investor involves looking at numbers and understanding them. But don't worry. You don't need a PhD in mathematics or rocket science physics. Much of the figure work involves nothing more complicated than looking to see whether something is going up or down. And most of the rest involves the simple task of comparing figures from one company with those from another.

The most difficult maths task is working out percentage sums, which you can do on a calculator that costs less than £10. Many investment decisions depend on knowing whether a figure is higher or lower than the figure from a previous year and by how much.

That's what this chapter is all about – being a successful share investor by looking at numbers from stock-market-quoted companies and then understanding what those numbers mean.

The Gospel According to the Market: Compare Apples with Apples

Stock markets don't have set rules. So whatever figures you come up with during your investment number crunching, you must compare them with other numbers that are around at the same time (instead of comparing them with some absolute).

For example, you may calculate or hear that profits at a company have increased by 10 per cent. Well, that's obviously better than profits going down – or even going up by just 9 per cent. But you can only see how important that 10 per cent gain is by referring to the market as a whole and to companies that compete with the company you're looking at.

If the market average gain is 15 per cent, your company is in house building, and rival construction companies have gained 20 per cent, then your share is doing very badly! The converse also applies, of course. A 10 per cent profits advance when most other firms are struggling to make any gains is really good!

Lots of people get basic percentage sums wrong because they input the numbers on their calculator in the wrong order or divide when they should multiply. The task is made more difficult because some calculators use different keys for percentage calculations. Thing is, getting it wrong can be very costly. So practise with sums that have answers you can easily check in your head. For example, a firm that earns £1.15m this year would be 15 per cent ahead of last year's £1m and has gained 15 per cent. Going down from £1m to £750,000 is a 25 per cent fall. A decrease can't be more than 100 per cent!

Profits: The Basic Building Blocks of Companies

Investors in shares have one concern that overrides all else. They need to know how much profit the company will make in the future.

Future profits are the great unknown, although investors try to estimate what they'll be and how they'll compare with those of other companies. Share values adjust to these expectations, and investors then compare their hopes or fears with reality.

When stock market experts forecast a 20 per cent profits increase at a company, they factor that expectation into the share price. They calculate whether 20 per cent is above, below, or on line with competitor companies and with the market as a whole. They also look to see how that compares with previous figures and expectations from the company. And outside the direct orbit of these experts and the firm she or he works for, other market professionals also consider the credibility of the forecaster. A forecast from a stockbroking analyst known to have a good record in the past and close contacts with the company counts for more than a forecast from a largely unknown source.

But the real test is the actual profit number when it's officially released by the company. If the reality is 30 per cent, the share price will gain on the news. But if the gain fails to reach 20 per cent or only scrapes by that figure, disappointed investors will sell, and the shares may fall in the absence of some other positive news. Targets in the stock market are there to beat, not just to equal.

Quoted UK companies must publish a five-year record of their profitability or loss-making in their annual report and accounts. These figures are also easily available on a number of company information Web sites.

Looking at profits from an accountant's point of view

If you buy a car for £1,000, repair it, and sell it for £2,000, you've made a £1,000 profit. Or have you? Although you have £1,000 more in your bank account, you need to count a lot of costs, including materials to repair the car, your time, and advertising the vehicle. And don't forget the cost of the £1,000. You either had to borrow the money, which cost you interest, or had to raid your savings account, losing out on interest. Go a bit further, and you have the rent on the garage you kept it in (or the amount you lost by not letting out that space to others), and the expense of the tools you needed.

If you were a big company, you'd go a lot further again, employing teams of accountants who can either make your profits look impressive for investors or minimise them for the tax inspector.

If you had to account for your car repairing venture, the £1,000 would be the gross profit and just the start of the process.

Examining a company's profit and loss account

Look at a company's annual report and its profit and loss (known as the *P & L*) account. Lots of different sorts of profit are listed. You need to find the right one to see whether the company is going forward or backward, but you also need to understand the others to see the message they give out.

Most company accounts are called *consolidated* because they bring together all the various subsidiaries that big firms have. You can ignore any other profit and loss accounts, although they can be found at Companies House and you can pay for a copy if you want.

All companies have to produce detailed accounts once a year. Quoted concerns also issue half-yearly statements to show their progress. And a growing minority come up with figures every three months. These figures are the key to what's going on.

Luckily, most sets of figures in the UK follow an established pattern, which starts with the biggest number at the top of the page and keeps taking away the further down you go. So the top line may be billions, but the bottom may be pennies. (When you look at a company account, note that accountants don't use minus signs. Instead, they use brackets to indicate items to be subtracted. Likewise, if a company makes a loss, that figure is also shown in brackets.)

Here's a breakdown of what you'll see on a sample company's account – from the top to the bottom with some figures and what they tell you. Note that most accounts show sums in millions (£m). Note, too, that this stuff is technical, even though I'm not explaining the most complicated versions. The latter are really impossible to follow unless you have a postgraduate qualification in company accounts from oil and insurance companies.

- ✔ **Turnover (£100m).** This is the very biggest figure. It lists the amount people spend with the company. For a high-street store, it's the amount that came in through the tills. For a bank, it largely consists of the income from interest on loans.

- ✔ **Cost of sales (£80m).** This is the amount the company has spent on raw materials as well as manufactured items it has bought to sell to customers.

- ✔ **Gross profit (£20m).** This is what's left after taking the cost of sales away from the sales themselves. It's the biggest profit figure, but there's a lot to take away from it.

- ✔ **Operating expenses (£15m).** This is the cost of running the company, including staff salaries and rent on premises. The pay that directors get is listed in notes to the accounts, the small print where quite a bit of the detail is hidden.

✔ **Operating profit ($5m).** This is what the company would make if it operated in a vacuum! If there were no tax to pay or interest on bank loans to count, this would be the actual profit. It's a good indicator of a company's management efficiency. If two competitor firms both sell $100m, the one with an operating profit of $5m is running itself better than the one with an operating profit of $4m.

✔ **Exceptional items ($500,000).** These are one-off items that really have nothing to do with the day-to-day running of the business – things like profits made from selling off a piece of spare land or the expenses of relocating the firm. They can be positive or negative. Firms often don't have any of these items.

✔ **Profit on ordinary activities before interest ($4.5m).** This tells you how much the company made before paying for bank loans. It's a useful indicator of progress because it does not involve a major external such as interest, over which the company itself has no control whatsoever. Don't worry. We're getting there but still a hurdle or two.

✔ **Net interest payable ($500,000).** This is the cost of bank and other loans needed to run the business less any interest earned on bank deposits. Occasionally, companies may have earned more interest than they spent. This is an important figure because it tells you how susceptible the company is to interest rate changes. Here, the interest charge is 10 per cent of the operating profit. Compare this with previous years and with competitor firms.

✔ **Profit before tax ($4m).** This is the big headline figure and the profit definition used in most media reports.

✔ **Tax ($400,000).** Everyone has to pay taxes, but companies have ways and means of keeping the figure low.

✔ **Profit after tax ($3.6m).** This is the amount the company has for ploughing back into the business and for paying out dividends. This amount is entirely at the control of the directors.

✔ **Minority interests and preference dividends ($200,000).** These are amounts companies must pay to special groups of investors before paying their own shareholders. Many companies do not have this item.

✔ **Profit attributable to ordinary shareholders ($3.4m).** This is what you and all the other equity holders have to share out.

✔ **Dividends ($1.9m).** This is the cost of the payments made to shareholders.

✔ **Retained profit for the year ($1m).** This is what's left to plough back into the company for future expansion.

✔ **Earnings per share (17p).** This is the profit attributable to ordinary shareholders ($3.4m) divided by the number of shares in issue – in this case 20 million. It comes at the end, but it's a key figure for working out how well your investment is doing.

Understanding what company profits and losses actually mean

The ideal scenario is for a company to make record profit gains every year and beat the expectations of the experts by a huge margin. Don't ever bank on this scenario, though. If such a paragon of virtue company existed, its shares would be really expensive because such amazing expectations would be built into the price.

The 99.99 per cent probability is that the companies whose shares you buy will have a variable profits record, doing better in some periods than in others. Your job is to understand what the figures mean.

Profits may not always be quite as real or as rosy as a company's investor and media relations teams like to make out. And although no one wants to make a loss, getting into the red may not always be a disaster or even a danger signal.

So headline profit figures may not be what they seem. Following are some key profit moves to look for and assess. And don't forget that many companies are great at creative accounting, which is the stock market equivalent of turning a sow's ear into a silk purse.

- ✔ **Rising profits year on year.** These sound really good. In most cases, they are. These are just the sort of companies investors love. But look out for comparisons with rival companies that may be doing even better; whether the company is doing anything more than just keeping up with rising prices in its product area; tricks such as massaging the profits upward with accounting devices; and whether the rising profits are due to the company buying other firms and incorporating their earnings into its own.

- ✔ **Profits reported each year but sometimes up and sometimes down.** This is a normal pattern, especially if firms can't rely on rising prices year after year to give paper profits. Check that the ups are as good if not better than competitor firms. Look at the reasons for the setbacks. Could they have been avoided? Did rivals do better? Did the company warn shareholders adequately that there might be problems?

- ✔ **Making neither a profit nor a loss.** Not a good sign, but if the company is in a healthy business with a good reputation, this status may say something about the failings of the management. Good companies with poor people at the top tend to end up with a takeover bid, good news for shareholders. Don't forget that breaking even when others are losing loads of cash *is* doing well. Check that directors aren't overpaying themselves.

✔ **Losing money.** Acceptable reasons include heavy research and development costs, a company starting up and needing to spend heavily before establishing itself, and economic slumps. Find out what the company is doing to turn itself around. If there's no reason or light at the end of the deficit tunnel, run a mile from the company. Don't forget, it's your money the company's losing, so there has to be some gain after your pain.

Published company figures are two to four months out of date when they're released. Circumstances by then may have changed. Companies take different times to add up the figures. High-street stores and banks tend to be quick. Firms with lots of different overseas offshoots and smaller companies are usually slower.

Bad figures take longer to add up than good ones. That's not literally true, but companies that delay releasing figures or are late compared with previous years are usually in financial trouble. Treat any postponement as a danger signal.

Earnings Per Share: The Thing to Look at First

You may only have one share in a company that has issued one billion. But that *earnings per share (eps)* figure at the end of the company's profit and loss account is what you get. And even if it's at the very bottom of the page, it's where in-the-know investors look first.

You can use the eps figure rather than the headline profit to see whether the company is really moving ahead. It may have issued millions more shares to acquire other firms, which could result in the profit it brings in boosting the pre-tax profits figure, but once it's divided up among more shares, the end result could be down.

For example, say that Company A has £10m profits attributable to shareholders who have 10m shares between them. So each earns £1 per share. Then Company A buys Company B by issuing 10m shares. Profits go up to £15m, but each share now only has 75p in earnings because the £15m must be divided out 20 million ways. The takeover has been bad (or to put it in jargon, *non-earning enhancing*). It might be better later on, of course. Or even worse. Owners of shares in companies that are bought tend to fare better than those who own shares in companies that are doing the acquiring.

The eps figure is also honest because it's after tax. It measures what's really yours and not a slice the taxman will grab.

What a price earnings ratio is

The earnings per share figure lets you compare one year with the next at the same company. But it's pretty useless if you want to rate one firm against another. Whether your earnings are high or low all depends on the share price.

A 20p eps sounds twice as good as a 10p eps. But it's not necessarily so. It all depends on the share price. Dividing the earnings into the share price gives a magic figure called the *p/e*, which stands for *price earnings ratio*, and it's widely used in working out whether a share is good value. It tells you how many years of earnings at the last published level you'd need to equal the share price.

Loss-making companies can't have a price earnings ratio because they have no earnings. That's why the p/e column in newspaper listings sometimes shows a dash.

If two companies have identical prospects, the one with the lower p/e number is the better deal. If both companies are going to earn, say, 10p per share, the one with the p/e of 12 equalling a 120p share price is more attractive than the share on a 15 times p/e because then you'll pay 150p for the same thing.

What a prospective price earnings ratio tells you

The p/e is a great comparative tool. It's widely quoted in newspaper reports, and it's carried in many share listings both on- and offline. It goes up when share prices rise and down when they fall. But it has one big weakness. The figure you see is based on the most recent accounts, it's called the historical p/e and it's unlikely that the company is going to make the same profits again. It might make more or less.

The way around this weakness is the *prospective p/e*, which is based on what the stock market thinks the company is going to make in the current financial year and sometimes in the year or two after that. For example, a company with earnings last year of 10p and a current share price of 100p has a p/e of 10. The forecast is for earnings of 20p per share, so the prospective p/e falls to 5. If the forecast were for earnings of 4p per share, the prospective p/e would rise to 25.

Take prospective figures with a pinch of salt. They are educated guesses with a bit of help from the company itself, which will steer or guide stockbroker analysts in the right direction.

How to use the price earnings ratio

So what can you really do with the price earnings ratio? Well, you can use it to:

✔ Compare the share prices of companies that appear to have similar prospects.

✔ Pick out companies that the market thinks will grow. Growth companies have higher price earnings ratios.

✔ Check whether you've spotted a growing company early on. If the p/e starts to climb after you buy, congratulate yourself.

✔ Determine whether to sell. Some investors sell shares if their p/e goes a certain percentage above the average.

✔ See which shares are in or out of fashion. A low figure suggests that other investors are ignoring the company. They may be right or their information may be out of date.

✔ Provide a framework. Ask questions if a p/e is much higher or lower than similar shares.

Beware of shares with astronomic price earnings ratios that imply you'd have to wait 100 or more years to get your share price back if earnings stayed the same. Mega ratios usually come with shares with more hype than hope, more faith than a fair future. Or they may simply be figures based on a previous year when earnings were much higher.

Dividends: What They Really Mean

Would you like a twice-per-year cheque from your share investments that you can spend or save or plough back into the stock market? Or are you happy to just rely on whatever your shares fetch on the day you decide to sell? Most UK investors opt for the first choice.

Companies pay out *dividends*, or share payments, usually around every six months, of so many pence per share. That price is multiplied by the number of shares you have, so you're sent a cheque or a bank transfer for the amount to the nearest penny.

Some companies offer re-investment schemes, so you can use your dividend to buy more shares. Because your dividend probably won't buy an exact number of shares, any leftover amount is carried over to the next dividend payment. (You can only buy whole shares, unlike units in unit trust funds, which subdivide each unit by 100.)

Dividends represent your share of the profits. And they're a major part of the UK share scene. But not all companies are expected to pay dividends. Exceptions are new companies, where investors expect all the profits to be ploughed into the business, as well as companies making losses, which can't afford to spare the cash. However, once companies are in the position where they can afford the payments, they're expected to do so. Holding back without an explanation is viewed with grave suspicion and a fast-falling share price!

Understanding what dividends tell about the company

Because the dividend is seen as a vital part of the share makeup in the UK (less so in many other countries), analysts look at its level as a vital sign of that firm's financial health or perhaps lack of health.

The essential figure is the *dividend yield*, a figure that requires all the dividends in a year to be added up. Some firms pay more than twice a year, and payments are rarely equal. Companies with seasonal businesses, such as package holiday firms, may pay only a token amount at one payment and nearly everything in the other payout. That's because the cash flowing in and out of the company is uneven.

Working out the dividend yield means working out a percentage sum. You need to divide the dividend in pence by the share price in pence and multiply by 100 (or press the percentage key). So a 50p share price paying a 1p dividend gives a 2 per cent yield. And a 100p share price paying a 10p dividend gives a 10 per cent dividend yield.

The price earnings ratio rises with share prices. But the dividend as a ratio falls when shares go up.

Looking at dividends, like everything else in the investment world, is comparison work. There are no absolute levels. For example, many companies that paid a 10 per cent dividend yield in the inflationary 1970s and 1980s went down to 2 per cent by the end of the 1990s.

You need to be concerned with two dividend yield figures. The current rate is the one you use for analysis. But the rate worked out for the price you paid for the share can also be important because it gives you an idea of what another investment would need to produce to give you the same amount of spendable cash. If the current share price at 300p offers you a 10 per cent yield, you'd have a 30 per cent yield on your cash if you bought the shares at 100p.

To look at dividends, you need benchmarks:

- ✔ **The average yield on the FTSE All Share Index.** See whether your share comes up with a higher or lower number. The higher the figure, the less the stock market thinks of the share's future growth prospects. Many newspapers carry this statistic.

- ✔ **The sector average.** This looks at companies in similar businesses to your own, such as breweries or software companies. This figure is also published in some newspapers and is available online.

- ✔ **The yield on a basket of UK government stocks, or *gilts*.** This helps tell you what you'd get for your money in the safest UK investment. If the dividend yield is lower than the one for gilts, you'll have to hope for future growth from the share to compensate. Otherwise, there's no point in taking the risk of equity purchase.

  Most shares yield less than gilts because they have growth possibilities; gilts can never return more than their face value. The greater the difference (known technically as the *reverse yield gap*), the more growth oriented your stock is. Shares with yields higher than gilts can be suspect! Look to see why such a big payout isn't rewarded with a higher share price. Remember, high yield equals high alert!

Deciphering the signs that dividends provide

Comparing a dividend yield or return with its benchmark, such as a sector average, and the amount paid in previous years gives a list of possibilities for investors looking for pointers to a company's future health. All the ideas here offer clues to the company and how other investors see it.

Rising dividend payments

Rising dividend payments are what investors expect. The ideal share gives a bit extra each time to reflect growing profits.

But investors would be worried if payments went up faster than earnings because it would show that the company isn't investing in its own future. Instead, it's trying to buy stock market favour, perhaps to ward off an expected takeover bid. The exception is when a company has a lot of cash and has announced that it thinks shareholders can make better use of it than the company management.

Static dividend payments

Generally, static dividend payments are viewed as bad news because the company isn't growing its profits. Static dividend payments are viewed as even worse news if the company has to dip into its bank account to pay the dividend. Firms shouldn't borrow to pay dividends.

Falling or no dividend payments

Falling dividend payments or no dividend payments are really bad news, but companies often prepare investors for this situation ahead of the announcement because it's even worse if the decision to reduce or cut out payments comes as a surprise.

As a rule, a company that says it's being forced to halve its dividend will see its share price fall by roughly the same amount over a relatively short period. Investors are more forgiving if they can see light at the end of this tunnel in the shape of a return to dividend growth in the future.

Very high dividend payments

When you see very high dividends, do a reality check. Dividend yields shown in newspapers are historic because they're based on the most recent payouts. The company may have announced a reduction or complete cancellation of its next dividend, so check Web sites and other news sources before relying on this yield figure.

Even if nothing has been said publicly, investors can often put two and two together and find out whether a company is going to have to cut dividends. If the company is about to cut or abandon (technically called *passing*) the dividend, then investors tend to sell.

Looking at the dividend cover

Dividing the dividend per share into the earnings per share gives something called the *cover*. For example, an earnings per share of 20p with a dividend of 5p gives a four times cover. This figure is the number of times the dividend could've been paid out from after-tax earnings. In this case, the 5p dividend could have been paid four times over, so the cover number is four.

Too low a number, especially less than one, tells you the company is pulling out all the stops and all the cash from wherever it can to avoid the indignity of a dividend cut. Companies can only get away with this if they have a really good excuse and a promise that they'll go back to a higher cover in the future.

There's also the danger of running near to empty. A company paying out most or all of its earnings in dividends has nothing to fall back on if times become harder and profits fall.

But too high a cover, perhaps more than four or five times, suggests that the company is hoarding cash. Nothing is wrong if you can see the reason, so find out whether its research, development, and other expansion requirements really need it to be quite so mean to shareholders.

Forecasts: Reliable Sources or a Lot of Hot Air?

Stockbrokers and investment fund management firms spend a fortune on highly paid analysts who are supposed to predict the future. Some firms employ people to research one or two stock market sectors, and smaller broking outfits expect their staff to look more widely.

Some of this research is available to small investors. A number of investment magazines print extracts as broker recommendations, and many stockbrokers dealing with private clients send out material. As a rule, big firms of stockbrokers tend to cover the biggest companies, leaving the Tiddlers to the brokers who specialise in individual investors. (Check out Chapter 7 for details on who the Tiddlers are.)

Most stockbroker notes list the share price when the research was finalised; essential ratios, such as the price/earnings and the dividend yield; the share's high and low points over the past year; past earnings; and – most crucially – what the analyst expects the company to report as a profit for the next full year or perhaps even the year past that. Obviously, the farther the figures point into the future, the less reliable they are.

The notes should also contain some detail on where the company is going, ranging from 100 words to 100 pages. In addition, good material then compares the profits forecast to the present share price and decides whether that price fairly reflects the prospects.

You should also see a recommendation, such as buy, sell, or hold. You'd think there'd be rough equality between the buys and the sells. After all, most investors don't have limitless money, so they want some guidance on what to sell so they can purchase something with brighter prospects. But very few broker notes these days are headed *Sell*.

The reason, cynics say (and they're probably right), is that too many brokers get their information on where a company is going from the company directors themselves in special briefing sessions. Some analysts don't want to bite the hand that feeds them! Broking firms may also have a special relationship with a company in which they represent the company in the stock market. In this type of arrangement, the broking firm is known as the *house* broker, and the firm may not want to jeopardise this arrangement with negative comments.

But due to the dotcom scandals in the US way back in 1999 and 2000, where some analysts were putting out company views as their own because they had a vested financial interest in puffing the company, analysts are now likely to have a clean act and stress how independent they are. Some no longer use terms like *buy* or *sell* but come up with targets for their expectations of profits or the share price and then leave investors to make up their own minds.

Looking at past records is the only way to check on whether your source of stockbroker information is any good. If the recommendations produce a bit more than the average or the fund invested in the stock market index, then you've hit on a good research analyst. Don't let go of her or him! You'll never get 100 per cent accuracy, so better than average is a winning proposition.

Much of what you read in newspapers comes from analysts. They don't always get name checks. Some don't want the wider publicity of media appearances, but it may suit them to talk up shares their clients already hold.

Takeovers: Good, Bad, or Ugly?

Takeovers occur when one company wants to buy another stock-market-quoted company lock, stock, and barrel. They happen because:

- The company making the acquisition thinks it can squeeze more profits out of the target company, and so it's worth paying for.

- The target company has profitable patents or products that the acquiring company wants.

- The target company is a rival, and a successful takeover bid would mean less competition. (Note that this scenario may have to pass Competition Commission hurdles if the result would place too much power into the hands of one company.)

- The target company has lots of assets, such as property, that can be bought for less than their true worth and then sold for a profit – a practice known as *asset stripping*. It's frowned on, but it still happens.

- The acquiring company is running out of steam and ideas, so it wants to bring in a smaller, more successful firm to rejuvenate it. This scenario is sometimes called a *reverse takeover* because the smaller firm ends up in charge.

Whatever the reason for them, takeovers generate big excitement and usually big share price gains for the target company. Takeovers are supposed to be top secret before the official announcement is made, but leaks and rumours are common.

There are at least ten takeover rumours for every real bid. So don't believe every one you see mentioned in newspapers and elsewhere.

The share price of the target company goes up for the usual reason of supply and demand. In this case, there is demand for every share from the bidder, so the value naturally goes up.

The company making the bid hopes that the directors of the target company will recommend the bid to their own shareholders. But the shareholders want to see a second bidder, counter-bidder, or rejection from the target company because it should send the price up even further. Investors with shares in the target company always benefit from an auction between two or more determined bidders.

Holders in the target company may be offered cash or shares (or a mix of the two) in the acquiring company. Cash is the best option because you know what you're getting; shares will go up and down. A loan stock option, which is a special device where the company keeps your takeover cash and pays you regular interest on the amount, may also be offered. The purpose is to help investors cut down on capital gains tax bills. They do this by cashing their loan options in instalments each year rather than the whole lot in one go.

Bids come with timetables and complicated rules to determine which firm emerges as the winner in a contested takeover. Shareholders in the target company must choose between accepting the bid, hanging on for a better offer, or selling their shares in the stock market. Sometimes, selling immediately can be the best idea. Bids fail, and the target's share price could fall backward again. It's a bird in the hand decision.

Takeovers are mostly good for shareholders in the target companies. Many academic studies show that takeovers are less good for acquiring firms. It's common for shares in the bidding firm to fall when it announces a takeover.

Technical Analysis: The Arcane World of Share Price Charts

Warning here: What I discuss in this section is so technical that it's called *technical analysis*. And it's not everyone's cup of tea. But those who use it swear by it, and fans include a number of stock market movers and shakers. So you need to know about technical analysis even if you dismiss it as mumbo-jumbo.

Most people look at the fundamentals of shares. The fundamentals include the general economic situation, industry-specific trends, interest rates and foreign currency exchange rates, how the company you're looking at is seen to be doing, balance sheet strengths and weaknesses, the company's products, the company's management, and a host of other financial and business factors.

But a sizeable minority of investors reckon that looking at the fundamentals is a waste of time. So these investors go back to basics – so far back that some don't even care what the name is of the share, bond, currency, or commodity they're looking at. Instead, they revert to one of the very early lessons investors have to take in. And that lesson is that you can't always explain what's going on except by saying that prices rise when buyers outnumber sellers and that prices go down when sellers outnumber buyers. So instead of looking at fundamental factors, they do technical analysis: draw up charts of prices, log the ups and downs, and look for patterns.

The theory of technical analysis is that markets move on expectations and sentiment rather than cold facts. Fans of price charts say that facts are usually known and taken into the price, but you need the *psychology* of market participants to get a real picture. And the only way you can get this psychology is via a chart showing the forces of buying and selling. Technical analysts believe that price charts show human emotions present in investors – emotions such as greed and fear, panic and elation – and that facts are often manipulated to suit these emotions. So when greed rules, all the fundamentals become positive.

During the dotcom boom in 1999 and 2000, every company seemed to have a guaranteed rosy future. In the stock market collapse that followed, every company seemed to have dismal prospects. With some recovery since then, maybe thoughts have become more balanced. However, fans of price charts say that their analysis showed that the good prospects during the boom were built on just a few share purchases that sent the shares soaring. And the gloom that followed the boom was just as thinly based. They say that they did better by looking at the real action in the stock market and ignoring all the hype and noise.

Technical analysts, or *chartists*, produce all sorts of patterns. Some charts cover a very brief time, and others look at decades. Here are some patterns and what they mean:

- ✔ **The moving average.** This is a line that smoothes out short-term fluctuations by averaging prices over the past (usually 100 or 200 trading days). The trick is to compare this line with the actual day-to-day ups and downs. The idea is to see whether the longer-term trend is moving up or down.

- ✔ **New highs and new lows.** This is not a chart at all, but is a list based on new tops and bottoms for a share over a period, usually a year. Some newspapers print the number of shares that have made new high or new low points for the year. They may also print their names. As the numbers of new highs or new lows increase, the likelihood is that prices are due to reverse. This isn't surprising. At the very top of a share market with lots of new highs, there's a panic to get in, so share values zoom up. At the bottom of a falling market with lots of new lows, there's a rush to get out, so a record number of shares hit new bottoms.

✔ **Head and shoulders.** This is one of many body-part patterns used in share price charts. The first shoulder is formed by a line as the price is ticking along. Then the line shoots up to form the top of the head as the price increases. If the line then comes down to form a new shoulder, the outlook is poor because the price has decreased. Chartists reckon that the head represents excitement from buyers, which has now ended.

✔ **Reverse head and shoulders.** This is the head-and-shoulders pattern turned upside down. If the head-and-shoulders pattern points to lower prices, then a reverse head and shoulders must look to better values.

✔ **Double bottom.** This is not a body part pattern! If a share hits a low point twice in a period, but the second low point is not as bad as the first, then chartists take it as a positive sign.

✔ **Double top.** This is the opposite of the double-bottom pattern and hence a bad sign. Nothing to do with darts.

If a method works for you, enabling you to spot more winners than losers, that's all you need. Whether you look for a reverse head and shoulders in a price chart, examine Japanese shooting stars (see the nearby sidebar for info on them), or concentrate on companies at the end of the alphabet (a theory from one investor – that no one looks at these companies until it's too late because most share buyers start with A instead of Z), the aim is to make more money. Never apologise if you manage this, even if the method you use sounds daft!

Burning the candle at both ends – the Japanese way

Three hundred years ago, Japanese rice traders wanted to have a better idea of how supply and demand was affecting the price of this staple food. But they didn't want rivals to know how they were thinking. So they came up with a charting method where the price action was disguised as a candlestick, complete with candle, wick, and shadow. These disguises are still used today.

These patterns have great names, like *shaven head* and *spinning tops*. In addition, when several candlesticks are put together, they form *hammers* (where the market is hammering out a bottom prior to a recovery). And the *hanging man* warns investors that they may soon lose their financial lives when the execution trapdoor opens. There are *shooting stars, morning stars,* and *evening stars* as well.

Does this method work? Fans say that it has lasted 300 years, so it must have something going for it.

Chapter 10

Banking on Bonds

. . . .

. . . .

During the 1970s, 1980s, and most of the 1990s, bonds were boring. Worse, they were guaranteed losers. They were no-hope purchases for no-hope purchasers. The only sensible investments during this time were equities. Shares in quoted companies made real gains even after the high inflation of much of this period. Even mediocre shares in boring companies earned their keep. It all had to do with something called the cult of the equity. Pension fund managers, who controlled more and more of the stock market during the second half of the 20th century, bought shares with their members' money. Their counterparts in the United States and Europe continued to buy bonds, but their performance didn't compare with that of the UK management firms. Equities ruled.

But then something strange happened that caught all the equity folks by surprise, even though it should've been seen a million miles off. The members of those pension funds got older. They were no longer a collection of 30-somethings who didn't worry much about pensions but a large number of retired or almost retired folks. They needed secure pension payments each month. And the only way they could get those monthly payments was through bonds. Shares with their big ups and downs just aren't suited for regular pay cheques.

Over the past ten years or so, bonds have come full circle. They were out of fashion when equities boomed, came back in fashion when equities slumped, and just when they reached the top of the popularity charts, equities or shares came back into favour again. But with an aging population looking for some security for life savings, bond salespeople, bond issuers, bond purchasers, and bond traders aren't likely to find themselves on the redundancy scrapheap anytime soon. Leaving aside whether they can beat equities or property or not, bonds do have a role. And even if you don't want to buy bonds, you need to know about them because their prices can determine other parts of the financial mix.

This chapter gives you the savvy about bonds so that you, too, can be a fashionable investor.

The Bottom Line on Bonds

Bond is one of those words that the financial services industry uses all over the place. Industry folks like it because it inspires confidence. In this chapter, though, I'm referring to the technical meaning of the word. At its basic level, a *bond* is a loan made by investors to a company, national government, or international body. In return, the company, government, or international body offers to pay the holder a set sum of interest on set dates and promises to repay a pre-established amount on a set date in the future. Because of all this certainty, bonds are often called *fixed-interest* or *fixed-income investments*.

Cash is the lowest risk investment idea around. Bonds are one step up from the security of cash in an established bank. The returns are a little higher, but you have to take a little more risk on board for the privilege.

In some ways, bonds are like cash. Here's the simplest bond deal: A company needs money, and you lend it £10,000. It promises to pay you 5 per cent interest (£500 a year) divided into six-monthly instalments, so you get £250 (less tax) twice a year. The company also promises to repay your £10,000 on a fixed future date – say, January 31, 2020.

This sounds very much like a fixed-rate mortgage where you promise to pay a set sum of interest at regular intervals and repay the capital borrowed sometime in the future at a date laid down in the home loan paperwork. For the company borrowing the money, that's a true assessment.

But for the investor, bonds have one big extra dimension over the bank-style loan. Bonds are traded on stock markets. Although the cost to issuers, such as companies or governments, doesn't change during the bond's life, the value to the holder can change all the time. The price goes up and down with economic variables, most importantly interest rates. But the amount the company has to pay when the bond reaches its payback, or maturity, date doesn't vary (except for a few index-linked bonds).

If the certificate says £10,000 (known as the *nominal amount*), then £10,000 is what the holder gets back on maturity, regardless of the price that the person paid.

'Do I need bonds?'

You need bonds if you think they will outperform equities and other investments, such as property or cash. But you also need them if:

- You're a cautious investor who wouldn't be happy with share price ups and downs.

- You have a defined aim for your money, such as you must pay education fees on fixed dates or you want to give a set sum to a child on graduation or reaching a certain age.

- You have investment funds for your retirement years, and you're within five to ten years of stopping work. Some plans allow you to move gradually into bonds from shares. This arrangement helps prevent your pension from being hit by a sudden fall in share values.

- You have retired and need certainty of income from your savings.

'Tell me the big differences between bonds and shares'

Companies that need to raise cash can issue equities – or *shares* as they're better known. They can also issue bonds (called *corporate bonds* to differentiate them from those put out by governments) and get the same amount. So what's the difference?

- Shares are permanent. Once issued, they carry on until the company ceases to exist, either because it goes bust, is absorbed by another company, or buys in its own shares to cancel them. Equally, investors have no time limit on their equity holdings (except for a few specialised investment trusts).

- Bonds usually (although a handful of exceptions exist) have a fixed life, which is shown on the paperwork you get. You know when they'll stop paying you a regular amount and give back the original cash instead.

- Shares pay dividends, which can go down as well as up. Sometimes dividend payments are missed altogether. The rate of dividend depends on the profits of the company and what it needs to do with the cash it generates.

- Bonds pay interest (known as the *coupon* because old bond certificates used to contain small squares that holders had to cut out every six months to claim the payment). This interest is fixed whether the company is doing well or not. Bond interest must be paid before any share dividends are issued.

- Shares give holders a say in the company proportional to their holding. Shareholders are the legal owners of the company, and they get to attend an annual general meeting where they can quiz the board.

- Bondholders, in most circumstances, have no ownership or annual meeting voting rights. Bondholders are only active when the bond issuer (company or government) is in financial trouble.

- Share prices can be very volatile.

- Bond prices vary less from day to day.

- Shareholders have to worry about how well the company is doing. Share prices depend on profits.

- Bondholders have to worry more about credit risk – the chance that a company will do so badly that it'll default on loan repayment or on an interest payment.

All That is Gilt is Not Gold: UK Government Bonds

Understanding the basics of bonds is easiest by looking at *gilts*, which are UK government bonds. In case you're interested, they're known as gilts or gilt-edged because the certificates used to have gold-coloured borders. That titbit aside, gilts are one of the ways the government pays for its spending other than by raising taxes. (It also borrows through National Savings.)

Gilts are super-safe. You don't have to worry about the issuing company going bust. Think about it: If the UK government fails to pay its legal obligations, then there will be a lot more problems than just some angry investors!

Gilts also appeal to cautious UK investors because they're in sterling. You can buy bonds in dollars, euros, or several other currencies, but you'll have to worry about currency exchange rate risks as well.

When the government decides to issue a new gilt, it advertises:

- ✔ **The amount it intends to raise (often £1 billion or more).** This info fascinates economists, but it's not very useful for investors.

- ✔ **Its name.** Most gilts are now called *Treasury* or *Exchequer*, but there's no difference between the two. Older gilts may have other names, such as *Funding* or *Conversion*, but they don't mean much of anything either. The figures are what are important. So in a title such as *Treasury 6% 2020*, look at the numbers, not the letters.

- ✔ **The coupon.** This is the headline rate of interest that forms part of the gilt's title. So in a title such as *Treasury 6% 2020*, the headline rate of interest is 6 per cent.

- ✔ **The redemption date.** This is the final date after which the gilt will be repaid. The date is typically 5 to 30 or more years in the future. It's also part of the title, so in a title such as *Treasury 6% 2020*, the redemption date is the year 2020.

- ✔ **An indication of price.** This is the tricky bit. Everything in bonds is based on the nominal value of £100 (or $100 or €100). But what you pay when the bond is launched and at any stage afterward may be more or less than the nominal sum. When launching a gilt issue, the UK government usually sets a fixed amount per £100 nominal for small investors. Big investors with millions may have to enter an auction and may end up paying a different price for the same bond at the same time.

Gilts (and all other bonds) can go up and down in value. But the shorter the remaining life of a bond, the more you can be sure of it. Government bonds react to interest rates above all. If your bond has only a few months before redemption, there's not much chance of a big interest rate change. If it has 20 years to go, then it's anyone's guess what will happen.

After you buy a gilt, either directly from the government at the very start of its life or in the stock market, you're on your own. You can't force the government to take it back until its final redemption date, which could be a few weeks to several decades from your purchase date. But you can sell it in the stock market through a stockbroker – just like a share.

Note, too, that no one can force the government to issue new gilts, so if the government isn't currently issuing gilts but you or other investors want one, you'll have to buy through a broker at whatever price is on offer at the time.

The gilt price you see in a newspaper or on an Internet site is the middle price. You'll get a little less if you sell and pay a bit more if you're a purchaser. You'll have to pay commission for the sale or purchase. But, hey, the government can sometimes be generous: You don't have to pay stamp duty when dealing in gilts (and many other forms of bonds), which saves £5 for every £1,000, or 0.5 per cent.

What Makes Bond Prices Go Up and Down

Put your £1,000 savings in the bank, and your money stays at £1,000. What you generally don't know, though, is how much interest you'll get. Most bank accounts have variable rates. Put the same money into a gilt or other bond, and your £1,000 could be worth more or less the next day. But you'll know how much interest you'll get. With a bond, your interest is fixed, but your capital value is variable.

Like everything else in stock markets, bond prices are driven by supply and demand. When people want to buy, the price rises. And vice versa.

Working out why people want to buy or sell shares is complicated. So many factors hit the average company that it's a real juggling act to get them all in the air and then make some sense out of them when they land. But bonds are simpler. Investors look at three main factors:

- Interest rates in the economy
- Credit risks or the chances of the bond issuer defaulting on obligations
- The remaining life of the bond

The interest rate gamble

Investors buy bonds to provide interest payments. Purchasing bonds is only worthwhile if the rate of interest is better than the rate you're likely to get from a bank or building society over the life of the bond.

It has to be better because buying a bond costs money in stockbroker fees, and the danger always exists that the bond will fall from the level you bought at or, if it's not from a stable government or company, that the issuer will go bust or have financial troubles. And even if you're happy about who you're lending your money to, the longer a bond has to run, the greater the chance that interest rates will change or something unforeseen will happen.

Bonds offer fixed interest and a fixed repayment of the nominal capital on a future date. But although they are a lower-risk investment, they aren't risk-free. Bonds are a balance between their capital value and the interest rate. When interest rates fall, bond prices go up. When interest rates rise, bond values fall. This scenario is like a seesaw, where both ends can't rise or fall at the same time.

A time when bonds were a disaster

Bonds were an investment disaster in the UK for most of the second half of the 20th century. A person who invested £100 into UK gilts at the end of the Second World War and re-invested all the income without paying any tax would've had £3,668 at the end of 2002, according to figures from Barclays Capital. Adjusted for inflation, that comes down to a real £151 value. The 57 years of savings only resulted in a genuine gain of just over half.

The same money put into equities would've produced £65,440, or £2,689 after price rises were counted. That's a gain of nearly 27 times.

Over long periods, equities should always beat bonds because they are more volatile. You get 'paid' for taking on the extra risk associated with shares. This is known as the *equity risk premium*.

When interest rates fall

Suppose that interest rates are 10 per cent and you buy a bond offering a 10 per cent coupon for £100. You get £5 twice a year, or £10 in all.

Now suppose that interest rates fall to 5 per cent. Bond values go up when interest rates fall, so the value of your bond to new investors would be twice as much, or £200. They'd continue to get the same £10 per year interest, but it would only work out at £2.50 every six months, or £5 a year, for each £100 they spent on the bond. You're getting twice the amount of interest compared with a new investor.

Now you have a choice. You can continue to enjoy your larger fixed-interest cheque every six months, getting more than you'd get as a new bond purchaser. Or you can cash in on your good luck. A new investor would pay £200 for your bond and get the fixed £10 per year. You can collect a £100 profit to reinvest elsewhere.

When interest rates rise

Suppose that rates rise from the 10 per cent at which you bought the bond to 20 per cent. No one would pay £100 for your bond because they could invest that money to earn £20 per year. So because the interest rate has doubled, your bond is only worth half as much. You have the tough choice of taking a loss on the capital value or accepting that you'll get far less interest than a new investor.

Interest rates often go up because the inflation index that measures rising prices increases. When you have high interest rates and high inflation, the paper value of your bond goes down. You're given a double hit:

> ✔ Interest levels rise so the capital value falls on the seesaw principle.
>
> ✔ The real value of each fixed payment and the final redemption amount also drops in purchasing terms because each currency unit (such as the pound, dollar, or euro) buys less at the shops.

The way around the interest rate gamble

Rising prices are bad news for bonds. The £100 they pay back for each £100 shown on the certificate isn't worth as much as when the bond was issued. A 5 per cent inflation rate halves the real value of money every 14 years.

And how do governments react to inflation? They try to control it with rising interest rates, also really bad news for bondholders.

Still, there's a way around this problem for investors who fear that rising prices will wreck their bond calculations. It's called the *index-linked gilt.* It's like an ordinary gilt because it pays income every six months and has a set future date for repayment – anything from a year or two to more than a quarter of a century. But that's where the similarity stops because each half-yearly coupon and the final repayment are linked to inflation using the government's retail prices index (RPI) as a measure.

Here's a simplified example (meaning it ignores compounding and the eight-month delay between the RPI figure's publication and its effect on your money): You put £10,000 into an index-linked gilt with a 10-year life with a 2.5 per cent pay on day one. Your first year's interest works out at £250 before tax. After the 10 years of 7 per cent annual inflation, prices have doubled. Your final dividend will be £500 per year, and you'll get back £20,000.

Sounds like magic, so what's the catch? You start off with a far lower interest rate than on a conventional bond, so it could take years of rising prices to catch up. And if price rises drop to nothing or go in reverse, you'll lose out.

The UK government has replaced the RPI measurement to a consumer prices index of the type used in Europe for many purposes. This ignores housing and mortgages and so should result in a lower headline figure. But the RPI will continue to be calculated for many years to come and RPI-linked government bonds will carry on using the RPI for calculations.

The credit rating conundrum

If only life for bond purchasers was as simple as second-guessing where interest rates and prices are due to go over the life of the bond. But, alas, life for bond purchasers isn't that simple. And that's why armies of highly paid analysts look over each bond with superpower spreadsheets.

Besides interest rates in the economy, a big factor for bond investors is whether the bond issuer will pay out the money on time or even at all. Bonds are issued by all sorts of organisations from the US Treasury to biotech or dotcom companies with a 1 in 20 chance of making it.

A bond is only as good as its issuer. There are no guarantees you can call on. In the past, bonds issued by big nations such as Germany, Russia, and Argentina all failed. They became worth as much as wallpaper, except for a few attractive-looking certificates sold to collectors who framed and displayed them. (I have a Russian bond certificate from 1916, which I bought for £1. The frame cost a lot more.)

Alphabet soup: Looking at credit rating codes

You can get some help with working out which bonds have a higher credit rating. Agencies such as Standard & Poor's, Moody's, and Fitch look at each bond issuer and the terms being offered, and then the agencies come up with a risk rating code.

The code isn't difficult to decipher. You just follow the alphabet. The highest level is AAA (or triple A), followed by AA, A, BAA, BA, BBB, BB, B, with plenty more points all the way down to D. Plus and minus signs are used as well, showing whether a bond has been upgraded recently and is now less risky or whether it has been downgraded into a higher peril situation. Each rating agency has its own little quirks, but the higher the letter in the alphabet and the more letters used, the lower the risk is.

Triple A means a minimal risk. The US and UK governments and the biggest and best-financed companies pick up AAA. All the A grades are good, and some of the Bs are acceptable as well. Lots of bond investors draw the line at BBB, which, they say, is the lowest level of investment-grade bonds.

All the rest of them, many bond investors say, are undependable rubbish. With C grades, you run a reasonable risk of problems, and with D grades or ungraded bonds, you're gambling. You may miss a payment or two, or you may never see your money back on the redemption date. But note that bond experts don't call these bonds rubbish. Instead, they call them junk bonds (or, more politely, *high yield* bonds).

The higher the rating, the lower the interest rate. Investors want something extra to make up for the dangers of a poor credit rating but are willing to give up interest for the security of a top rating, such as triple-A or AAB. The rating looks at how long the bond has to pay out. A government or company may be good for a year or two, but will it still be paying out in 20 or 30 years' time? Risk ratings are regularly revised by agencies. What starts out at AAA can fall to junk levels while rubbish can rehabilitate itself and move up the scale.

Junk bonds: Where there's muck, there's brass (maybe!)

Why invest in junk bonds when the rating agencies say they're below investment grade? The obvious answer is the risk/reward equation. Junk bond investors hope to spot bonds that are due for an upward re-rating, that should push prices up.

Issuers of junk bonds pay higher interest rates to make up for the risk. And you can often buy the bonds at far below their face value. You pay, say, £30 for a £100 face-value bond from a company that may or may not live long enough to repay investors as it should. If the company survives, you've made £70 plus bigger interest payments all the way along the line. If it fails completely, you've lost your £30, but if you've had a few years of above-average payments along the way, then your loss doesn't look so bad. It might even work out that you've received your £30 back and more.

One junk bond may be a recipe for disaster. But put together a diversified collection in your portfolio, and there's a good chance that some winners will more than make up for the losers.

Look at the following example portfolio to see how a diversified collection can sometimes work out in your favour. Assume that all the bonds have five years left to run and that you've invested £1,000 face value in each. The examples ignore tax and compounding of re-invested income.

- ✔ Bond A is bought at £60 for each £100 (£600). It pays 8 per cent nominal and survives intact. After five years, you have interest totalling £400 (£80 × 5) plus a £400 profit (£1,000 that you get less the £600 you paid). *You make £800 in all.*

- ✔ Bond B is bought at £25 for each £100 (£250). It pays 4 per cent nominal and lasts for three years before going bust. You collect £120 in interest but lose your £250 capital. *You lose £130 overall.*

- ✔ Bond C costs £50 for each £100 (£500). It pays 6 per cent nominal. But the issuer gets into trouble and never pays you a penny. The bondholders form a committee and force the firm into early repayment of the bonds at £75. You receive £750. *You make £250.*

- ✔ Bond D costs £70 for each £100 (£700). It pays 5 per cent nominal. The credit agencies decide to take the bond issuer off the junk list because it has new management, and the agencies put it on the quality list. The 5 per cent is about right for the market, so the price shoots up to £95. You sell and take a profit. *You make £175.*

- ✔ Bond E costs £10 for each £100 (£100). It pays nothing and goes bust within weeks. *You lose £100.*

How low can you go?

At the top end of the quality scale, credit ratings are only for the ultra nervous. The gap between AAA and AA or A isn't really that crucial for most bond buyers. But anything below BBB is speculative. Investors have to pay more attention to junk bond ratings as the risk of loss is real. So how low can you go?

✔ BB is probably still fine, but there are long-term fears over the issuing company or government. The company is more likely to be a bit late with the cash rather than not pay out at all.

✔ B should be okay as well, but if the economy or the business turns down, you may face problems. There are no guarantees, but you should get your payments. You can expect to get around 3 per cent per year extra on these bonds compared with AAA.

✔ CCC, CC, C is for caution. There's a current problem in the business or country issuing these bonds. An improvement on what you see now needs to occur before you can rest easier. You can expect around 4 to 7 per cent extra per year on these bonds.

✔ DDD, DD, D is for distress, disaster, and default. Default is the bond dealer's shorthand for anything going wrong. The bond issuer is already in severe trouble, has missed out on payments, and may be heading toward an early death. D-style bonds are only worthwhile buying if you're prepared to take a big gamble. You should aim for at least 10 to 15 per cent per year more here to make up for the ultra risky rating.

Some winners, some losers. But here the gains more than outweigh the losses.

Credit ratings apply to bonds from countries as well as companies. Countries can go bust or have problems repaying interest or debts. But some countries, such as former parts of the Soviet Union or nations in Africa, are young and don't have much of a credit record, so they get low marks. Always remember bond buyers are naturally cautious. If they weren't, they'd be buying something racier.

The redemption calculation

Assuming that you're happy with the credit rating and the interest rate, you need to look at the redemption date of the bond. That's the day on which you'll receive, say, £100 for each £100 nominal on your bond certificate. It doesn't matter what you paid; you get £100.

The redemption date may be anywhere from days to decades away. Bonds fit into three main categories according to their final date:

> ✔ **Shorts or short-dated.** Anything up to 5 years.
>
> ✔ **Mediums.** From 5 to 15 years.
>
> ✔ **Longs.** From 15 years upward.

With the passage of time, a Long becomes a Medium and then a Short. The US is different (natch!). Over in New York, a long bond is called a long bond from day one all the way to the date it is finally repaid.

The date matters because the longer away it is, the greater the risk of either a default (the issuer missing a payment or not being able to repay) or an interest or credit rating change. Not much will happen over the next 30 days, so a very short-dated bond is unlikely to change much in price. The next 30 years, however, is a different matter. Bonds with a very long date can be very volatile, although that's only by bond standards! Shares can and do move up or down 10 per cent, 20 per cent, or more in a day. Bond moves are small by comparison, but bond investors, more used to fractions of a percentage point, don't think so.

Longer-dated bonds should pay more interest to reflect the greater risks. This arrangement is called the *yield curve*, and the pay rate should go higher the further a bond has to run. Investors often look at why they're buying bonds and choose a life to fit. Someone with a 12-year-old child looking to fund educational fees may opt for a 10-year bond because it should coincide with a hoped-for university graduation.

I want to briefly share one more thing related to this whole redemption calculation business. Bonds have two interest rates:

> ✔ **The running yield.** This is the amount you receive on your bond divided into the price you paid. So someone paying £90 for a £100 nominal value bond and earning £9 a year in interest would get a 10 per cent running yield.
>
> ✔ **The yield to redemption.** This one takes the running yield and then adjusts it for the gain or loss you make on final repayment. If you buy at over £100, your yield to redemption will be lower than your running yield; and if you buy at under £100, the redemption yield will be higher (assuming the bond will not go into default). A complicated formula exists for working out the yield to redemption, but most mortals just believe the figures they see in newspaper bond listings.

Taxpayers are better off with gains on maturity than high running yields. That's because bonds that are under £100 should give a tax-free capital gain on redemption. Income is taxed unless it's in an Individual Savings Account (ISA).

'What is this? No date is listed for repayment!'

Some UK government bonds don't have a date for repayment. That's because the government never has to pay them back – ever! These bonds have wonderful names, such as *Consols* or *Treasury After '61,* but the best known is *War Loan,* which was raised to help pay for the costs of the First World War.

If you buy these types of bonds, you should get the same return forever. Their prices go up and down according to interest rates at the time.

But although the UK government guarantees your interest, it makes no promises to repay your bond in the future. However, if interest rates fall so low that the government is paying out more than it has to, then it might repay the bond. The small print says it can.

War Loan was a disastrous investment for the patriots who bought to help out the inter-war government. But the big interest rate falls of the 1990s made big money for those bold enough to take a plunge. Some investors tripled their money.

Which Way to Buy Your Bonds

Two main routes are available for buying bonds:

- ✔ **Purchase individual bonds through a stockbroker.** You'll pay the normal commission. Alternatively, if you're buying UK government bonds, special low-cost facilities are available through the Bank of England brokerage service, which is designed for small investors. The Bank of England Web site has details.

- ✔ **Purchase bonds through a fund.** Hundreds of unit trusts specialise in bonds. They range from gilt funds, where the yield is low, to speculative junk bonds and bust-country bond funds.

The choice is yours. To help you make an informed decision, here are the pros and cons of the two options:

- ✔ Individual bonds come with set conditions. You know the payments you'll get as long as there are no defaults. This setup makes them ideal for paying items such as educational fees, where you know there will be a start date and an end date.

- ✔ Unit trusts offer less certainty. Even if all the bonds survive, you're never promised your original cash back. The price of the units depends on market levels when you buy and sell.

- ✔ Individual bonds have one charge when you buy them through a broker. There are no charges for bonds bought when they're issued. Nor are there any annual fees.

- ✔ Unit trusts charge an initial fee of around 5 per cent, and between 1 and 1.5 per cent as annual fees after that.

✔ Individual bonds mean you're on your own unless you can persuade a broker to help you for a fee. When the bonds are repaid on maturity, you'll have to think afresh about what you're going to do with the cash.

✔ Unit trusts offer management, so you don't have to be so involved.

✔ Individual bonds send you interest on fixed dates.

✔ Unit trusts offer a choice of interest on fixed dates or rolling the money into new units if you don't want to spend it at that time. And some trusts offer monthly facilities, so you get a regular income.

Bond funds are the most worthwhile components in an Individual Savings Account (ISA) plan. Unlike with equities, you get the full tax-relief savings – saving 20 per cent if you're a basic-rate payer and 40 per cent if you're in the top category. You can invest up to £7,200 per year into an ISA from April 2008. The taxman gives a trust a bond-fund label if 60 per cent of its value consists of bonds. On top of this, the interest on most bond funds is greater than the dividends on equity funds. So you get a bigger ISA bang for your investment bucks.

Chapter 11

Building Your Information Bank

. . . .

In This Chapter

▶ Using your eyes and ears for information

▶ Searching the Internet

▶ Analysing tipsheets

▶ Examining press coverage

. . . .

The Rothschilds' financial fortune and banking empire was founded, so it is said, on the family receiving news before all others of the defeat of Napoleon at Waterloo by the Duke of Wellington, with the British having some last-minute help from the Prussian army. The Rothschilds had organised a series of messengers and carrier pigeons so that they'd know the outcome first.

The stock markets of the time believed that the French would win and priced investments accordingly. But because the Rothschilds knew the real result first – that the opposite outcome had occurred – they were able to take big financial bets against the markets and make the early 19th century equivalent of billions.

Now, as then, investment markets revolve around information. If your information is quicker, more accurate, and better understood than that of others, you'll prosper. So this chapter explains how to build your own personal information bank. The Internet, the media, and ever-increasing disclosure rules for stock-market-quoted companies can give you more facts, figures, and opinions than you'll ever want or be able to use. On top of that, companies produce annual reports and other documentation that grows weightier with each passing year.

Before you build your information bank, you must decide what you want from it. You can't file away everything available on financial markets, so limit yourself to looking at the shares and bonds you already hold or at an area of the market that interests you, such as government stocks or bank shares. And after you build your information bank, you have to make up your mind what to do with the info. Know that if you're still confused, it's okay to keep your money in the bank. Know, too, that there's no such thing as an unrepeatable offer. You don't have to 'buy now while stocks last' because another deal is *always* coming along.

Be careful when it comes to price-sensitive info

Acting on some forms of information you may receive is actually illegal these days. There are laws against *insider trading*, where you buy and sell shares based on information that's only available to you or a select few as a result of having a secret source within a company or organisation.

The law can come into action if the facts you know are deemed to be *price sensitive*, meaning that the info would move a price up or down if it was known to the general public.

Very few successful prosecutions for this crime have occurred in the UK, not because the crime doesn't happen but because finding sufficient evidence to prove it to a jury is difficult. However, the Financial Services Authority is getting tougher. It has, for example, warned quoted football clubs that they must announce potentially price-sensitive information, such as a transfer of a star player or the appointment or sacking of a manager, to the stock exchange before they tell the sports media.

Taking a Look Around You

To build an information bank, your first move requires neither a computer nor a filing cabinet. It requires merely your eyes and ears.

You're surrounded by the products and services of stock-market-quoted companies. The high street is full of them. So too are your food cupboards, wardrobes, and home leisure areas. The fortunes or otherwise of these firms are ultimately based on the purchasing decisions made by millions of consumers. And that includes you. Acting on gut feeling can be a valid start to a share buying or selling decision.

All the boasting and blustering of a firm's top management are meaningless if the employees nearest to the consumers fail to deliver good service or if the consumers themselves aren't interested or prefer a rival.

Here are some potential investing areas to look at:

> ✔ **Fashion retailing.** If you and your friends stop going to a store or start buying a lot less, then it's probable that others in a similar position are also shunning these outlets. Alternatively, you may start buying at a store that you previously thought had a poor design or bad value. For a real example, consider that shoppers started putting Next back on their style agenda in the mid-1990s. And by the end of that decade, fashionistas shunned Marks & Spencer (especially the women's clothing). In both cases, it took a long time before the stock market caught up with consumer taste changes. And then it took time again before investors realised that Marks & Spencer, for instance, had turned the corner and was acceptable once again. Companies can continue to churn out good

profit figures for some time after customers have deserted them and may fail to reflect an increase for a year or two after consumers vote with their feet in favour.

✔ **Publishers.** Look at the Harry Potter phenomenon. Whether you like the books or not, millions of readers do, turning publisher Bloomsbury from a small niche firm into a major player. But investors want to know where Bloomsbury goes now that best-ever seller has reached the end of its series.

✔ **Food retailers.** The state of the car park and the length of the checkout queue at key times, such as Saturday mornings, can speak volumes about the success or otherwise of a superstore firm.

✔ **Financial firms.** Regardless of how many fancy deals big banks do abroad in esoteric markets, they depend on ordinary savers and borrowers for their long-term bread and butter. Attractive branches full of people are good signs.

✔ **January sales.** Whether they're selling cars or clothing, watch out for companies that have too many sales. Winter sales and summer sales should be more than enough. When the company gets to pre-Christmas, half-term, spring, and autumn sales, start to worry. These firms aren't efficient.

Going Online

I have a chunky bookshelf lined with volumes on how to invest online. They're all very worthy and offer large amounts of useful information, and they stress how the Internet has revolutionised share buying and selling for the individual. True. They also point out how much information there is to be found online. True again. But most of them fail to make these vital points:

✔ A huge amount of duplication is on the Internet, so concentrate your searches to a few sites that you know how to navigate and where you trust the content.

✔ Information on the Internet isn't guaranteed to be accurate unless it comes from the company whose fortunes you're putting into your information bank.

The chat rooms or so-called investment communities that played a big part in the dotcom boom and bust are a waste of time. Why? They consist of clueless people posting messages to those looking for clues, or, more dangerously, they consist of chat from people with a position in the shares looking to give their investments a boost by persuading others to join them. Some of this information is downright misinformation – and often the very opposite of the truth. Ask yourself why a total stranger hiding behind a pseudonym should be so anxious to help you by sharing thoughts.

✔ The Internet doesn't change the fundamentals of investment. It just speeds up some of them.

✔ Using the speed of the Internet to make buy or sell decisions can deprive you of those vital few seconds when you pinch yourself and double-check that you're doing the right thing.

✔ Thousands of financial scam sites exist, and they're devoted to parting you from your money.

Those are the warnings. But the Internet has great value in building up your personal investment information bank as well, especially if you use it counter-intuitively – in a way that most other investors don't think about doing because they're too busy confusing themselves in the noise and rubbish of investment communities. This section helps you use the power of the Internet to build your information bank.

Web sites come and go. Their names change. Their services are altered. Their policy on what is free and what you have to pay for also varies over time. So although any inclusion of a Web site is accurate at the time of writing, there's no guarantee that any of the information will remain correct. This news may not be as worrisome as it sounds. Much of the info on the Internet that's useful to investors is repeated over and over again on various different sites.

Exploring the company's Web site

The dotcommers' vision of a world free of shops, where all products and services are traded online, has, as of yet, remained a pipe dream. But although most people still stick to traditional ways of buying, the Internet has a big influence on their decisions.

Exploring the Web sites of companies can give you a great deal of insight about the companies themselves. To build your information bank, you need to assess the actual site, read the company's online report, and read between the proverbial lines.

Assess the site itself

Your eyes and ears should always play a big role in your information-bank building, so when you're exploring a company online, take a look at how well designed the Web site is.

Start off with the product or consumer area. Act as though you want the product or service. If the site is easy to navigate, then it's likely to attract extra business. A bad site will send potential customers to the competition.

Assuming that the assessment passes your personal quality-control barriers, head off to the corporate section of the firm's site. Here, you should find a large amount of information about your target company, including press releases (usually doctored so that the press office phone number is left blank), company statements, recent stock exchange filings, and annual and interim reports. In addition, you should find information on what the company does, its directors and senior managers, and how to contact the firm for more information. Also usually included is an investor relations section. (Investor relations is as much interested in would-be share buyers as in those already on the register.) While reading through all the information, again assess whether the company has made its info easy to access, navigate, and understand.

Read the company's online report

Companies are legally obliged to produce an annual report and accounts, which they must send to shareholders (even if it's only an abbreviated version). These reports form an essential part of any information bank.

Although firms are not obliged to make these reports available on the Internet, view with scepticism any company that doesn't. The reason the company doesn't make its report available online may be that the company doesn't want you to see the report or to be aware that the company is late filing it.

Most online company reports are presented in a format called pdf, so you need Adobe Acrobat Reader software to read them. The software is easily available at no cost from many sites.

Read between the lines

Understanding the nuances of a company Web site is akin to understanding a bank reference or a school report. It's what's missing that counts!

Don't expect Web material from a company to mention the negatives. Where these bad points have to be revealed publicly, the firm may well try to place them in a report in such a way that only the most wide-eyed reader will find them. In any case, no quoted company is yet obliged to keep a Web site.

So look out for:

- One person listed as both the chief executive and the chair of the company. This setup runs contrary to present-day standards for company governance.
- Too many mentions of the company boss. Egomaniacs usually fail.
- Inadequate explanations of past problems.
- Glossing over director-level resignations.
- Promises of future growth without sufficiently good explanations as to how it will be achieved.

Your information bank contains both positive and negative points on companies. No firm is faultless.

Exploring other sites for more info on the company

After you fully explore the company site, go back to your favourite search engine. Now you're looking for:

- ✔ **Sites such as Adfvn, Bloomberg, Citywire, iii, Motley Fool, or Yahoo.** These sites offer a brief company history, up to five years of past results, charts of past share-price performance, names of company officers, directors' share dealings, comparisons with rival companies, and present share-price information. You should be able to look at past performance over a number of timeframes with reference to the market as a whole.

Most sites give share prices delayed by 15 minutes unless you pay for a premium service that gives real-time numbers. Paying for real-time prices is probably only worthwhile if you're a short-term trader rather than a longer-term investor. Many share prices don't change that much from day to day, and those that are frequent movers often go up and down within narrow limits.

- ✔ **Industry comparison tools.** Try typing *company name + company sector* in the search engine. (Don't actually key in my generic example! Type the actual company name and sector, separated by a plus sign.) Here, you should find all the firms that compete with each other, such as department stores or car importers.

- ✔ **News stories on your chosen company.** At your request, some sites, such as Citywire and iii (this strange run of letters probably once stood once for Internet investment information before the branding people got their hands on it!), will e-mail you any market information on selected firms. You may have to pay for this info, or it may come bundled in a stockbroker package so there's no extra cost involved. These and similar sites may have chat rooms, so note the Warning paragraph about chat rooms at the very beginning of this whole 'Going Online' section.

- ✔ **Media coverage.** Broadsheet newspaper articles are usually archived and should be easy to find. Access to these articles may be free, although many newspapers, including the *Financial Times* and *The Wall Street Journal*, now charge a fee. (*The Wall Street Journal* is considering free access so try it and see.) Even those that don't charge you may demand that you register.

Information sites and other areas you look at online have a strange way of disappearing. Never be afraid to print what you want. Otherwise, you may never find it again!

Bookmarking your favourite sites

Despite the bursting of the dotcom bubble, literally dozens of information bank sites are available for you to choose from. Many are look-alike sites with listings of quoted companies and mainstream unit trusts. There are also some in-depth sites, such as Standard & Poor's for unit trust performance figures and its online site for investment trust material.

Your best bet is to try out as many of the general sites as possible and then bookmark two or three as your favourites.

Sites appear today and disappear tomorrow, change their emphasis without notice, and alter their charging structure. So no Web site listing can be fully guaranteed.

Following are some general sites to try out. Don't forget to add the prefix *www* to all of them:

- ✔ **find.co.uk.** This site does what it says on the label. It finds other sites for you, including news services, stockbrokers, unit and investment trust company Web sites, and banking and loan information.

- ✔ **etraderuk.com.** This is a portal leading to many other sites. It is mostly focused on share trading and is intended for investors moving up the sophistication ladder. It has more than 400 finance and business Web sites divided into more than 40 categories, now including contracts for difference, spread betting, foreign exchange dealing, futures and options, unit trusts and OEICs (Open Ended Investment Companies, a technical name for a type of unit trust), investment trusts, broker forecasts, ethical investing, technical analysis, courses and seminars, and details on investment clubs.

- ✔ **moneyextra.com.** This site is now run by an independent financial adviser firm that is a subsidiary of a major bank. But the essential features of a useful tool remain. Most of the emphasis is on packaged investments with lots of comparative performance tables, but for individual share fans, there's a handy online stockbroker comparison tool. Investors who register can use a personal portfolio tracker so they can easily follow the progress of their chosen funds and shares.

- ✔ **moneynet.co.uk.** This one is aimed at data rather than news or online guides to products. It's focused on personal finance issues such as pensions and mortgages, but it has good sections on investment funds, the stock market, and investing in traded endowment policies.

- ✔ **Hemscott.net.** This site has a basic free service with news and some access to share prices and information, including five-year abbreviated balance sheets and profits figures. Also available are more sophisticated levels that you must pay for.

✔ **funds.morningstar.com.** This site leads to Morningstar's unit trust and mutual fund database. This is the one the newspapers quote. It sorts out the performance of up to 80,000 funds worldwide over a wide variety of timeframes. Also available is information on fund management groups.

✔ **Trustnet.com.** This site is best known for its investment trust database where you can find charts, performance figures, and links to sites run by the trust managers. It has most of the funds but is not complete. It also has unit trusts and a useful feature that lets you set up your own portfolio onscreen so you can monitor its progress. Also available is a section where you can check out stock market indexes from across the world.

✔ **citywire.co.uk.** This site is great at breaking news. It should be because it's staffed by experienced financial journalists who look for originality instead of merely re-running the material sent in by news services. So you get (depending on your level of subscription, although some services are free) directors' dealings, secret buying (which looks at financial institutions and individuals who are building up or getting rid of stakes), and other revelations. You can also get alerts on shares you hold or are interested in. Also available are the usual mix of prices, information on companies and funds, and price charts.

✔ **digitallook.com.** This site gives you a weird mix of stock market news and football! The site is helpful for those looking for a good source of company news and financial data from both the UK and the US. It is linked to an investor education centre. And it carries lots of news and tips.

✔ **theaic.co.uk.** This is the official site of the Association of Investment Companies, which is a trade association for the investment trust world. It has news and views from the Association and member companies (not all the investment trusts on the market because membership is optional), Web site links to members' own online offerings, leaflets on how to understand the trusts, a trustfinder that narrows down the selection according to your own needs, and risk indications. It also provides a link to splitsonline, which has facts and figures on split capital trusts.

✔ **Investmentuk.org.** This is the site of the Investment Management Association, the trade body for the OEIC and unit trust industry. The site has facts and figures including past performance statistics for unit trusts as well as details of its member companies and information on how to invest. The site also has links to the IMA's fact sheets, which are a great help to beginners (and to more advanced investors as well!).

✔ **fool.co.uk.** This is the UK site of the US Motley Fool phenomenon. Although it has been cut back over the past few years, the site still has lots of education features and sets out to show how you can invest without paying commission or fees to professionals. It's good on direct share investment and on why the professionals add little or no value. The site is very investment oriented, but sometimes it's too self-reverential and referential for many people's tastes.

✔ **fsa.gov.uk.** This is the official site of the Financial Services Authority. It has comparison tools for Individual Savings Accounts, pensions and unit trusts, advice sheets, and the all-important check on whether an adviser, broker, or fund manager is authorised in the UK. Shun those not on its list.

✔ **proshare.org.uk.** This site mainly publicises the pro-share mission of encouraging private investors into direct share purchases, including investment clubs and employee share schemes. Also available are a selection of news services, share prices, annual reports, details on stockbrokers, and material on risk.

✔ **bestinvest.co.uk.** Okay, this stuff comes from a financial adviser. But this is the firm that produces the Dog Funds publications, which tell you all about the very worst fund managers. And that's a big change from the usual trick of just publicising last year's winners. You can buy funds online through a supermarket structure. It's also good on with-profits bonds and structured products such as guaranteed bonds.

Examining Tipsheets

Tipsheets and specialist share magazines, such as *Investors Chronicle* and *Shares*, can be part of your information bank.

The weekly magazines won't burn too much of a hole in your pocket. You can expect to spend £150 or so a year on each one. *Investors Chronicle* also has a Web site aimed specially at subscribers. These publications are good as archive material because they often cover results from companies that are not big enough to make it to the pages of daily newspapers. They can be helpful in portfolio building, often running their own selections with the reasons for each choice. They can sound authoritative but be warned that many of the articles are written by junior staff who are unlikely to write anything other than the orthodox view at the time.

Tipsheets can be far more expensive. Some charge up to £1,000 a year for a few pages each month. Literally dozens of tipsheets are on offer. They're regulated by the Financial Services Authority, although so far the watchdog has done little to ensure that those behind the tipsheets don't already have holdings in the shares recommended. Tips do tend to push up prices, especially because most of the sheets concentrate on tiny companies where one buy or sell order sends the price soaring or sinking. They usually ignore bigger companies.

Here are a few additional titbits about tipsheets:

✔ Most tipsheets have low-cost introductory offers. You sign up for a direct debit for three to six months at a bargain rate, which, unless you cancel it, automatically moves to the far more expensive rate after that.

✔ Some go for a scatter gun approach and tip a large number of shares in each issue, hoping that one or two are bound to be winners. Others are more careful.

✔ There's no evidence that any tipsheet is consistently good. But if you like the idea, try a few to find one that suits your risk/reward profile and the sort of share you like to invest in. One or two tipsheets specialise in sectors such as technology or investment trusts.

✔ Tipsheets advertise their successes and ignore their failures. They aren't obliged to reveal the date when the tip was made in any advert or when the sheet suggested selling, so know that the successes may be several years old when market conditions were quite different.

Looking at News Coverage

All UK quoted companies have to report at least twice yearly to shareholders as well as issue statements on a number of other occasions, such as during takeovers, the issuing of new shares, and significant director-level changes. This information is all revealed to the stock market via the Regulatory News Service (RNS), which gives equal prominence to an announcement from a company worth £10 billion or more and to one worth £10 million or less.

Big stockbroking firms and investing institutions subscribe to this service. You can do so, too, but it costs a fortune and delivers little in return for the cost.

One way to find out what's going on is to join one of the online news services listed earlier in this chapter. Many of these services will e-mail you alerts on those companies in your portfolio that you've registered with the Web site; they will often also send you alerts about companies in which you've indicated an interest. This approach is fine for serious investors who can spend all day in front of their screens.

The rest of us tend to rely on newspapers as a primary source of information and also for comment on the stock market and other investment issues. But even the most comprehensive newspapers only cover a proportion of a day's RNS output. It's vital to know how City pages work, the decisions editors make, and why some companies receive so much more coverage than others.

Rule 1 is that City pages aren't just written for investors. They have to attract at least some other readers to justify their expense. Companies with a high street presence, such as retailers and banks, get more coverage than manufacturing concerns or mining companies, no matter how important these companies might be, because non-investor readers like to know how famous names are doing.

Rule 2 is that reporters can't be everywhere at once. They concentrate on companies they consider sexy. They may even take that word literally. For example, reporters write about some companies because they're in the fashion world – a cue for a picture of a scantily clad model. A firm making millions of pounds by making billions of nuts and bolts doesn't make a pretty picture. Reporters also concentrate on controversial companies, including those whose directors are deemed to be greedy fat cats or where big losses are occurring. All this coverage is at the expense of other firms that simply grow a little each year. There's generally little coverage of small companies unless they're especially newsworthy, perhaps because of a celebrity involvement.

Rule 3 is that public relations agencies play a role. Most quoted companies hire PR firms whose job is to ensure that good news gets into newspapers and bad news is hidden away or, preferably, ignored. These firms try to influence the comment columns most City pages run.

Newspapers available in the UK fall into four categories, at least for investor purposes:

- ✔ **Specialist newspapers, such as the *Financial Times* and *The Wall Street Journal* (read online for the US edition rather than the European version).** The specialist papers are worth reading not just because they offer more of what an investor wants but also because they're influential and taken seriously by City movers and shakers. They can directly impact share market values.

- ✔ **Broadsheets (even if they're now all different shapes), such as *The Daily Telegraph, The Guardian, The Independent*, and *The Times*.** The broadsheets have some influence on a regular basis but come into their own when they do investigations. They also tend to have their favourite sectors, such as transport or investment trusts.

- ✔ **Tabloids, which are the rest of the dailies.** Don't expect too much from the tabloids because their stories rarely move a share price.

- ✔ **Sunday newspapers, including *The Independent on Sunday, The Mail on Sunday, The Observer, The Sunday Telegraph*, and *The Sunday Times*.** The more serious Sunday newspapers sometimes play a controversial role. They're often used for breaking news. Public relations companies acting for firms but legally independent of their paymasters phone journalists they know and trust on these newspapers to give them whispers about forthcoming takeovers or to offer stories that run down the firm's competitors. But there's no such thing as a free lunch. In return, the journalists write something complimentary about the companies in question or their directors at a later date. These are known as *puff pieces*.

Watch out, too, for the results of the *Friday night drop*. This refers to PR companies offering snippets for the share tipping columns most Sunday newspapers run. This stuff isn't supposed to happen but it does.

Most newspapers now have online archives so you can look at how a company was reported in the past.

Chapter 12

Choosing a Stockbroker

· ·

· ·

*S*tockbrokers used to have an image – deserved or not. They supposedly wore pin-striped suits and bowler hats, arrived at work in the City from their large country homes around 10.15 a.m., went out for a long lunch at their club around 12.45 p.m. (where they started with several large gin and tonics and ended with several large brandies), returned to work at 3.30, and went home again around 4.30.

Even if that image were ever true, these days most stockbrokers work very long hours and take a sandwich lunch. Regardless, few investors ever meet their stockbrokers because most stockbroking is done online. Having a real flesh-and-blood broker is a rarity and can be an expensive one at that.

Regardless again, investors need the services of a stockbroker or other financial adviser for most buying and selling transactions in shares, bonds, investment trusts, and unit trusts. This fact applies even when investors don't want or require any help or advice in coming up with decisions. So this chapter explains what you need to know in order to choose an adviser or stockbroker to best meet your individual needs.

The few times when you don't need a stockbroker

For most buying and selling transactions in shares, bonds, investment trusts, and unit trusts, investors need the services of a stockbroker – even if an investor doesn't want or require any help or advice.

But a stockbroker *isn't* needed with these particular investments:

✔ Shares purchased during a flotation (also known as an initial public offering, or IPO).

✔ UK government stocks bought at the time of issue.

✔ Investment trusts purchased through savings plans, which can be sold back to the scheme.

✔ Shares bought through a dividend re-investment scheme.

✔ Unit trusts bought directly from a fund manager, including those bought via regular savings schemes.

And regarding that last item, here's a little tip for you: Never buy unit trusts from fund managers directly unless they offer a big discount. Otherwise, you'll end up paying more but receiving a lower level of service than a financial adviser will give you. Most financial advisers will offer a big up-front discount. How can they do that? They get a 0.5 per cent payment each year from the fund company. This is known as *trail commission*.

Would You Like That Service with or without Advice?

Any firm involved in advising the public on investments in the UK must be authorised by the Financial Services Authority (FSA). The FSA Web site (www.fsa.gov.org) enables you to check on this matter. The firm should only employ qualified individuals who've passed a series of exams to offer advice.

Never deal with any firm that's not authorised. This warning includes financial concerns whose marketing material is authorised by an FSA-approved adviser when the firm itself is not on the list.

All advisers split their work into two compartments:

✔ **With advice.** *Advice* here means you get individualised buy and sell recommendations that are designed to take in a whole range of your personal needs, including your attitude to risk, family circumstances, overall wealth, investment aims, and any other investments you may already have. So here, you have some sort of contact with the adviser or broker, either face to face at your home or their office, on the phone, or, more rarely, in writing.

✔ **Without advice, or** *execution-only.* Here, you fill in a form in a newspaper or magazine, or reply to a mailshot the adviser or broker has sent. It doesn't matter how targeted the mailshot is. It may include terms such as *strongly advise*, for example, and your name may even be printed on it so that it appears personalised, but it's still without advice according to the FSA.

The Levels of Service Available

Many advisers offer general help on a wide range of topics, including pensions, insurance, and investments. These advisers generally fall into two categories:

✔ Independent financial advisers (IFAs) who can advise on a wide range of products.

✔ Tied agents who usually work for banks or insurance companies and can only sell their own limited selection of products, although some now sell a number of other investments from other providers to fill out their range.

A mid-way level known as *multi-tie* also exists, but that need not concern real investors. Multi-tie is mainly concerned with selling insurance.

Whatever their status, most advisers confine themselves to packaged products such as unit trusts and investment-based insurance plans. But stockbrokers and some IFAs go beyond, so you can buy and sell individual shares.

Stockbrokers dealing with private investors offer up to three levels of service. Two of the levels, advisory and discretionary, have been around for decades. The third, execution-only, is more recent and is the level most frequently needed by small investors.

Advisory service

The advisory level of service is where the broker contacts you personally and recommends a course of action. You're free to accept or reject this recommendation.

Brokers earn their fees from commissions on purchases and sales. These are likely to be based on a percentage of the value of each transaction if you're a very large investor. Smaller investors (the definition of this can vary from those investing anything under £500,000 to those with £25,000) are generally charged fees on top. Giving advice in this way is very costly in stockbroker time.

Discretionary service

With the discretionary level of service, you discuss your needs with a broker, such as a need for longer-term capital growth or a need for income now. Your stockbroker takes your money and then puts it into shares on your behalf.

The advantage is that someone is doing the work for you and is able to reduce the costs of individual share dealing by dealing for a number of clients requiring the same sort of portfolio at one go. The downside is that you aren't told of every transaction, although you receive regular updates.

With this level of service, you usually pay an annual fee rather than pay commission on each trade. The advantage of a fee over commission is that it removes any temptation for the broker to *churn* your portfolio – to make money from unnecessarily frequent trading.

Discretionary services are often a good idea for those with around £100,000 or more to invest and who want to hand either the whole amount to a professional or perhaps a large proportion so they can concentrate on managing the balance themselves. Some brokers offer discretionary services for those with smaller sums, but they're often based on investment and unit trusts rather than individual shares.

Execution-only service

This service has nothing to do with capital punishment! Instead, it means you decide exactly what you want to do based on your own research and your own understanding of your needs. Once you have come up with a buy or sell decision, you contact the broker who will then execute the deal for you via the stock market. This is the most frequently used service level by small stock-market investors.

Most execution-only services are online, but many brokers still offer phone dealing (likely to be more expensive) and a few deal by post. Postal buying and selling is usually confined to infrequent traders – perhaps those dealing once or twice a year.

If you deal by post, the share price is determined when the broker carries out your order, not when you sent the instructions.

What You Can Expect to Pay

Financial advice and stockbroking services aren't free. Advisers and brokers generally expect a good lifestyle, irrespective of whether their input into your investment planning is successful. Only a tiny minority work on a success basis, and even then, you're still likely to pay some costs.

Commission

All tied agents and most IFAs work for *commission*, a percentage of the amount you invest. A typical unit trust deal will pay the adviser 3 per cent of your money when you invest and a further 0.5 per cent per year in *trail commission* thereafter. Lump-sum insurance investments, including with-profits bonds, pay the adviser up to 8 per cent.

Advisers have to disclose these amounts. Many IFAs rebate part or all of the amount, especially if you're dealing with a large sum. Tied agents, such as those working for banks and building societies, rarely rebate.

There's no more work involved in arranging a £100,000 insurance bond deal than one for £1,000. But on standard commission arrangements, the adviser could earn £8,000 on the larger sum and just £80 on the smaller amount. So there is scope for haggling.

Fixed or by the hour

Some IFAs work on a fee basis. Here, you agree to a fixed charge or per-hour fee beforehand. If it's per hour, ask for an estimate of how many hours the work should take. The IFA then rebates any commission to you.

This arrangement avoids allegations of product bias, where the adviser tries to sell you the investment deal with the highest commission. A fee-based adviser could equally suggest National Savings (zero commission) or insurance bonds (high commission).

Per-hour rates range from £50 to more than £100. Fixed fees are more commonly used with defined jobs, such as moving a pension plan from one home to another. Here, you may pay £500 or £1,000 depending on the complexity of the job.

Based on the level of service

Stockbroking costs also vary based on the level of service you choose:

- ✔ **Advisory service.** Expect to pay around 2 per cent on each purchase or sale deal. After that, you could pay up to £100 an hour for the broker's time. Unless you're a very rich client, you're likely to be given a junior broker as your personal adviser.

✔ **Discretionary service.** There's a wide range, but typical charges are around 1.5 per cent on each transaction, plus a 2 to 3 per cent annual management charge.

✔ **Execution-only service.** If you're reading this book, this is the most likely service level you'll aim for. You'll almost certainly deal on the Internet, although less choice exists than there once was. At the height of the dotcom boom in 1999–2000, some 40 firms were chasing business. Many have now joined forces out of necessity or just gone out of business. So the result is the end of some of the cut-throat competition where many brokers offered free (other than stamp duty) dealing for a fixed period. Those that are left usually charge the same amount no matter how big your buy or sell order is.

Expect to pay £12 to £25 on each transaction. The few that base charges on the size of the deal have a ceiling charge of between £25 and £50. Some offer frequent trader packages where you pay a fixed sum, such as £10 to £20 per quarter, but then pay a lower sum on each deal. You generally have to deal at least once a fortnight for these packages to be worthwhile. There may also be a fee for holding your shares in a dematerialised form (without a share certificate and through a nominee holding arrangement). The lowest cost dealings are through the post, where you can pay as little as £5 because there's no guarantee exactly when your order will be carried out.

It's all too easy to get carried away by online dealing. At its simplest, you click a button and have either bought or sold. But you're dealing with real money (and your *own* money). It's not Monopoly money. Execution-only stockbroking means no one's around to say, 'Stop! Think before you act because you could be making a big mistake!'

What to Look At When Selecting a Stockbroker

If you come from a fabulously wealthy background, you probably already have a family stockbroker. If not, read on.

Considerations with discretionary and advisory services

Discretionary and advisory services rely on at least some face-to-face contact between you and a stockbroker and the broker's need to find out exactly what you want out of your investment strategy. So you may need to do some shopping around to find a stockbroker who's right for you. Areas to look at include:

✔ **Size of portfolio.** Make sure that your personal wealth is well within the broker's parameters. If the broker wants a minimum £25,000, then having £25,001 isn't much help because you could easily fall below the line if markets turn against you. Ask what happens if your fortune shrinks either through bad decisions or because you choose to spend some of your money.

✔ **Level of service.** Consider the experience of your contact or account executive, as well as whether e-mail alerts and regular newsletters or other forms of stock recommendation will be sent out. Find out whether the broker offers a portfolio based on unit trusts, investment trusts, or exchange traded funds.

✔ **Costs.** This shouldn't be your first consideration, but it's essential all the same. Excessive costs can wipe out gains from a clever investment strategy. Very excessive costs can turn good decisions into instant losses.

✔ **Protection from churning.** Unscrupulous brokers try to earn more from your investments by over-frequent buying and selling. You could agree to a limit on their trading activity.

For a listing of potentially suitable brokers, contact APCIMS, the Association of Private Client Investment Managers and Stockbrokers, at www.apcims. co.uk.

Considerations with execution-only services

Investors who want to make up their own minds don't need advice, but they do need a broker to carry out the transaction. Most dealing is on the Internet.

The advantages of online dealing are obvious: being able to buy and sell anytime, from anywhere; seeing how your portfolio is performing in real time; and getting up-to-date prices, charts, and news. But drawbacks exist too. The obvious one is backup if your computer or Internet connection fails. Some online brokers have a telephone alternative. In addition, security can be a worry, although most sites are now encrypted to a high degree. In fact, very few instances of online fraud and security lapses have occurred. That said, you may still want to check out the nearby sidebar about online security.

Of greater concern should be your need to use one broker for all your transactions. This isn't a legal necessity, but the way online brokers operate and charge makes it difficult to have more than one broker. Many online brokers offer terms that make it cheaper to stick with one organisation. You'll have to set up a bank account if you do anything more than occasional dealing. And it's very difficult to set up portfolios that reflect your trading at another broker.

Build a firewall for online security

Newspapers love stories about online security lapses, and that's because they are very few and far between. All sites are password-protected and have 128-bit encryption.

But, still, it's best to be safe rather than sorry. You should build a firewall into your computer system to protect it from hackers. The best-known and most easily available program comes from Norton. But also available is a free firewall you can download from ZoneAlarm at `www.zonelabs.com`.

Remember this, though: Most Internet broker security breaches occur because investors – while at their workplace – leave their computers connected to the broker site or leave password details lying around for anyone to find.

Online charges are low because very little paperwork is involved. You won't normally receive certificates because your portfolio will be in a nominee account with Crest (the London Stock Exchange centralised settlement system) so the broker can instantly buy or sell on your behalf. Most online brokers insist on a nominee account and an associated bank account so that cash for purchases can move out without fuss and you have a receptacle for money you generate on a sale.

Most online brokers hold your money in an account in *their* name, so the company you're investing in doesn't know that you're a shareholder. You may lose your rights to shareholder material, such as annual reports (but you can usually find these online at the company's Web site), to voting privileges, and to shareholder perks. If these points are important, your broker may offer you an individual nominee account, but it could cost more.

Additional considerations

If you're considering an execution-only service, here are some additional points to consider:

- **Computer compatibility.** Not all stockbroker sites support Mac- or Linux-based machines. Some sites don't work that well on Netscape or other non-Microsoft Internet connections.

- **Trading range.** All brokers cover mainstream UK shares. But if you fancy the tiny UK companies on PLUS, traded options, or overseas shares, then your choice may be more limited.

- **How many extras you get.** Look for easy-to-use EPIC code finders (these are the letters used by professionals – for example, Marks & Spencer is MKS), a good stock history facility, easy access to company statements and stock exchange filings, research reports, and analyst ratings. Are these things free?

- **How much money you need to open a trading account.** Some brokers are only interested in the very wealthy and will demand you deposit big sums. But all will want something to cover your trades otherwise they cannot deal for you. The days when a 'gentleman' would be allowed to run up big bills are over, except maybe for the most blue-blooded brokers and their wealthiest clients.

- **Extra charges.** These charges may be for statements of dividends and capital gains (or losses) so you can file your annual tax return more easily. There may also be a fee for sending proceeds of sales to another account.

- **Whether the broker is set up to offer another service channel.** Does the broker offer phone or post service if the Internet breaks down or if you want to deal occasionally on an obscure overseas market?

- **Whether the service is in real time.** Is your decision acted on at once, or does it depend on e-mail? It matters if you're a frequent trader.

- **What interest, if any, the broker pays on your cash balances.** You will have cash balances with your broker either because you have deposited cash ahead of purchases or because you have cash from a sale of shares or bonds. Either way, many brokers offer you interest while the money is under their roof. But don't expect too much. Often it is a derisory 0.5 per cent or less.

- **Whether there's a fill or kill facility.** With this kind of arrangement, you set a maximum price for a purchase and a minimum acceptable price for a sale. If the broker can't fulfil your instructions, the deal is automatically terminated.

 Many brokers have a sampler service, meaning you can try out the site on a dry-run basis. You may find that you're willing to sacrifice some services and pay more for a broker that offers a site that's easy to navigate. Once you click Go, you've dealt, so don't make mistakes.

The Process of Signing Up with a Stockbroker

You can't just use a stockbroker either online or in any other form in the same way as a grocery store. There are forms to fill in and bureaucracy to satisfy.

After you choose an online stockbroker for execution-only services (where you make all the decisions, leaving the technical bits of buying and selling to the broker), you will need to open an account.

Brokers have to follow rules designed to combat money laundering, so they need to check that you are who you say you are. This process involves sending in your national insurance number online and may be followed by a request for hard-copy documentation, such as your passport and proof of address from a utility bill (gas, water, electric, fixed-line phone). If you've moved recently, you may have to provide details of past addresses for the previous three years. In addition, the broker needs details of your main bank account and needs to know whether you're a UK citizen.

After you complete these formalities, which can take two weeks or more, you need to send cash to open your trading account. The minimum varies from £100 to £50,000. Most brokers arrange for the cash to be moved electronically from your bank account. Some want a cheque, primarily as a further security check. The cheque may take up to two weeks to clear if it comes from a building society. Allow a week otherwise.

You may also want to transfer investments into your new account. If you're moving all your stocks and shares from another broker, then the broker you're ditching and the new broker whose services you're signing up to should be able to sort everything out after you've given permission.

Getting a new broker is a good time to dematerialise all those old share certificates and put them on an electronic basis so all your purchases and sells are recorded on a computer by the broker. You end up with a statement which you can print. It's just the same as dealing with your bank where you get an electronically generated statement and not the actual bits of paper. Share certificates are nothing but a nuisance, especially if they get lost.

A few old share certificates have collector-item value. You can arrange to have them cancelled and returned to you.

Part III
Collective Investments

'Actually my business card's in there if you're interested in investing your money . . .'

In this part . . .

With packaged investments, professional fund managers look after your money in return for a fee. Often, a bewildering variety of funds is available for you to choose from. And the management companies behind them spend a fortune trying to convince you that theirs is top dog.

The best fund managers are experts, but with the worst, you'd be much better off keeping your money under the bed! So don't expect gift wrapping or one of those reassuring guarantees. Never forget the professionals have their own agenda. This part tells you to take nothing at face value and always look at everything with a big pinch of salt.

Chapter 13

Looking at Fund Management

. . . .

. . . .

*Y*ou can identify a fund management advert from a mile away. It features a huge graph with the line heading to the stratosphere. It may even include a rocket heading for outer space just in case you're too dim to understand the concept. (Some fund managers push the point home even further by naming themselves after planets or stars.) And the warnings, of course, are listed in tiny print.

As a potential investor, you're supposed to pay attention to the positive upward image and ignore or dismiss the negatives in small print as just regulatory noise. The fund promoters hope that you'll just send them your cheque as mindlessly as you'd buy a packet of crisps.

Not if you're reading this book, you won't!

At the end of the last century, not that long ago, many big fund managers were launching technology funds with wonderful high-tech names, such as Techtornado and NetNet. The only problem was that they were one-day wonders (some didn't even last that long). And the tornado blew away investor cash that hadn't been netted by the other funds. You don't want that scenario to happen to your cash, so you need to be mindful of whom you send your cheque to. The technology story won't get a re-run any time soon, but do expect some other flavour of the month to get picked up, reproduced, and eventually battered to death. It could be mining, farming, Africa, or anything else where the managers think they can spin a good story.

Packaged, or *collective*, investments (the terms are interchangeable) – where a professional fund manager mingles your money with that of many others to run a portfolio of stocks and shares – have their place for most investors. In fact, some people don't want anything else but packaged schemes, such as unit and investment trusts. There's nothing wrong with that, provided you know why you're doing it and can deconstruct all the advertising and marketing tricks. That's where this chapter comes in. Read on.

Why Packaged Funds Are Worth Considering

More years ago than I care to remember, I used to edit a publication with an amazingly high subscription price but ultra low circulation – *Fund Management International.* Thanks to a keystroke mistake somewhere along the line, this publication became *Fun Management International*, which was enough for the magazine to be listed under *Leisure* in media guides. Dealing with leisure industry publicists became a daily task until I managed to correct the spelling.

But fund management and fun management do have something in common, so here's one reason to put some of your money into collective investments: You want to have fun, and you want to have a life. If that's you, then you probably don't want to spend your life poring over share price graphs, annual reports, and an online dealing facility. You'd probably rather pay someone else to take care of your investment money so you can read a good book or head down to the pub/gym/cinema/football ground/casino/other leisure venture.

Millions of folks are like this, and if you're one of them, don't think you've wasted your cash on this book. Choosing the right funds can be just as tricky as selecting the right individual shares. More managed funds of one sort or another are listed in the back pages of the *Financial Times* than individual shares.

Buying a fund is like supporting a football team. There's a professional manager controlling the individual players (or shares), but unless you know what's going on, you won't get the best out of your season ticket.

Wanting to have a life is just one reason for looking at packaged funds. Here are additional reasons:

✔ **You don't want all your investment eggs in one basket or even a few containers.** Diversifying so you get a good spread of stock market sectors, foreign companies, big and small companies, is really important in risk reduction. You may own 5 to 10 individual stocks, but to get good diversification, you need a minimum of, depending who you ask, from 15 to 25. (Some say 50 to 80 is better, but I think anything more than that is just ridiculous.) Buying worthwhile amounts in another 10 to 15 investments may be more than you can afford. Buying a collective fund gives instant results for an affordable price. You can add more cash later to your portfolio and either buy an individual share or go further into packages.

✔ **You want to fill in gaps in your investment spread.** You may fancy US or Japanese shares, but fancying is as far as it goes because you can't afford to, or can't be bothered to, buy individual US or Japanese shares in sufficient numbers to get diversification. Buying a well-selected and well-managed fund can plug that portfolio hole!

✔ **Seeing how the professionals operate can give pointers to which shares are in favour with the big buyers.** You can then either try to follow their lead or bet against them because your own belief is that the fund management herd nearly always charges in the wrong direction.

How Fund Management Companies Operate

The packaged funds industry in the UK controls hundreds of billions of pounds in unit trusts, investment trusts, and insurance funds. (Note that unit trusts are also known as *open-ended investment companies*, which is a bit of a mouthful, so the term is often shortened to OEICs. And, okay, technically, a unit trust and an OEIC have different legal structures, but show me anyone outside a specialist lawyer who cares.)

All packaged funds work in the same basic fashion. You hand over your money to a fund management company, which can be a stand-alone company, a life insurance firm, or a bank. The fund management company generally hires managers who try to maximise your investment, which is added to that of many others to produce a multimillion or even multibillion plus fund. Generally? Yes. Some funds track an index by purchasing all of the companies that are its constituents (such as the hundred shares in the FTSE 100 Index) in their correct ratios (so your biggest holding is the largest company by stock market size in the index). Some of these funds are run by automatic computer programs, saving on costs.

Flesh-and-blood fund managers look at the same factors as any potential investor. But because they control millions or billions, they get preferential treatment from brokers and research houses. But they also have to go further in their work than individual shareholders because they must keep a number of juggling balls in the air if they want to keep their usually very well-paid jobs. And what's written on those juggling balls? The following words:

- ✔ **Performance.** The manager must beat the majority of direct rivals or come up with a very plausible excuse.

- ✔ **Liabilities.** Many funds, especially those from insurance companies, have rules which insist they balance the desire to shine with a responsibility to produce a basic return for investors and policyholders.

- ✔ **Cost controls.** Some fund management companies can spend money like it is going out of fashion. Most funds have constraints to prevent managers from dealing all day long, eroding the collective's value in stockbroker fees.

- ✔ **Publicity.** Managers want an eye-catching performance to attract more money and hence push up the value of their personal employment contract.

Your deal is with the fund management company, not the individual fund manager who may leave for a better job (if he/she's good) or get the sack (if he/she's bad). Over recent years, there's been a lively transfer market in good managers and a big turnover of those who can be outplayed by a five-year-old picking shares with a pin. Less than half of all funds have had the same manager for five or more years. Funds can also be shut down or amalgamated.

Calculating their crust

Most fund management companies earn their money by taking an annual percentage fee from your holding. This fee can range from 0.3 to 2 per cent or more of your money. They earn this percentage whether your fund is rising or falling. Obviously, the more it goes up, the more they get. They also receive a boost when new investors join in, assuming that they outweigh those who want their money out.

Investors argue that it costs little more to manage a £200m fund than a £20m fund, so why does the management firm get ten times as much? It's a good point, and a small minority of fund management companies, mostly in the investment trust sector, offer lower fees as the amount grows – a feature called *economies of scale* and one worth looking out for.

A new way of looking at fund expenses and costs exists that does recognise economies of scale as well as the set annual fee. This new way is called the Total Expenses Ratio, or TER, and takes in such items as custody fees, the money the fund spends on buying and selling securities, and various legal costs. The TER is a better way of looking at which fund offers the best value because a fund with a 1 per cent annual charge could have 2 per cent in other expenses, giving a 3 per cent TER, whereas a rival might have a 1.5 per cent annual charge but only 0.5 per cent in other costs, so it would have a 2 per cent TER. And with costs, 2 per cent of your money is better than 3 per cent. Look out for the TER in information about unit trusts.

A handful of managers also get success fees on top of a percentage. These are extra payments based on a formula such as beating the averages or coming in the top ten funds. The idea is that managers deserve something more if they produce a better result. Success fees mostly operate in hedge funds, although some investment trusts feature them.

What's the big downside of success fees? Lousy performers still get to keep their basic contractual fee, which may be high anyway. The managers don't have to give you money back in non-success fees if they mess up. And many success fees are linked to a shares index. So if the stock market goes down 20 per cent and the fund only drops 15 per cent, they can claim to have outperformed their benchmark and grab extra cash. They get paid more for losing your money. Great job!

Swapping collective funds can be very expensive. Some fund management companies charge you up to 5.5 per cent as an up-front entry fee, so your investment must grow by that amount before you break even. Changing your mind twice a year over ten years would more than wipe out all your original money in costs unless your fund grows. Funds are for the long term, so budget to stay with a collective for at least five years. Constant swapping of funds that are successful may land you with a large capital gains tax bill.

Examining the role of the marketing department

Running a fund management company is all about taking in money and keeping it in your collective investment vehicle. But at the same time, fund management is a unique product. No one else takes in big sums of money and hands back a piece of paper and a promise to do their best. And there's no guarantee that the fund product you buy will do what it says on the tin. So good marketing is vital to the success of the company. Marketing is also vital because fund management firms can't rely on word of mouth or an attractive display in a store to sell their products.

Investment product advertising is constrained by a rule book the size of a telephone directory. But at the same time, it's virtually unregulated. There's no point complaining that the advert appeared to promise you'd make money when the manager lost yours. The company will have that angle covered. The Advertising Standards Authority (motto: legal, decent, and honest) barely makes a token attempt to control fund publicity. Of course, the marketing director's job is to know just how far to go before some regulatory authority or another does get angry enough to order a halt to a sales campaign. Regardless, don't be afraid to ask questions and query what you're told. It's your money after all, not theirs.

There's nothing wrong with buying collective funds, but you should know some tricks of the marketing trade. Here are some:

- Dividing all publicity between the big print designed to get effect and the small print, which absolves the fund management company of any responsibility if things go wrong.

- Launching a flavour of the month. Fund management companies love bandwagons. They see that a sector, a stock market, or an asset has per-formed very well over the past 6 or 12 months, so they launch a fund to market that flavour. That's great if rum and praline are still going to wow them for the next five years. But they won't. They'll be replaced by ginger and honey or coffee and chocolate chips. Avoid this problem by going for plain vanilla. Keep strawberry and chocolate chip for more daring moments.

- Always making sure that the publicity says *top* or *best* of something even if it's the fund management equivalent of best marrow at the local gar-deners' show. So you get publicity like 'the top quartile in its sector over three years'. Note that marketing people love *quartiles*, where you divide a list into four. But top quartile in a list of 400 funds could mean 100th position.

- Boasting about awards given by investment trade publications. Thing is, so many categories exist that almost everyone gets a prize. There are even prizes for best administration or adviser service, which means these firms are fastest with the commission cheques. Anyway, these awards are dished out, so managers dress up and show up at £200-a-head award dinners where they can drink and be entertained for 20 min-utes by a TV personality (who picks up £20,000 for the gig).

- Always being optimistic. They relegate to small print any possibility that the fund could lose (or be less effective than a rival's fund in rising markets).

✔ Ignoring risk. Some fund managers go for a high-risk strategy in rising markets on the basis that if they get it right, they can boast about it, and if all goes wrong, they can hide the fund and get on with marketing another.

✔ Taking media-friendly independent financial advisers for a few golfing afternoons so they'll praise the products the next time a journalist calls for a quote or sound bite.

✔ Taking journalists on all-expenses-paid trips to exotic places, such as South Africa, Morocco, and Hong Kong, with business class travel and five-star hotels. That guarantees acres of favourable coverage.

Am I being excessively cynical? The investment industry would say I am. But you can't take an investment back to the shop because you don't like it once you get home. So be a savvy investor by being prepared for marketing tricks.

The Worth of Performance Tables

One of the most controversial issues in fund management is past performance and whether it has any relationship to the future. Academics have said that you have as much chance of picking a future winning fund by selecting the best from the past as you have of winning at roulette by looking at where the balls ended up earlier.

The Financial Services Authority (FSA) has said that the past has no serious predictive value. At one time, the FSA wanted to ban past performance figures because the FSA said they just confuse investors. But the fund management industry put up a spirited defence of the practice (without which it would have to rewrite all its adverts), and its view has prevailed.

Whether your collective is an investment trust, OEIC, or insurance bond, performance tables are available for you to scrutinise. The tables are subdivided into sectors, such as UK bonds or Pacific equities excluding Japan. The idea of sector tables is to compare apples with apples, not oranges or pears.

Keep in mind, though, that comparisons don't always work that smoothly. Some funds are mobile. They move their asset mix over time and change sectors, usually to make the collective look better.

And sometimes the sector boundaries or even the name is altered, making it tough to follow a fund over the years. An even bigger problem occurs when funds merge. Usually, the fund with the better record continues, and the other is air-brushed out of history.

When examining performance tables, which are subdivided into sectors, keep in mind that coming in fifth in a sector of 200 is a real achievement, but coming in fifth in a sector of 10 is just average.

The ideal collective isn't one that's currently topping the table. Too many fund managers have succeeded in heading the league one day and propping it up the next. Instead, look for consistency over the years. The fund that generally beats 60 or 70 per cent of its competitors on a regular basis is the one to aim for. If past performance shows anything, it's that managers who are consistently ahead of the majority provide better value for investors than those with flash-in-the-pan genius.

Tables that show cumulative figures

My favourite tables come from Morningstar and Trustnet. You can access them online or find their figures in specialist investment magazines (but be aware that printed figures can be way out of date). Going online is easier because most sites let you sort funds according to your criteria, usually over a set time period.

These tables assume that you start off with a set amount (usually £1,000) and re-invest any dividends received after a basic tax deduction. Then they show what you'd have after six months, one year, two years, three years, five years, seven years, and ten years.

Most unit trust and insurance fund tables are on an *offer to bid* basis, meaning they deduct the up-front charge to give a true idea of the total return to a real investor. But some tables are *bid to bid*, meaning they only show how effective the fund managers have been and ignore the hit investors take from charges. Investment trust tables are less accurate because they fail to take purchase and sale charges into account, although the best will still be best.

Performance tables showing the cumulative result of investing a set sum over a set period, such as £1,000 over five years with net income re-invested, give no idea of consistency. The good or bad performance may have been due to one great or one atrocious patch nearly five years ago. Going down to the three- or one-year tables may show the fund manager in a different light altogether. A fund may show that it doubled over ten years. But scratch that a bit, and you'll see that it tripled during its first year and then lost money ever since! The reason may be due to a change of manager, a change of style from risky to cautious or vice versa, or, most likely, a change of market conditions. Some fund managers work best in fast-rising markets; others shine when stock markets are less alluring.

So if you want to judge consistency, you may want to scrutinise a different type of table – one using discrete figures (see the following section for more info).

Tables that use discrete figures

Besides examining tables that show cumulative figures, you can examine tables that use discrete figures. They show every single year for the past five or ten years, so you see the results for a number of 12-month periods taken individually. If your table were dated June 2004, for example, you'd have the 12 months from June 1, 2003, to May 31, 2004, as well as the year from June 1, 2002, to May 31, 2003, and so on.

Discrete figures let you judge consistency and when the out- or under-performance occurred. A fund with a ten-year cumulative performance that was superb eight, nine, and ten years ago and then reverted to average would still look good over ten years. But the discrete figures would show this up, and you could look at its average performance since then.

Out of the ten best US collective funds in 1990, five years later, only two funds were still in the best 10 per cent on a one-year discrete basis. Three were in the worst 10 per cent of all funds, and four others were below halfway. Fast-forward another ten years, and the funds were scattered all over the table. Only one was still a real winner, a second had fared well, but many of the rest were also-rans. There's nothing special about the US. The same exercise in any other country and over other time periods would come up with similar findings.

Discrete period tables are a powerful past performance tool that most marketing departments would rather you didn't see. As a result, discrete tables are usually less available and more difficult to find online or in publications. The easiest place to find them is in *Money Management* magazine, a monthly publication available at newsagents. It's read by both serious investors and the packaged investment trade. Over longer periods, the tortoise beats the hare.

What tables are strongest at showing

The debate over past performance and its relevance to the future will doubtlessly go on forever, with each side marshalling its own version of statistics (don't forget that statistics come after lies and damned lies in the list of untruths) to back its viewpoint. But, oddly, the strongest argument showing its relevance marshals statistics that would never be used to justify a collective fund purchase.

Get savvy with fund performance table talk

A *quartile* means that a table has been divided into four subsections. First-quartile performance is the top 25 per cent of the table, which may be anything from a few funds to more than 100. Anything from average upward appears in the top two quartiles. Third and fourth quartiles are for the also-rans.

A *decile* means that a table has been divided into ten subsections. The top decile of a table of 100 funds is the first 10. So top decile is better than top quartile, and bottom decile is worse than bottom quartile.

Past performance is most accurate in predicting really bad fund managers. Collectives that have spent most of their life in investment's equivalent of the fourth division relegation zone tend to stay there. You can use this info to eliminate the no-hopers. Good funds may go down, and average funds may go up. But rarely does the total rubbish ever throw off that poor performance mantle and shine.

Ways to Separate the Good Managers from the Bad

To divide the wheat from the chaff – the good fund managers from the bad – you need to ask lots of questions. If you don't get straight answers, move on to another fund.

Here are some pointers to test the fund management company and its managers:

- ✔ What's the fund's purpose? Is it all-out growth irrespective of risk, total caution, or something between the two?

- ✔ How will the company's fund managers work to fulfil the fund's purpose in practice? Look at the present holdings to see how they fit. Is the portfolio a ragbag, or does it have coherence?

- ✔ How frequently does the manager buy and sell? If the manager of a collective investment is forever buying and selling, costs will drag down performance. The practice may also show that the manager has no idea what to do, so the fund lurches here and there. But if there's very little activity, what are you paying for?

✔ What markets will the funds work best in, and what's the strategy for a change of market conditions? Fund management companies are great at giving you a best-situation scenario. You want to know what will happen if the worst occurs.

✔ Who's in charge? Is it a named individual, and, if so, who's the backup?

✔ What happens if the manager quits? How easy is it to get rid of a poorly performing manager? Or is there an anonymous team of managers?

✔ Does the fund management company impose on individual managers a central philosophy or even central lists of shares to buy? Or does it let the managers think and act for themselves?

✔ If the fund is new (and most marketing tends to be around new funds), then what is the purpose? What new thinking does it bring to the party that previous funds do not?

✔ What is the history and track record of the lead fund manager? Experience is important. Don't get confused by statements such as 'Managers have 40 years of experience in markets.' Some funds may have ten managers; that's an average of just four years each! Or the average may hide that there's one experienced fund manager with 20 or 30 years in the business and a team of college leavers.

The Worth of Fund Manager Fees

The collective fund industry would rather not focus on costs. Instead, it'd prefer to concentrate on benefits. But you can't separate the two. Whatever gains professional management may bring, you may lose them, and then some more, if you pay too much in fees.

The costs of buying into a fund aren't too much of a problem. They're not far different from those involved with purchasing individual shares. You generally aren't charged an exit fee from a unit trust or an insurance fund, so think of the initial charge as a round trip in-and-out fee. Many independent financial advisers rebate part of the up-front fee. Frequent traders are harder hit by entry costs.

Annual fees are where you're hit hard. These fees are often shown at 1.5 per cent, but the counting doesn't stop there. Fund fees attract *VAT* (Value Added Tax), making the real figure nearer to 1.75 per cent. Add on some compounding, and, in rough terms, a fund held for ten years would give its managers around 20 per cent of your money. About 9 per cent over five years.

To show value, the fund manager must add more than 20 per cent to a ten-year investment and around 10 per cent to a five-year holding for the holder to break even. Managers who can consistently deliver good results with the costs handicap can congratulate themselves.

Investment Clubs: Do-It-Yourself Fund Management

This section gives you the best of two worlds – fund management *and* fun management. You can do both, getting the advantage of diversification while adding to your personal amusement level, through an *investment club*, where a group (usually not larger than 20) gets together at set intervals to pool part of their financial resources as well as share their ideas in a social environment. Several thousand investment clubs operate in the UK.

The concept can bring together friends, families, neighbours, work colleagues, and other like-minded people. All you need for membership is a mutual desire to increase your understanding of the stock market and improve your personal investing ability. Decisions are (or should be!) made democratically by members at meetings, which are normally monthly.

More for entertainment than enrichment

Most investment clubs aren't intended too seriously. They tend to work on a monthly subscription basis – often £50 to £100 – which is invested in the market. Clubs work better if everyone has the same stake, but this setup can be difficult after a time if members change. There should be enough to buy one or two shares economically at each meeting. The shares are then owned collectively.

Over a year or so, you should get a balanced portfolio, or, if you wish, an extreme portfolio of high-risk shares. After all, what's the point of just investing in the big companies like the big fund managers?

An investment club isn't meant to be a person's only stock-market involvement but an extra amount over and above his or her core investments.

Don't imagine 10 to 20 people deeply engrossed in the pages of the *Financial Times* or commiserating on the latest results of the club's investments. Instead, for many people, the club is a chance to chat with others on topics other than home, family, and work. Many meet in pubs. And most clubs encourage a little light-hearted 'I told you so!'

How to start an investment club

A minimal amount of legality is involved in setting up an investment club. The easiest source for this framework and all the other things you need is Proshare, an organisation working for wider share ownership and the UK's only dedicated promoter of services for investment clubs. Virtually all investment clubs are set up using the materials and templates provided by ProShare. Getting the basic ProShare information is simple. Log on to its www.proshare.org Web site.

The *ProShare Investment Club Manual*, details on the Web site, is a useful guide to setting up and running an investment club. It's based on the experiences of clubs on both sides of the Atlantic. The manual also tells you how to ensure that no one runs off with the funds. (No such incidents have yet been reported, but there's always a first time!)

All you need to begin a club is one or two friends who share your enthusiasm and are happy to recruit a couple of friends each. Even if only a handful of people are at the first meeting, you may find that numbers grow quickly, and as the idea captures people's imaginations, you'll probably find that you'll soon have plenty of members.

Here are a few additional tips and titbits about investment clubs:

- ✔ Gaining recruits is far easier when markets are rising. And where you meet is important. An easy-to-find location in a pub seems to work best, but some clubs use village halls or move around members' homes.

- ✔ Better and more sensible investment decisions tend to be made collectively. The research work involved in investigating companies can also be shared between members, as can the cost of information.

- ✔ Experienced investors often find that an investment club is a good way to get ideas for their own private portfolios, and in time new investors will often use the knowledge they gain through an investment club to begin an individual portfolio of their own.

Tax and the Investment Package

Collectives such as unit trusts and investment trusts are taxable. Sorry.

Income tax

You pay income tax on dividends, although under present rules, there's no more tax to pay if you're a basic-rate taxpayer (roughly earning under £40,000 a year). The reason is because under complicated tax legislation, dividends are paid after a tax deduction.

If you pay at a higher rate, you must declare your dividends on your self-assessment tax return. You then must pay the difference between the basic rate and the top 40 per cent level. If you use a tax software package, such as Microsoft Money or TaxCalc, the computer does the sums for you. The official self-assessment site run by HM Revenue & Customs also does the calculations for you.

If you pay no tax at all, you can't reclaim the tax on collectives investing into shares. (Nor can you do so if you buy the shares directly for yourself.) Zero per cent rate taxpayers can ask for a tax refund if they buy into bond funds or mixed bond and equity funds if the bond element accounts for at least 60 per cent of the total.

Capital Gains Tax

Capital Gains Tax, or CGT as the accountants call it, is normally payable on profits made when you sell an asset. In most cases, you can offset losses. The good news for unit and investment trust holders is that CGT isn't paid by fund managers on the ins and outs of their portfolios.

The bad news is that you may have to pay CGT when you exit the fund. The good news is that you have nothing to pay until your gains (what you get less what you paid) top your personal annual allowance. This allowance changes every year with rising prices but is around £9,500 at the time of writing. From 6 April 2008, a previously horrendous system of complex sums for calculating profit has gone, as has the previous top 40 per cent rate. From that date onwards, you just pay CGT at a rate of 18 per cent on your gains (less, of course, your personal allowance).

How to invest tax-free: The Individual Savings Account

An Individual Savings Account (ISA) gives tax-free investment into funds on the first £7,200 in each tax year (April 6 to April 5) unless you've also opened a cash ISA. If you have a cash ISA, even just £1, the maximum you can put into investment funds automatically falls to £3,600. Virtually all unit trusts and many investment trusts will put your money into an ISA at no extra cost.

But although tax relief is a good idea, ISAs aren't as good as they used to be. There is tax freedom on dividend income from shares, but only top-rate tax-payers now benefit from it. There's a better deal for bond investors (or those in a mixed bond and equity fund where bonds make up at least 60 per cent of the total) because all the tax is refunded, giving benefits to the majority on basic rate.

The ISA also offers freedom from Capital Gains Tax, no matter what the investment or the period held. But what the taxman giveth with one hand, he or she can taketh away with the other. The other side of the CGT freedom coin is that you can't count losses on ISAs against profits elsewhere in your holdings.

Sadly, when an ISA investor dies, the tax freedom also dies. ISA holdings are subject to inheritance tax just like everything else left behind, and that could grab 40 per cent. So spend it while you have it!

Chapter 14

Getting into Unit Trusts

In This Chapter

▶ Understanding how to own lots of shares for little cash

▶ Learning about unit trust charges

▶ Sorting out active from passive unit trust fund managers

▶ Looking at ethical unit trusts

▶ Visiting an investment supermarket

▶ Dodging tax bills legally

*U*nit trusts are one of the ways UK investors have of buying a ready made portfolio of shares or bonds backed by professional management. The trusts are the most widespread form of collective investment in the UK. Approximately £310 billion rides on their success.

But, if £310 billion is not an easy figure to understand, you can get started for as little as £50 (occasionally even £25) if you sign up for a monthly investment scheme, or £250 to £500 as a lump sum. Doing so gives you access to a professionally managed fund that diversifies your money into anything from some 30 shares to more than 200 holdings. You get a huge number of shares for not much money.

Don't get too impressed by funds with the longest list of holdings. There's no correlation between a large number of holdings and management success. In fact, some people think that having too many shares just spreads research and other fund manager functions a bit too thinly.

This chapter tells you what unit trusts are and how they work, to help you decide whether investing in them is right for you.

Understanding What Unit Trusts Are

Unit trusts are so called because you hold a number of units in a fund that's legally set up as a trust. Simple. But don't get too hung up on the word 'trust' as you can't always trust them to come up with the investment goods.

Unit trusts are sometimes referred to by other names. *Mutual funds* is the title preferred in the United States, and it's becoming more common in the UK. *Open-ended funds* (because the number of units has no limit) is also a US term that's moving across the Atlantic. And in the UK, more and more funds are, strictly speaking, defined as *open-ended investment companies (OEICs)*. But almost everyone still calls them unit trusts.

If you're really interested in all the legalistics of a trust, you can get a copy of the trust deed. But don't bother (unless you're a fan of legalese). It won't help you in your quest for investment gains.

Unit trusts are a simple concept. A fund management firm advertises a trust, and lots of investors send in money. After the firm subtracts around 5 per cent for setup costs and commission to brokers, the rest is invested in whatever assets the managers are promoting. The assets can be anything from global equities to UK gilts.

For example, suppose that a person invests £1,000 when the units are priced at £1 each. The investor now has 1,000 units, the value of which goes up and down in direct proportion to the underlying fund. The size of the fund obviously depends on the success or otherwise of the managers in picking the right investments. But it also depends on whether money from the other investors is flowing in or out because they're buying or selling. No matter what happens to the size of the fund, however, you always have your 1,000 units, which can change in price.

Examining One Big Difference between Unit Trusts and OEICs

Technical differences exist between unit trusts and OEICs, but most of them only interest lawyers. The exception is how you see prices quoted.

Unit trusts have two prices – one around 5 per cent higher than the other. The higher price, or *offer price*, is the one you pay when you buy. If you sell, you receive the lower price, or *bid price*. The gap between the two, known as the *bid-offer spread*, goes to the fund management company, which uses some of the cash to pay the broker or other seller.

OEICs have only one price whether you're buying or selling, a setup called *single pricing*. Does that sound like you're free of the bid-offer spread? If only. Although OEICs have only one price, brokers can load the price by around 5 per cent when you buy, so you're back to where you were with unit trusts. Some OEICs in fund listings have far lower charges. They're available to anyone with a minimum of £250,000 to £500,000. And that's probably not you.

Note that holders of OEICs also receive half-yearly reports in a different format. Instead of getting a thin leaflet just detailing one unit trust, OEIC investors get a fat book listing all the various funds offered by the management company. In law, what you've bought into is a subfund of the OEIC. The one advantage is that you can see details of how the manager is coping with other assets.

Knowing How Much Unit Trusts Cost

You can't expect collective investment for nothing. Unit trusts have up to three charges – an initial charge, annual charge, and exit charge. That can be complicated, but here's a simple word of advice. The worst deal you will get is to buy your unit trust (or OEIC) directly from the fund management company. It's throwing money down the drain as you'll see later in this chapter where I compare 'direct' with the discount or investment supermarket routes.

The initial charge

The up-front, or initial, charge is levied when you buy the fund. The charge can be either built in via the bid-offer spread or added on as a brokerage charge when you buy an OEIC. With most funds, you're charged about 5 per cent no matter whether you buy through a broker or directly from the fund company. But some exceptions to the 5 per cent level exist:

✔ Funds aimed at charity treasurers and professionals (such as brokers) who can invest large sums have no or low charges.

✔ Funds investing in UK government stocks and some other bonds generally undershoot the 5 per cent line, with some charging 1 per cent or even 0 per cent.

Many brokers rebate some or all of the 3 per cent commission they receive from the up-front charge on most funds. They're not working for nothing, however. Funds are now structured to pay *trail commission*, which means the seller receives 0.5 per cent of the value of your fund every year as long as you hold it. Brokers are supposed to give something back in terms of service and advice. Many don't.

The annual charge

All unit trusts have a yearly charge. It can vary from 0.295 per cent or 0.3 per cent for the best-value UK tracker funds to 1.75 per cent for some esoteric trusts. Most trust rules allow for higher charges, provided that you're given some notice. Over the years, annual charges have tended to rise. Managers have to pay the trail commission out of something.

The exit charge

A few funds hit investors on the way out, often as an alternative to up-front charges but sometimes as an addition.

In a number of cases, exit charges apply for the first five years of the invest-ment. These are often on a sliding scale: 5 per cent in the first year moving down to 1 per cent in the fourth year.

Hidden charges

With most funds, the annual charge is taken from the dividends received. So if the underlying fund earns 4 per cent and your charge is 1 per cent, you end up with 3 per cent. (This is a simplified example ignoring VAT.) Funds are gen-erally managed to ensure that there's some income to meet the costs.

But with a minority of funds, mostly investing in bonds and other high-income assets, you're given all the income. This is not generosity but sleight of hand. Instead of the charge being taken from the income, it's shaved away from your capital. The result? Fund management companies can proudly pro-claim a higher return on your cash than those going the conventional route of hitting your income. Looks good in adverts! Clever, huh?

Provided that you re-invest your income, the end result can be the same. Still, this route is not a good idea. You get marginally more income to pay tax on. And if you spend the income cheque (and that's the main purpose of a high-income fund), your capital goes down year on year. Here's how (using very simplified maths):

You invest £10,000 after up-front charges in a fund yielding 10 per cent. Your first annual payment ignoring tax is £1,000. After ten years of 1 per cent annual deductions from capital (and assuming no gains or losses in the fund), your investment is now worth about £9,000. The 10 per cent yield now pays £900 a year.

Check on charges. Some funds are better value. There's no relationship whatsoever between high annual charges and better-than-average performance.

Selecting the Best Unit Trust for You

To select the right unit trust for your needs, you need to follow this step-by-
step guide:

1. **Work out your asset allocation strategy.**

   You need to calculate how much you can afford to put into the different
   investment types. It ultimately depends on how much you have, how
   much you are willing to risk, and how long an investment period you
   have.

2. **Decide on the proportion of your cash that you want in collective
   investments.**

   Once you have worked out your long-term asset allocation moves, you
   don't have to carry them out all at once. This may be a good time to buy
   shares or bonds through a collective investment. But if it is not, then
   there is nothing wrong with holding your money back for a period. A
   good idea is to put this cash in a bank or building society account which
   you keep apart from your other savings.

3. **Select your investment objective.**

   For example, is your objective income, long-term capital growth, or a
   mix of the two?

4. **Refine your options by working through unit trust sector listings,
   where you'll see all funds with similar investment patterns, such as
   corporate bonds, North America, or Europe excluding the UK.**

   All trusts are classified in sectors so that you can see funds pursuing
   roughly similar investment objectives. The sectors change from time to
   time, but there are currently around 30. An unwieldy number, yes. So the
   unit trust statisticians break down the list into two main divisions:
   income and growth. And those two divisions are further subdivided. On
   top of that, there are a few that are 'half-way houses', a mix of income
   and growth. Sometimes this mix comes from one set of shares which are
   chosen to be midway between going gung-ho for growth and working all
   out for income. Other times, unit trust firms set up 'managed funds'
   where they mix 'n' match income and growth funds either from their
   own range or from other management groups. This section provides
   details of the various sectors available.

5. Ensure that the fund you choose will accept your level of savings.

Some trusts, for example, are aimed at large investors and broker firms with six-figure sums.

Income sectors

These are the fund types for investors looking for a higher than average income but who are unconcerned about growing their capital.

- ✔ **UK gilts.** These funds invest at least 90 per cent of their assets in UK government securities and are considered low risk. Around 30 funds are available.

- ✔ **UK index-linked gilts.** These are an even lower risk because they must invest at least 90 per cent into inflation-proofed UK government bonds. You have a choice of some ten funds.

- ✔ **UK corporate bonds.** These invest at least 80 per cent of the assets in investment-grade sterling bonds with a rating of at least BBB (see Chapter 10 for info about rating codes). They're less risky than funds investing in the shares of the same companies. About 85 funds are available.

- ✔ **UK other bonds.** These put at least 20 per cent of the assets into riskier bonds with below-investment-grade ratings. They also invest in riskier convertible bonds and preference shares. About 54 funds are available to choose from.

- ✔ **Global bonds.** These invest at least 80 per cent of the assets in bonds of all types from all over the world. The risk here is the pound getting stronger. About 50 funds are on the list.

- ✔ **UK equity and bond income.** These put anything between 20 and 80 per cent of the assets into bonds and 20 to 80 per cent into higher-yielding shares, so the result is at least 120 per cent of the dividend return on the FTSE All Share Index. The idea is that the bonds reduce the risks in an all-equity fund. You have a choice of about 30 trusts.

- ✔ **Money market.** Around 30 funds try to maximise returns from cash deposits and short-term interest-rate securities. Most funds have no initial charges, and most keep their annual fees to 0.5 per cent or below. Investors get speedy access to their money. These are often used to park cash between investments.

Half-way house

These fund types are really a half-way house between our two main sectors, having some characteristics of income trusts and some of the growth sectors.

✔ **UK equity income.** These invest at least 80 per cent of the assets in UK shares with the object of beating the yield on the FTSE All Share Index by a 10 per cent margin. Here, fund managers try to find shares that'll produce a rising dividend income combined with some long-term capital growth. Many investors buy into this sector and re-invest the income (most trusts do so automatically if the investors want) with the expectation that they'll do better than going for growth trusts. It works most years. You have a choice of approximately 100 trusts.

✔ **Cautious managed.** These invest globally but can't put more than 60 per cent in equities. The rest goes into cash or bonds. At least half the fund has to be in euroland and the UK. You have a choice of around 40 funds.

✔ **Balanced managed.** These must have at least 15 per cent in bonds or cash as well as 50 per cent or more in UK or euro-based assets. You have a choice of around 100 funds.

✔ **Active managed.** Around 100 funds have substantial freedom to move from global equities to bonds and back again.

Growth sectors

This is where you go if you hope to see your money grow over time and are unconcerned about dividend cheques. It's probably the place to invest if you can live on your present income but want to build up a nestegg for the future.

✔ **UK all companies.** These go for capital growth by investing at least 80 per cent of their assets in UK equities. Tracker and ethical funds are in this big sector of more than 250 trusts.

✔ **UK smaller companies.** These put at least 80 per cent of assets into the smallest 10 per cent of UK-quoted firms. This is a risky sector of around 60 funds.

✔ **Japan.** You have a choice of 50 trusts investing primarily in Japan – not the greatest home for your money over most of the last two decades.

✔ **Japanese smaller companies.** These funds specialise in the small end of the Tokyo market.

✔ **Asia-Pacific including Japan.** These 12 funds can put up to 80 per cent in Japan, but most invest less. The balance comes from the Far East, Australia, and New Zealand.

✔ **Asia-Pacific excluding Japan.** These nearly 60 funds go for Pacific region countries. This has been of increasing interest to Global fund managers as they remain cautious of anticipated returns in the United States, the UK, and Europe.

- ✔ **North America.** About 80 trusts invest primarily in the United States and Canada.

- ✔ **North American smaller companies.** These 12 trusts aim at the smallest 10 per cent of mainstream-quoted US and Canadian companies.

- ✔ **Europe including UK.** Nearly 20 trusts can invest up to 80 per cent of assets in the UK. In practice, the proportion is far lower. This sector reduces currency risks with its UK exposure.

- ✔ **Europe excluding UK.** Nearly 100 trusts focus on the eurozone.

- ✔ **European smaller companies.** These invest in the smallest 10 per cent of mainstream companies. The 15 funds can invest in the UK but are more likely to aim for central and eastern Europe, including the former Soviet bloc.

- ✔ **Global growth.** These invest anywhere in the world, so the asset allocation is up to the fund managers. There's a choice of around 130 trusts.

- ✔ **Global emerging markets.** These invest at least 80 per cent in emerging markets using the World Bank definition. The idea is that markets from Brazil to China and from Russia to South Korea have the potential for rapid growth but at a higher risk.

- ✔ **Protected and guaranteed.** These 12 funds protect your investments against falling (or against falling by more than a specified percentage) while offering some growth. The greater the protection against price drops, the less the gain when or if stock markets rise – a swings or roundabouts situation because you can't have it both ways.

- ✔ **Specialist.** A confusing title giving an umbrella to one-country funds that don't fit easily into other categories, such as South Korea, Switzerland, Germany, Thailand, and Australia, along with single-industry funds covering mining, healthcare, biotechnology, and financial services. This is a ragbag because there's no way you can compare a Swiss shares fund with a worldwide natural resources trust. About 40 trusts are in the sector. But they all aim at growth and are generally rated a 'scary risk'.

- ✔ **Technology.** Some are survivors from the dotcom boom, when fund managers launched into what was then the latest craze. But their managers and others say that an interest in backing technology will always exist, whether for communications or to help deal with global warming. Risky to very risky.

- ✔ **Property.** A small number of funds invest in property shares or in property itself. The property is commercial such as shopping centres or office blocks, so is not the same as owning or buying a house. Less risky than average.

Comparing Active versus Passive Fund Managers

Active fund managers buy and sell shares and other assets hoping that they'll perform at least better than average and preferably hit the big time. Most funds are actively managed.

Passive fund managers don't care. The reason is that they're usually computers, not people, without too much in the way of sentimental feeling. They buy all the constituents of an index in the right proportions (or occasionally come up with sampling methods to ensure that a fund doesn't have to cope with hundreds of tiny company shares).

The result of passive fund management (this is another name for the tracker fund concept as no one has to do anything to select the shares as they are automatically chosen) is that what you get is what you see. If the fund tracks the Footsie (the FTSE 100 share index of the UK's biggest stock-market-quoted firms), then your fund will go up and down each day along with the index. You'll get an income calculated as the average yield on the basket of shares your fund follows, less the annual management charge. You'll also know what level of risk you're taking.

Most passive funds in the UK track either the Footsie or the wider All Share Index. But you can buy passive funds that follow markets in other countries; that buy into sectors worldwide, such as technology or pharmaceuticals; or that only invest in an index of ethically and environmentally approved companies. A growing area of passive investment is to buy the replication of an index through Exchange Traded Funds. Exchange Traded Funds are traded via stockbrokers just as if they were real shares. They're big in America but largely confined to professionals so far in the UK.

Active versus passive is the big fund management debate. Both sides can come up with good (and sometimes bad) arguments:

✔ Active managers say that they can add value because they can sift out the wheat from the chaff.

✔ Passive managers say that they don't have to second-guess the future.

✔ Active managers say that they have a wider range of investments, including smaller companies with a great future.

✔ Passive managers say that most of these small-company bets fail. And even when they do well, they have little effect on the overall fund because holdings are minuscule.

✔ Active managers say that they offer strategies that vary with market conditions.

✔ Passive managers say that the market as a whole automatically adjusts to different conditions.

✔ Active managers say that passive funds end up with too many shares that have peaked. The trick is to look for shares that are growing fast enough to knock on an index's door.

✔ Passive managers say that a lot of active managers just buy big index stocks but charge up to five times extra for the privilege – a practice called *closet indexing* in the investment trade.

✔ Active managers say that passive funds often fail to track their chosen index properly.

✔ Passive managers say that they win on costs. They reckon that active managers have to do about 1.5 per cent better a year than the index – a tough call year on year.

✔ Active managers say that they can spread their investments more efficiently. They don't have to buy and sell whenever firms go in and out of an index. They can talk to companies and sometimes influence the stock market. But, they say, passive fund managers must buy stocks they have no control over and at whatever price the market dictates.

✔ Passive managers say that although they'll never top a table, they'll never be below halfway for long either. They say that active funds which beat them one year probably won't do so the next. Due to costs and other factors, a good index fund should always end up around 38th to 42nd place in a group of 100 funds over a typical year. Performing this way consistently is better than rocket performance one year and rubbish performance the next.

Active and passive fans will continue to swap insults and statistics to prove their cases. Don't get caught up in their ego trips. Instead, go for a core and satellite strategy. Put the bulk of your money in low-cost index funds and leave it there. This is your core. Invest the rest in selected managed funds that don't closet-index, such as smaller-company trusts, or go for specialist areas overseas.

Taking Ethics into Consideration

'Ethics? That's a county to the east of London!'

That's an old City joke and probably not one of the brightest. But all jokes have some element of truth, and this one says that the mainstream neither invests nor even cares about selecting investments with a green or ethical tinge.

But many private investors and members of a growing number of pension funds to feel that their money is backing firms they approve of. The ethical investment market has gone from zero to about £30 billion over the past 25 years. Some £6 billion of this sum is in unit trusts representing 5 per cent or so of all equity investment in mutual funds. We've got a long way to go to catch up with the US, however, where 12 per cent or more of equity funds are managed ethically.

Ethical investors want to avoid investing in companies involved in tobacco, armaments, hardwood logging, animal experimentation, nuclear power, gambling, and pornography, or in organisations that support repressive regimes or that manufacture goods using sweatshops in less-developed countries. Equally, ethical investment (often called *socially responsible investment*, or *SRI*) is buying into firms involved in positives, including alternative renewable energy, such as wind farms, and recycling and waste management. SRI also includes buying into firms at the forefront of good employment practice and those providing high-quality services or goods that clearly benefit the wider community.

Shades of green: Ethical unit trusts

SRI enthusiasts with a large investment pot can go to a specialist stockbroker for a bespoke portfolio. For the rest of us, a specialist ethical or environmental unit trust is the only serious route. These funds come in two shades of green.

Dark green funds work on an exclusion basis. Stocks of companies involved in any of the forbidden activities are dubbed *sin stocks*. They won't appear in the SRI trust portfolio, which cuts out about half the stock market. If a company moves into a sin stock zone, then the fund sells the shares.

Even dark green funds have a threshold. If a sin activity accounts for a very small proportion of a company's sales – say tobacco in a big supermarket group – then the fund managers or their ethical advisers look for positives to balance off the banned activity. (Investment supermarkets are covered later in this chapter, if you're wondering what they are.) Some dark green funds invite unit holders to take part in meetings that debate where the fund is going. Also note that negatives change over time. Twenty-five years ago, alcohol sales were a definite no-no. Now, there's more tolerance to alcohol. Likewise, attitudes to global warming and deforestation have toughened.

Light green funds take a different line. Their fund managers say that dark green funds exclude too much and too many sectors of the business world. So although they cut out the worst of the sin stocks, they're willing to look at the least reprehensible company in each sector. Searching for firms that are trying hard to upgrade their SRI credentials is known as investing in the *best in class*.

Fund managers of both shades engage with companies by telling directors how they could improve. For example, fund managers of light green funds don't sell if a company strays into sin. Instead, these managers try to use their voting power as shareholders (they, and not the actual investors who put up the cash, hold the voting rights in a collective) to change matters for the better.

Balancing act: The pros and cons of ethical investing

Some investors are passionate about SRI. They should skip this section. Others believe that a sin stock portfolio of tobacco, armaments, and pornography publishers works best. They should skip this section as well. You can read what you like into past performance statistics, depending on the period you select and the funds you look at, so it's really a matter of balancing the pros and cons of ethical investing:

- ✔ **Pro:** Stocks screened out come from dinosaur old-economy industries, such as mining, tobacco, chemicals, and armaments, where growth is more limited and government controls are stricter.

- ✔ **Con:** Fund managers can't perform their job if they're limited by non-investment criteria imposed by non-investment people.

- ✔ **Pro:** SRI-approved stocks tend to be young, dynamic firms that benefit from the general move away from dirty industries toward a cleaner future.

- ✔ **Con:** SRI companies may be less profit-conscious because they're too concerned with their employees or the neighbourhood they work in.

- ✔ **Pro:** Companies that show the management abilities to move to a more sustainable way of doing business are probably brighter and less stick in the mud-ish elsewhere.

- ✔ **Con:** SRI concentrates too much on volatile smaller companies.

Going with a Fund of Funds

Most unit trust investors start off with a UK fund, often a tracker. Then they add to it with more UK-based trusts, and then they venture overseas. But as they build up their portfolio, they have to make decisions. They have to choose the best in each sector that they select and then monitor their holdings.

The do-it-yourself approach has two big failings. Massive costs are involved every time an investor switches from one fund to another. And there's Capital Gains Tax on profits.

The alternative is to hand over money to a fund of funds manager, who invests in other funds but in such a way that minimises switching costs and has no Capital Gains Tax worries within the fund.

Do funds of funds beat a buy and hold strategy? The jury's out. But the fund managers must be specially gifted to overcome the drag of two sets of charges. There are annual fees on the fund of funds and yearly charges on the underlying funds. If you pick a manager badly, you'll end up paying more for less investment performance.

So far, no one has come up with a fund of funds of funds!

Don't confuse fund of funds, where one manager buys and sells units in different trusts to come up with an overall package that matches the amount of risk you want or the area you are interested in, with *manager of managers*.

With manager of managers, a fund, usually a poor performer, sacks its own managers and hires in others to do their job. The stated plus points include the fact that you can hire and fire managers very quickly in this way, maybe as little as with a month's notice, and that you can find specialist managers for each part of your fund. So if you had a European fund, you could take on a specialist for France, another for Spain, a third for Germany, and so on.

This all sounds great in theory, but in practice it's been a bit of a flop. By the time the manager gets around to hiring the 'best' managers on their past performance, they might well have passed their peak! Investment managers should come with a use-by date, just the same as groceries.

Checking Out Investment Supermarkets

Buying a unit trust directly from a fund management firm is a waste of money. You'll be charged the full up-front charge, including the 3 per cent paid to brokers, which is supposedly their reward for providing you with individualised advice. But you won't get this advice unless you're a really big customer.

If you know what you want by filtering down the 1,600 or so trusts to a short list and then studying the information on each via online sources, then you can buy your trust and get all or nearly all of the commission back into your bank account via an Internet investment supermarket.

Here, you select your fund, decide whether you want it as an Individual Savings Account (ISA), and pay for it with a debit card. The supermarket site should have links to the funds you're interested in. Easy.

The best-known investment supermarkets are Fidelity Funds Network (run by fund managers Fidelity, but offering a wide range of managers' funds), Hargreaves Lansdown, and Cofunds (available through independent financial advisers). A number of stockbroker sites also offer similar facilities, sometimes via a branded link to one of the main sites.

Investment supermarkets are like Sainsbury's or Tesco. They don't stock everything, instead concentrating on a pile-it-high, sell-it-cheap philosophy. If you need specialist funds from smaller providers, you may not find them on the fund supermarket shelves. And also unlike the high street, these supermarkets have a strict no-refunds policy.

Examining Monthly Investment Plans

Most funds have investment plans for regular savers, with some starting as low as £25 a month. These take your money from your bank account through a direct debit on a monthly basis and buy units in the plan (or shares in an investment trust) at whatever the price is on the day of purchase.

They are sometimes called 'savings plans' although, unlike bank or building society savings, you are not guaranteed ever to get your money back. These are risky investments.

Although some have very low minimum amounts, the majority of plans insist on at least £50 a month, and a few aim as high as £250. Savings plans have no minimum savings periods, so you can stop when you like and either cash in or leave your money to grow (hopefully!).

Besides the ability to fund a scheme with small sums, you also benefit from not having to worry so much about timing. Your regular sum buys more units when prices are low and fewer when they are high, so you iron out the ups and downs of investment prices. Stopping or selling will need a positive decision, however, as you will have to decide on what time is best for your needs.

Regular investment plans are very flexible as you can change your amount each month (as long as it stays above the minimum for your plan). You could, in theory, stay in for just one month. In practice, people invest affordable sums for many years. It's often money they don't really miss each month. But when they do cash in, they are often amazed at how well they've done.

Note that savings plans are rarely available through discount brokers or supermarkets.

Taking a Tax Break

January, February, and March make up the winter season for most people. But for the unit trust industry, those months comprise the Individual Savings Account (ISA) season. An ISA gives you tax freedom on up to £7,200 worth of investment every tax year (ending April 5 each year). You don't pay income tax on dividends, and you don't pay Capital Gains Tax on any profits. The investment must be with one funds firm, although it can be through one investment supermarket if you want to mix and match trusts.

Investment firms see tax freedom as a major selling tool. But during the dotcom boom, many investors who were suckered in with marketing lines of 'tax free' and 'if you don't use it, you lose it' regretted their decision.

An ISA is only worthwhile if you were going to invest anyway, because the income tax savings on some trusts are minuscule. You only get the full income tax relief on dividends from bond funds. There's no income tax advantage for basic-rate taxpayers on equities or equity funds, although there are still some savings for those in the top 40 per cent band.

An ISA makes best sense if:

- ✔ It's your first £7,200 of investment.

- ✔ You're a higher-rate taxpayer.

- ✔ You're investing in a bond fund.

- ✔ Your holdings are large enough to give you a potential Capital Gains Tax bill.

- ✔ You don't want to have to bother about declaring your dividend income to the taxman each year or calculating your gains when you sell.

Remember that you can't claim any losses you make on ISAs against any Capital Gains Tax payments you might need to make elsewhere.

Finding Out More about Unit Trusts

If you'd like to find out more about unit trusts, a good place to start for general information is the Investment Managers Association (IMA), a trade body taking in most unit trust management firms. The Web site is www.investmentuk.org; the phone number is 020 7831 0898. The IMA publishes a number of useful booklets.

In addition, every fund manager has a Web site, and most fund managers post their monthly thoughts about investments as well as details of how to invest. Many independent financial advisers (IFAs) simply repeat this material to clients as if it were their own.

Chapter 15

Gearing Up with Investment Trusts

. . . .

In This Chapter

▶ Knowing what investment trusts are

▶ Building up a portfolio

▶ Deciphering savings schemes

▶ Examining split capital shares

▶ Checking out venture capital trusts and their tax-relief deals

▶ Looking at the perks you get as a shareholder in investment trusts

. . . .

*I*nvestment trusts are the oldest form of collective investment in the UK –
and probably in the world. Many investment trusts date back to the
Victorian period. Foreign & Colonial, the oldest and now the largest fund, was
set up in 1868. Scottish American dates from 1873. They've outlasted world
wars, booms and slumps, and huge technological changes. And they've survived the indifference of independent financial advisers. (IFAs rarely recommend these trusts because either they don't understand them or, more likely,
the trusts generally pay no commission.)

Investment trusts share a lot of similarities with unit trusts. They give professional management in return for an annual fee, and investors get a portfolio
of shares. These trusts are intended for longer-term investment, and choices
range from global growth to specialist areas, such as Latin America, Thailand,
and start-up companies.

But differences between investment trusts and unit trusts exist, too. The
most important for typical investors are the low charges associated with
investment trusts. Alliance Investment Trust, one of the biggest and oldest
established funds, levies around 0.35 per cent a year in fees. That's less than
a quarter of the 1.5 per cent level from many unit trusts that have a similar
worldwide investment remit. Many other investment trusts keep their costs
below 0.5 per cent. Over five to ten or more years, those savings mount up to
a useful sum, with the gap growing in the investment trust's favour the more
the market rises.

Got your attention, eh? This chapter tells you what investment trusts are and
how they work, to help you decide whether investing in them is right for you.

Understanding What Investment Trusts Are

The Americans call unit trusts *open-ended* (or *mutual*) funds, which makes sense because the amount a unit trust manager has to invest depends on day-to-day purchases and sales of the fund. But investment trusts are different, and likewise the Americans call investment trusts *closed-end funds*. The reason? An investment trust is effectively a stock-market-listed company with shares and a fixed amount of money on its balance sheet. But instead of using its capital to buy assets (such as factories or shops) and to fund research (like GlaxoSmithKline does) or to buy the latest fashions (like Marks & Spencer does), the managers use the trust's capital to buy shares in other companies.

When you buy a Marks & Spencer share, the company itself doesn't get the money. The money ultimately (and indirectly) goes to the shareholder selling. Likewise, if investors decide to sell Glaxo, the firm itself doesn't shut down part of its research or manufacturing network. The company can look at the longer term, past the day-to-day concerns of individual shareholders.

Investment trusts are the same. Buying and selling moves the price of the trust share on the stock market. But it doesn't affect the underlying assets that are used to buy investments in other companies. So investment trusts can look to the long term. This fact may explain why so many investment trusts have been around for decades.

Looking beyond the Trust's Title to Determine Its Objective

Unit trust titles have a twofold purpose. They tell the name of the fund manager and the trust's investment objective. ABC Japanese is an (obviously fictitious) example.

But investment trust titles are different. Although some of the names give unit trust types of information, such as Aberdeen Asian Smaller Companies, other names mean nothing at all. Incomprehensible names include Albany, Alliance, City of London, Brunner, Claverhouse, Mid Wynd, Strata, and Witan. A further class of investment trusts have really confusing names. For example, Foreign & Colonial doesn't invest in the colonies; Scottish Mortgage has little investment in Scotland and none in mortgages; and Electric & General probably sounded like a good idea when founded in 1890, but the company invests in a lot more than electricity nowadays.

Because investment trust names are often so meaningless, investors must look at the sector to determine the trust's objective. The sector labels are roughly comparable with unit trust labels. However, relatively few UK-only trusts exist, and the biggest investment trusts are the Global Growth sector, which invests anywhere in the world.

A good place to start is www.theaic.co.uk. This is the Web site of the Association of Investment Companies (AIC), a trade body that speaks for most trusts. You can also get information from the www.trustnet.com site.

Examining the Discount: Market Value < Actual Assets

Quoted companies never have a stock market value that's exactly in line with the value of their underlying assets:

- ✔ Some sell at a premium, where the total share value (or *market capitalisation*) is greater than the underlying assets. A typical example is a chemical research company where the market is valuing the hope of a future breakthrough over the worth of its assets (probably not much).

- ✔ Some sell at a discount. Property companies, for example, usually have a stock market value below what all the individual properties may fetch if sold. This discount is a safety barrier or breathing space in case things go wrong.

Premiums go up and discounts tend to disappear when markets are optimistic. The same happens with investment trusts. Their market capitalisation is usually below their break-up worth (known as the *net asset value*, or *NAV*), although there are occasional premiums.

The discount tends to magnify market movements. When the underlying portfolio goes up in value, demand for the shares tends to shrink the discount, so holders benefit twice. In a bear market, discounts widen as the portfolio drops, giving investors a double hit.

Should you worry? Not nearly as much as unit trust sellers and some commission-crazed independent financial advisers (IFAs) suggest. Over time, discounts tend to stabilise. Investment trusts can adjust their own discount with share buybacks. So you can ride out the ups and downs in discounts.

The discount has some advantages. If you pay 90p for a share with a NAV of 100p, you receive the dividend income on 100p worth of assets, an 11 per cent boost.

Knowing What Gearing Means

Because they are stock-market-quoted companies just like Barclays Bank or Vodafone, investment trusts can behave in ways that differentiate them from other forms of collective investment.

For example, they can borrow money either through a bond issue or directly from the bank, a process called *gearing.* Trusts take loans because they believe that the stock market return will be greater than the interest costs. The loan enables them to get greater stock market exposure to the benefit of shareholders. In this way, trusts are rather like a cyclist who uses gears to go faster in good conditions (such as on the flat with the wind behind).

But as any cyclist knows, high gears are a pain going up steep hills. It's the same with trusts. Funds that gear up and then face a falling market lose out twice because they have to keep paying the interest to the bank or bond-holder.

Investment trusts publish their gearing levels. Many limit gearing to modest amounts, such as 10 per cent or under. A few try more sophisticated deals, such as borrowing in one currency and buying assets quoted in another. Here, the managers are betting on getting the foreign exchange dealing right as well.

Gearing is a risk but can be a reward when market conditions are right. Buy investment trusts with above-average gearing compared with similar funds if you think markets are going to rise. Don't worry that you've spotted something that the market as a whole has ignored (thus thinking that you're wrong). Trading in many investment trusts is sporadic and inefficient, leading to opportunities wised-up investors can grab.

Starting with the Global Growth Sector

Most investors start out with the Global Growth sector, which is all many people ever invest in or need. Others use Global Growth as a core portfolio and then buy more specialist funds.

The sector is worth in excess of £14 billion including some 15 trusts with assets over £250 million. Among the biggest are Foreign & Colonial, Witan, Alliance, Scottish Investment Trust, and Scottish Mortgage.

The Global Growth sector is defined as trusts whose objective is to produce a total return to shareholders from capital and some dividend income. The trusts have less than 80 per cent of their assets in any one geographical area, with at least 20 per cent in UK-registered companies. They can also hold cash and fixed-interest securities.

These non-specialist trusts are suitable for beginners, and they usually form the basis of long-term savings plans for children. They can also be useful for others, however, because the format can provide a widely diversified core for any widespread portfolio. Because many London-quoted companies are really international giants, don't be taken in by the proportion invested in the UK.

Global Growth also gives an opportunity for you to spread into newer investment areas that would otherwise be difficult for private investors to research and buy. These areas can be anything from Singapore to Switzerland to start-up companies but without the constraints a more specialised portfolio may have.

Note that a number of super-selective trusts exist. Pubs, tea plantations, alternative energy, gold mines, property, and traded endowment policies are just a few examples. Most of these trusts are so specialised that they're one-offs. They exist in a sector all by themselves without any comparisons.

Saving Costs through Savings Schemes

Twenty-five years ago, investment trusts were flagged as doomed to disappear quickly. They were seen as superannuated hangovers from a bygone age.

Then Foreign & Colonial set up a low-cost savings scheme, which was soon copied by most other trusts. Replication is a sure sign of success. Now much private investment into the trusts is through the savings schemes, although you can buy trust shares through a stockbroker as well at the same rate as ordinary equities.

A seriously good idea

Savings schemes offer bargain-basement dealing facilities both for regular payments and for one-off lump sums. After you're registered for one payment, you can start, stop, restart, and change the sum (provided that you keep to the minimum) whenever you want.

You don't have to worry about timing because your money goes regularly into the market every month. You get more shares when prices are low and fewer when they rise.

Monthly payments benefit from *pound-cost averaging*, a continuous drip-feed method of purchasing your investment. It means that the average purchase price paid over any given period is going to be lower than the arithmetical average of the market price.

And what does that mean in plain English? Consider this example: If the shares were quoted on three successive months at 30p, 50p, and 70p, the arithmetical average would be 50p. If you invested £300 at 50p, you'd get 600 shares. But suppose that you invested £100 every month for three months. In month one, you'd get 333 shares. In month two, you'd get 200 shares. In month three, you'd get 142 shares. This strategy would give a total of 675 shares (ignoring fractions and costs).

Pound-cost averaging takes the worry out of investment decision making. You don't need to panic when the price falls because you will merely be buying more of your chosen investment. And because you are committing funds on a regular basis, you need never worry you are investing all of your funds at the top of the market either.

Pound-cost averaging can reduce your risk, and the more a share value swings, the greater the benefit. For example, if the market swings down every other month, then on each downturn you buy more shares or units, which will be worth yet more on each upturn.

In a bear, or falling, market, pound-cost averaging allows you to build up an investment poised to benefit from a recovery without having to worry about trying to work out when the bottom of the market will occur. However, this strategy means you'll lose out on the best of the growth in a rising market. But this may be a small price to pay for the added security that pound-cost averaging brings to investment trust savings-scheme decision making. In the example earlier in this section, you would've fared best investing the entire £300 when the trust stood at 30p. But would you have known that or been put off by a low price and adverse media coverage?

What to look for in a savings scheme

Here are some things to check into when considering a savings scheme:

- **Minimum monthly amount.** The amount is usually £50, but some schemes have a minimum monthly amount of £20. A few schemes want £100. Anything higher than £100 indicates a trust that's not really serious about a savings scheme.

- **Minimum lump sum.** Many investors like to start off with a lump sum or add one when they have some extra cash. The standard minimum is £250 or £500.

- **Dividend re-investment.** Most trusts automatically re-invest your dividends in more shares. Dividends on most investment trusts tend to be small sums every six months, so you won't miss them. But over time, re-invested dividends add up to lots more shares, which then create higher dividends. That's a virtuous circle. A few income-producing trusts will send the dividends if you ask.

✔ **Purchase date.** The bigger trusts tend to invest your money into new shares on the day it's received. Others only do so weekly or monthly. If you invest £5,000 or more as a lump sum, most trusts invest for you at once. As monthly payments eradicate timing problems, it probably matters little when your money goes into shares. But you should find out so your direct debit arrives on the right day each month.

✔ **Charges.** All funds must charge 0.5 per cent government stamp duty on a purchase. After that, some funds charge nothing for purchases, many have a 0.2 per cent fee, and some go as high as 1 per cent. There's also the bid-offer spread, so you'll pay a little more than the published price to enter the trust and receive less when you exit (see Chapter 14 for more about the bid-offer spread).

✔ **Adviser commission.** Some trusts pay 3 per cent of anything you put into savings schemes if they know you've received advice from a registered independent financial adviser. This only applies to a relative handful of savings scheme members.

✔ **Selling facilities.** Almost all trusts arrange sales as well as purchases. If you're selling a large amount, timing will be crucial, so find out first how long it'll take. It should be the next day at the very worst. Otherwise, use a broker. Selling costs range from a flat £10 to 1 per cent plus a £10 charge. Most trusts cap sales expenses at a maximum £50.

✔ **Other features.** Look for trust transfers within a manager's scheme, declaration of trust facilities if you're investing for someone under 18, and share exchanges so you can convert your unwanted shares in other companies into investment trust holdings. Share exchange is a great way to get rid of small parcels of shares that would be uneconomical to sell through a stockbroker.

✔ **Individual Savings Accounts (ISAs).** You can put up to your £7,200-per-year ISA allowance into an investment trust through savings schemes. This arrangement has tax benefits. But most investment trust schemes impose extra costs on ISA plans, which can wipe out the tax benefits, especially for smaller investors. Spending £60 a year to gain £5 in tax relief is pointless.

✔ **Pension plans.** Some trusts market themselves as personal pension scheme components through Self Investment Pension Plans (better known as SIPPs). Expect to pay an administration charge for this.

And here are a few additional titbits you need to be aware of:

✔ Never invest in a trust just because it has the best-value savings plan. It may turn out to be a disaster.

✔ Because you're buying shares (and not units in a unit trust or OEIC), you can't buy fractions of a share. There will nearly always be some change from your regular amount. This change is carried over to the next month and added to your new contribution.

> ✔ HM Revenue & Customs treats re-invested dividends the same way as dividends paid by cheque. You have to declare the payments. If you are a higher-rate taxpayer, you'll have an additional tax bill to settle.

Knowing the Real Deal about Split Capital Shares

Split capital shares sound like a good idea. You divide up the underlying portfolio so that those who want income maximise their dividend cheques while those who want flat-out income growth get what they want, too. Super! Everyone is happy.

So why is *split-cap* a dirty word in large parts of the investment press? Because the idea was pushed and pushed, and then pulled and pulled, and finally stretched and stretched until it failed, flopped, and fizzled out into disaster.

Government hearings took place where fund managers admitted that everything depended on a wing and a prayer. Many investors were left with tiny fractions of their money instead of the safe long-term income they were promised. Some investors did manage to get compensation.

So what happened? If you've read earlier parts of this book, you know that high returns and low or no risk is an unsustainable combination unless you're very lucky. Well, for the previous 20 years, the investment trust world *had been* lucky, thanks to the long bull market of rising prices.

The original idea was to split the underlying capital of an investment trust into two classes of shares. The income class would provide high income for a set period until the trust was wound up. Whatever was left on that date would go to the holders of the capital shares.

Then along came the zero dividend preference share. If all went well, this share offered a set sum when the trust ended its life. So if a zero dividend preference share was originally sold at 100p with the promise of 200p after ten years, the compounded return was about 7.2 per cent. Investors had to compare that deal with other deals on offer. Because the gain was capital and not income, there were tax benefits.

Zeroes, as these shares are called, should've been safe. Their holders were first in line for payments. And because the fund manager would've taken in enough money in the first place to pay out the zero holders (even if it meant others ended up with nothing), then making the payments should've been easy. But investment firms like to push a good idea to destruction, promising more and more even when the outlook points to less and less. And they often do this by coming up with more and more obscure bits of financial engineering.

Not all splits were a disaster. Those that went under had invested in other zeroes, which in turn were probably into still more. This was a circle where it would have been easy enough for a fund to have ended up investing in itself. But since the early part of the decade, some splits have recovered. Some split capital shares exist that produce good returns for investors. Some investors have done well out of others' losses, picking up worthwhile investments at bargain basement prices. And the split debacle doesn't mean that conventional investment trusts are a disaster.

Don't invest in split capital shares on a whim. The www.splitsonline.co.uk Web site has up-to-date information and specialised help.

Getting Tax Relief through Venture Capital Trusts

Some investment trusts, such as 3i and Graphite Enterprise, put money into small, unquoted companies. Their managers try to spot firms with good growth prospects. Otherwise, these investment trusts behave in the same way as any conventional fund.

Another group of investment trusts, called *venture capital trusts (VCTs)*, looks for small, unquoted start-up companies as well, but because these high-risk trusts owe their existence to some tax-saving legislation, they have special rules.

Provided that you buy shares in a new trust directly from the promoter (not through the stock market), you're a UK taxpayer aged 18 or over, and you're prepared to hold the shares for a minimum of three years, you can invest up to £100,000 a year into a venture capital trust (VCT) and qualify for these tax-relief deals:

- ✔ You can have 30 per cent of your subscription money back as tax relief (if your earnings are great enough to generate sufficient taxable income), whatever your tax rate.

- ✔ You can defer elsewhere capital gains of up to £40,000 to help you make better use of your annual exemption (around £9,500 – it changes each year), but only if you bought the shares before 5 April 2004.

- ✔ Dividends from the VCT investment are tax free (this also applies to shares you buy that have already been issued).

- ✔ You pay no Capital Gains Tax on any profits you make (this also applies to 'second hand' shares that you buy in the market from other investors).

VCTs can invest in any unquoted companies, including those listed on the Alternative Investment Market (AIM) and on PLUS. Investments in AIM and PLUS trusts are easier to follow than those in companies whose real share worth is virtually impossible to value.

Examining Shareholder Perks with Investment Trusts

Investment trusts are quoted companies. Shareholders receive annual and interim reports, and they can attend annual general meetings where they can raise issues and vote.

The trusts have boards of directors who are independent of the fund managers. The directors should stand up for the shareholders, not the fund managers. If the managers are inefficient or charging too much, the directors can sack them. This power is being used increasingly. At the same time, directors now work to ensure that managers no longer have long-term sweetheart styles of contracts.

The directors can be voted out by shareholders, including big institutional investors controlling large numbers of shares. This has given rise to the 'activist' investor. Here, a well-off investor or an organisation with substantial financial backing buys into an underperforming investment trust, tries to unseat the board, and either attempts to install new managers or to bring the trust to an end, liquidating its assets. The activist hopes that either course (and some variations exist) will facilitate an exit at a big profit.

Chapter 16

Examining Investment-Linked Insurance Plans

*L*ife insurance sounds like such an easy idea to understand. You buy a policy that promises to pay out a set sum if you die, provided you keep up with the monthly premiums. Some policies, called *term cover*, have a limited time span. You may take up cover for 10, 15, 20, or 25 years, or whatever other time period you choose. If you stay alive, you receive nothing at the end. Other policies, more rarely sold, are called *whole of life* policies. You pay every month until you die, at which time your family receives a payout. You may pay for one day if you die immediately or for 60 or 70 years if you enjoy a really long life.

What could be more simple than that? Not much, but back in the 1960s, some bright insurance company executive came up with a new idea that would prove to be worth millions to his company and zillions to the life insurance world. As a result of that idea, a new version of collective investment emerged: Investment-linked life insurance plans. The clever trick was that hardly anyone really knew they were investments with risks. Insurance sounded so safe.

This chapter examines these insurance plans, explaining how they came to be in the first place, how the costs work, and what options are available.

The Birth of Investment-Linked Life Insurance Plans

During the 1960s, two light bulbs illuminated in the head of an insurance company executive. The first light bulb was that life insurance came with tax relief, which had been around for decades to encourage people to take out policies. Specifically, there was tax relief on the premiums paid every month, and payouts were tax free as well.

The second light bulb involved the *endowment*, a facility that gave policy-holders an investment-linked payout at the end of a term plan even if they didn't die. Endowments were painted as a win-win situation. The policyholder won because the family was guaranteed a payout on death, and the policy-holder won because there was a return on the premiums if there was no death.

Now endowment policies had been around for more than 100 years. Their beauty for the insurance company was that customers didn't understand that the balance between the life cover protection element and the amount given over to investment were bundled into one package. (In those days, no one asked questions about it.) I'll explain why that was a beautiful thing for the insurance company in a minute. But first, you need a little more setup info.

The mystery was deepened because all endowments were originally with-profits, a concept that is still around with us today (even if policy buyers are less enthusiastic for them, they sound a great idea). Policyholders share in the profits of the life company, which smoothes out the payments through annual bonuses. The insurer invests money and keeps some of the gains back in good years to pay them out when markets are weaker. After an annual or reversionary bonus is declared, it is added to the value of the policy and cannot be taken away.

But this caution was thrown to the wind in the 1970s and 1980s. A mix of inflation and competition from new companies pushed the *terminal bonus*, the bonus paid when the policy matured, to the fore. This was just as shrouded in mystery as the annual bonus, but it was far larger, sometimes accounting for more than half the final payout.

Many insurers artificially boosted terminal bonuses to ensure that their firm topped payout tables. Doing so was easy. In some years, even a big firm may have had only a handful of customers completing a 25-year policy. It cost little to give them extra because the firm knew it would more than recoup the cost from new policyholders sucked in by the publicity.

Insurance company taxation

Life company taxation is a real nightmare, capable of filling many volumes. But here are some general pointers:

✔ All life funds are taxed internally. So your investment has suffered both income tax and Capital Gains Tax at special rates. Your policy is hit by these deductions whatever your personal tax rate. Most people don't pay Capital Gains Tax because the first £9,500 or so of gains is exempt (the exact amount changes each year). And now, above that, the one and only tax rate is 18 per cent.

✔ As a rule, you lose if you're not a taxpayer. And you gain if you're a higher-rate income taxpayer or have large capital gains.

✔ Single premium policies allow annual withdrawals of up to 5 per cent of the initial investment without an immediate tax charge. You can add up the 5 per cent slices from year to year if you don't use them all the time. But you don't dodge the tax. Instead, you defer it. That can be a useful investment tool if you know your personal tax rate is going to fall. This is really aimed at top rate (40 per cent) taxpayers who expect their tax level to fall to 20 per cent when they retire.

✔ Basic-rate taxpayers have nothing extra to pay on lump sum insurance-linked plans.

Top-rate taxpayers are subject to *top slicing*, which is terribly complicated. It's the mechanism used to average out long-term gains to work out tax payments in the year the policy is surrendered. You take the average gain over the total number of years the bond has been in force.

Say, for example, that a £50,000 investment has grown to £130,000 over the past 12 years. The gain is therefore £80,000, and the slice is calculated by dividing it by 12, to £6,667. This sum is added to any income accruing in this tax year and the marginal tax rate calculated. For example, somebody with a £10,000 annual income would be deemed to have a notional income of £16,667. The tax level would be 22 per cent, but it has already been paid. Someone with an income of £50,000 would have £56,667, making all the gain liable to higher-rate tax at 40 per cent. But tax at 22 per cent has already been paid, so the bill would be 18 per cent of the total gain (in this case, 18 per cent of £80,000, which equals £14,400). I warned you: It's terribly complicated. And, anyone reading this book from 6 April 2008 needs to change the sums a little because the 22 per cent rate falls then to 20 per cent, so the sum is then 20 per cent of the gain. As I said, it really is complicated.

Now you may still be wondering why it was such a beautiful thing that customers didn't understand that the balance between the life cover protection element and the amount given over to investment were bundled into one package. Well, no legislator had ever defined the balance between the protection and investment. So our clever insurance folk came up with the investment-linked life insurance plan. It could be a regular premium deal, so the policyholder paid the same each month, or a lump sum.

The life cover was limited to a minimal 1 per cent extra on top of the policy's value, but the package still qualified for all the big tax savings. So if your policy was worth £1,000 and you died, your estate would receive £1,010. It was a wonderful loophole, especially because it cost insurance companies nothing! They built the risk of paying out this 1 per cent into the costs of these maximum investment plans, or MIPs. MIPs were directly linked to investment funds, which increased the clarity over with-profits and allowed lots of new very sales-oriented companies into the market.

Although most of the tax deals have been plugged over the years, enough remain to keep a whole army of salespeople in very profitable business. (I've put a technical bit in a nearby sidebar to detail how the tax breaks now work, if you're interested. But suffice it to say that they are only valid for a small handful of people, whatever your adviser might say.)

To end this little history lesson, I want to pass on a couple of final notes here: The terminal bonus isn't guaranteed even though policyholders are given indications of what it might be. Recent stock market problems mean some indicated terminal bonuses have gone down or been abolished altogether. And the with-profits concept is now seen as tarnished, but millions still have plans, often tied to their mortgage.

How the Costs Work Out

Take a look at some typical life-insurance-linked investment publicity. To encourage bigger sums, the company may promise a beguiling 102 per cent investment allocation if you put £10,000 into its maximum investment plan or 105 per cent if you can afford £25,000. It may only give 98 per cent if you put in the minimum £1,000. Obviously, these allocation rate figures vary from company to company, and there may well be intermediate points. But whatever the actual figures, this sounds like a great bargain. You invest £10,000 and get 2 per cent, for example, so you end up with £10,200.

How can they do this? The answer is they don't. As soon as they get your money, they deduct initial charges and a bid-offer spread, which pays the broker, who may get as much as 7 per cent of your money. No wonder brokers like insurance-linked investment! The commission is much higher than the 3 per cent on unit trusts and the 0 per cent on most investment trusts.

Suppose that the initial charge is 8 per cent. (Some are less.) Your £10,000 is now down to £9,200. Now give that a 102 per cent allocation rate, and you go up to £9,384. You lost more than £600 on the way in, but you feel better because your allocation rate is over 100 per cent. Insurance has a lot to do with peace of mind but never mind the value.

Some brokers rebate part or all of the up-front charges, so you may end up with more. They can afford to do so because the policies they sell have higher annual fees, and as the policy progresses they can collect the commission they gave up at the start. What you gain on the up-front roundabout, you lose on the yearly swings.

Managed Funds

Insurance companies offering investment-linked policies (often called unit-linked funds) display an impressive array of funds in their publicity. There's everything from cash to global bonds to UK equities to Japanese smaller companies. But about 98 per cent of insurance-linked investment goes into managed funds.

This arrangement sounds reassuring. You have the image of some clever fund managers moving vast collective funds, including your own, around – moving from equities to bonds to property to cash and back to equities as world economic and stock market conditions change. The reality is different. What usually happens is that new money is allocated to the good idea, leaving the rest of the fund wherever it was.

Fund managers argue that moving a £1 billion fund around makes steering a super tanker on your local park pond an easy task. Investors say that the fund managers should at least be more honest and take lower fees, because they charge management on the entire fund and not just the small part where they make decisions.

The typical managed fund might be 50 per cent UK equities, 15 per cent overseas shares, 20 per cent bonds, 10 per cent property, and 5 per cent cash, no matter what the conditions.

You can, however, switch into other funds even if you started in the managed fund. You can usually do so at low or no cost. Because of life company charges and taxation, you're generally better off investing in another form of collective fund. But if you've been in a fund for years and suffered the pain of the up-front charges, you may want to stick with it for some future gain.

If you go into a property fund, you may be stuck for six months if you want out again. And some more specialist funds have higher annual management charges.

Single Premium Bonds

The single premium, or lump sum, bond is an insurance plan with minimal life cover but where the entire amount is paid in one go. In most cases, single premium bonds are a waste of time for the investor and a boon for the seller, who can get more commission than with a rival collective. Single premium bonds do have some tax advantages for a small minority, however.

They can also come in flavours, such as cautious managed or aggressive managed, which aren't available easily from one unit trust, although putting an equity unit trust with a bond trust or two gives much the same investment result. In addition, some insurers sell distribution bonds, which are intended to give a regular income from a lower-risk investment mix of bonds and equities.

With-Profits Bonds

Put the lump sum insurance investment idea together with the with-profits concept, and you get the with-profits bond. Most of the big, well-established life insurance companies have issued these bonds, mainly to elderly or risk-averse investors, who have bought them in amounts adding up to billions.

These bonds offer a mix each year of a guaranteed bonus, which can't be taken away, plus a form of terminal bonus, which is added as you go along to give you an idea of the worth of your investment but which is not guaranteed (so it can disappear just as quickly as the insurance company bosses can say 'with-profits'). Past-performance figures can look good, with advisers touting 8 to 12 per cent a year. And companies selling the products often make them look even better with a guaranteed first-year growth rate. The cost of the guarantee is, of course, recouped later on with lower bonus rates. And just to make sure that no one takes too much advantage of up-front special payments, most bonds have extra early-cash-in penalties over the first five years. They're usually on a sliding scale – typically 8 per cent penalty in the first year falling to 1.5 per cent in the fifth year.

In common with all with-profits plans, bonus sums are up to the insurance company. There's no way of knowing whether you've been treated generously or short-changed.

There's an additional sales line too. The safe route they offer to annual growth can be used to fund living expenses, thanks to a special tax law known as the *five per cent withdrawal rule*.

Note that following years of disappointing investment markets after 1999, the same advisers who were happily selling the bonds are now telling customers to cash them in (although not refunding the commission they earned). This about-turn comes because although, in theory, values on with-profits hold up, in practice those who want to cash in get clobbered.

Understanding the market value reduction

The *market value reduction*, or *MVR*, is a penalty on withdrawals or partial withdrawals from with-profits bonds. (It used to be called the *market value adjustment* until even the insurance companies conceded that the value was only ever adjusted downward.)

The MVR is hidden in the small print. And even those who notice it are told it'll never be applied. It negates the can't-lose promise of a with-profits bond.

The MVR is a percentage that changes, sometimes day to day, with market conditions. The date you start the bond is also important because many companies quote MVR on an individual basis within high and low points. Those who buy when the market is high face higher penalties.

For an example of MVRs in action, suppose that a £10,000 bond grows to £11,000 over two years, and the owner wants to cash in. But there's a 25 per cent MVR. Subtract 25 per cent from £11,000, and the amount returned will be £8,250 – a loss of £1,750 on the original money.

The MVR does not apply:

- ✔ If the bond is not cashed in.
- ✔ On regular withdrawals when listed in the bond contract.
- ✔ If the bondholder dies or if the second of two named on the policy dies.
- ✔ On MVR-free cash-in dates, which are offered on some bonds. Often, these dates are birthdays, such as the 10-, 15-, and 20-year anniversary of taking out the bonds.

Knowing what to do if you're in a bad situation

Bondholders facing a with-profits investment that's turning into a without-profits or with-losses investment have a number of choices. But realistically, they should first find out the cash-in value of their plan.

The options are:

- ✔ Do nothing and hope for an improvement. Insurers know that these bonds are popular and will want to restore the image of a low-risk, high-sales product.
- ✔ Make regular penalty-free withdrawals where possible.
- ✔ Cash in and pay the penalty. Then switch to a low-risk alternative, such as a lump sum investment in gilts, property, or cash. Distribution bonds are a slightly higher-risk option.

Many advisers who have sold the bonds are now telling clients to sell and move to another investment. Doing so could earn the adviser or broker a second slice of commission. Insist that all commission on the second bond is rebated back to you in order to prevent *churning*, where advisers tell investors to make moves that are unnecessary to create commission-earning situations.

Here are a couple of final notes to keep in mind on this subject:

- ✔ Few with-profits bond investors are likely to want to switch into riskier equity funds.
- ✔ New purchasers aren't subject to existing MVRs.

Traded Endowments

Most regular premium endowments are cashed in long before they reach their maturity date. Some people can't afford the premiums any more; others want the money to finance a project or to help settle a divorce. Only a few endowments end early through death.

The usual cash-in method for those who want the money and don't die is surrendering the policy to the insurance company. With a unit-linked policy, the calculation is easy. The insurance company works out the bid value of each unit. Often, there may be more than one class of unit, each with different values.

But with-profits policies are more complicated. The life company offers as little as it thinks it can get away with. Because with-profits policies are shrouded in mystery, those surrendering can't be sure that they're getting a good deal.

Instead of surrendering their with-profits policy, the holders can try to sell it to a traded-endowment policy dealer, who may offer around 10 per cent more. These second-hand policy traders must then sell the plan to someone who'll continue with the monthly payments until the policy's maturity date. And that's where the investment element comes in.

Traders mark up the policies they buy and then sell them, often to individual investors who can afford to fund them. The advantage for the new owner is that the original holder has taken the hit of the early years, when costs are high, leaving the subsequent investor to take the hoped-for gains of the latter years.

The way to value the policy is to compare the amount you pay for it and the cost of the monthly premiums with the guaranteed sum assured and any extra you think it could make. You need to look at the financial strength of the issuing company. Mutual companies tend to pay out more generously than those owned by stock-market-quoted companies.

Second-hand policy investors don't lose complete touch with the original owner. If the first owner dies, the policy comes to an end, and the investor collects the death payment. Note, too, that in most cases, there's no extra tax to pay when the policy matures.

You can build up a portfolio of second-hand policies with varying maturity dates and from different insurers to spread the risk. You can also invest in a range of second-hand policies through a specialist investment trust, where the holdings are managed.

Do these specialist funds work? The jury is out. People who bought into these specialist funds when they were first launched have seen annual returns of under 2 per cent in many funds. One fund went bust. However, anyone buying into a mature fund with just a few years left could see returns of around 8 per cent a year.

Bonds with Guarantees

Investment is tricky, so the word *guaranteed* in big print across the front of a prospectus can be a powerful attraction. A number of products from insurance companies based both in the UK and in tax havens such as the Isle of Man or Dublin make this boast. But you have to scrape the small print to know what exactly is guaranteed. The *precipice bond* (a term used by regulators, commentators, and investors but not finance companies) guarantees the income in big print. But it offers no warranties as to the eventual capital value. Some can fall very quickly once the stock market drops below a set point, sometimes twice as fast as the market itself.

As many investors in precipice bonds have found out to their cost, guaranteeing the income without making assurances about the return of the capital can be the route to quick ruination.

Guaranteed capital and income

Guaranteed-income bonds, which invest in a portfolio of UK government stocks for a fixed number of years, from one year to six years, promise to return the original capital intact plus pay a regular income. These bonds come from a number of insurance companies, often those specialising in this area. The income is tax-free for basic-rate income taxpayers, but non-taxpayers can't reclaim the tax paid by the insurance company. Some income bonds, called guaranteed-growth bonds, allow investors to roll up the payments so they get a lump sum on maturity.

These bonds are suitable for investors wanting total security for their cash.

Guaranteed capital but variable growth

A number of insurance companies (and banks as well) sell can't-lose investments based on the stock market. They usually have a five-year life. If the FTSE 100 (the Footsie) index rises over the period, you receive the gain. But if it falls, you get your original money back. Some of these investments average daily results over the last 30 days or 3 or 6 months so you don't get caught by a sudden fall (but nor do you win out from a quick rise).

These investments sound ideal, where heads you win and tails you don't lose. So where's the catch (or catches)?

- ✔ You're locked in for five years.

- ✔ Some offer all the return in the Footsie. Others cap it so you can't make more than a set percentage.

- ✔ Some bonds from banks make you pay income tax on gains. Those from insurance companies are usually structured so you pay no tax.

- ✔ You receive no income.

- ✔ You lose out on dividends. Over a typical five-year period, re-investing dividends is worth around 15 per cent of your money.

- ✔ You need to re-invest at the end of the period, whether you want to or not. And doing so involves new costs even if they're hidden.

- ✔ The guarantee is only as good as the financial institution backing it.

Because you don't receive any income, the index on which your investment is based must fall around 15 per cent or more before the guarantee starts to have some value.

Guaranteed income with no capital guarantees

Take a deep breath here. These bonds are really complicated, although they don't seem so from the literature sent to prospective investors. They show a huge 10 per cent on the cover plus a guarantee to pay that level of income each year for three to five years. It can be tax free as well for most taxpayers. The deal sounds really generous when bank and building society investments struggle to pay income one-third of that level. Warning! Warning!

Now read the small print. Yes, the income is guaranteed. But what about the return on maturity of your capital, the savings you've spent a lifetime building up? That part is *variable*. And that's Weasel word 1. *Variable* here means it can only go down, never up.

Your capital return will be lower than your investment if the underlying investments fall over the period. But don't worry, the literature says. In 'back testing' 1,000 (or some really big number) periods in the past, this situation has never happened. Weasel phrase. Savvy investors know that the past is no guide to the future.

And even if the market were to fall, the literature says, there is a safety zone of 20 per cent. More weaseling. When markets drop, they can fall by as much as 70 per cent, so the protection is soon wiped out.

After the 20 per cent zone on maturity is breached, your losses can mount up. You go straight to giving up 20 per cent of your money. This is the start of the precipice. In some bonds, you go straight down, losing 1 per cent for each 1 per cent. But in others, you drop even faster, sacrificing 2 per cent for each 1 per cent fall in the underlying portfolio. Here, a 50 per cent fall wipes out all your money, although you should get your income.

There's worse news. If the market recovers, you only get back to your original cash if the portfolio goes all the way back to its starting point. A partial recovery is some help, but that's all. And you don't get the advantage of the so-called safety zone after it has been breached.

Oh, and by the way, if equity markets go up, you lose out on any gains. They don't tell you that either.

Heading for the precipice

Precipice bonds can be based on a number of investments:

✔ The simplest are based on one index. But watch out if it's a specialist index such as the US high-technology NASDAQ or one few have heard of, such as the Eurostoxx.

✔ Nastier are those that depend on three indexes from different countries. Think you're gaining from diversification? Think again. What you get back depends on the worst performing of the three. Any outperformance in the other two is ignored.

✔ Nastiest are those based on a basket of shares. Almost everyone uses this phrase (including me) to indicate that an investor has a diversified portfolio where the winners balance and, hopefully, outweigh the losers. But in the world of precipice bonds, you can have 30 separate investment contracts based on 30 different shares. Each one accounts for 3.33 per cent of the whole. After a share loses 20 per cent, it starts to go down big time. If it goes bust, that's 3.33 per cent of your capital lost forever. It doesn't matter whether the other 29 double, triple, or quadruple. You've lost that slice of your money.

Precipice bonds are often sold as high-income stock market plans. What they are really is a bet on the volatility (or rather non-volatility) of the underlying investments. The derivative contracts on which they're based are a gamble on the market remaining largely unchanged over the period.

If the assets on which the fund is based move no more than about 15 per cent higher or 20 per cent lower over the period, you've probably done as well as or better than leaving your money in the bank. Any bigger movements, and you either lose out on your capital return or fail to make money in a rising market.

These bonds are for suckers.

As a final insult, bonds that promise you a fixed return for three years or five years pay you the annual amount three or five times. But they keep your money for two or three months longer without making a payment! How's that for mean?

Offshore tax havens

You can invest your money in an offshore insurance bond. Many of them are offered by the tax haven offshoots of UK life companies. You'll find them in places such as the Channel Islands or the Isle of Man. You can make some tax savings. But unless you're going to live outside the UK tax net, you'll be caught for tax when you cash in the policy. In the meantime, the advantages of rolling up dividends and other income tax free are often wiped out by higher charges.

Chapter 17

Hedging Your Fund Bets

In This Chapter

▶ Understanding what hedge funds are

▶ Understanding the strategies that are available

▶ Checking out a fund of hedge funds

▶ Knowing about some new ideas based on hedge funds

▶ Looking at some do's and don'ts when investing in hedge funds

*T*he reputation of hedge funds is appalling. Every media article on them includes an almost obligatory reference to Long Term Capital Management, the multibillion hedge fund that went spectacularly bust in 1998, threatening to take the whole world financial system with it. Subsequently, a whole load of other hedge funds went belly up but with a lot less publicity. Some of them lost in the region of half a billion pounds each. That's an awful load of dough.

So why are they worth looking at? Because you can't ignore them. They are often extremely successful, making fortunes for their big investors and even bigger fortunes for the managers who run them. They can affect all sorts of other investments, including those whose owners run a mile at the very words *hedge fund.* And they're becoming more mainstream and acceptable as time advances. Your pension fund may invest in them. Some investment trusts include hedge funds in their portfolios. Your future fortune may be riding on one without your knowledge. They are the genie that can't be forced back into the bottle.

To boot, hedge fund managers are lobbying the Financial Services Authority watchdog to be allowed to sell more hedge-style funds to more people in the UK. If the rules are freed up, you probably won't be able to escape hedge funds as a collective investment choice. They'll be thrown at you from all angles, including your local bank.

For all these reasons, you need to know about hedge funds, even if you can't or don't want to invest in them. That's where this chapter comes in.

Hedge Funds Defined

Hedge funds – sometimes (and confusingly) called alternative investments even though they have nothing in common with old-style alternatives such as classic cars or stamp collections – have been around since the late 1940s. Literally tens of thousands of them exist around the globe. No one knows quite how many of them are actually out there because there's no listing everyone agrees on. And new ones are born and failures die each year.

Strictly speaking, the term *hedge fund* only refers to a specialised legal structure. Hedge funds are private partnership contracts where the manager has a substantial personal interest in the fund and is free to operate in a variety of markets using a number of strategies. It's best to think of a hedge fund as a collective where the manager has substantial freedom to invest in areas other funds can't reach. These freedoms include the ability to:

- ✔ Be flexible. Most hedge fund managers can do what they like within wide parameters. They're not restricted by trust deeds to a narrow range of equities or bonds like other collectives.

- ✔ Go short. Ordinary fund managers only select shares they think will do well, a technique known as *going long*. Hedge fund managers can also choose equities they think will sink, making money as the shares fall, a technique known as *going short* or *short selling*.

- ✔ Employ derivatives, such as futures and options. There are stacks of strategies here – enough to fill a whole shelf with *For Dummies* books on them.

- ✔ Move in and out of cash and property as well as other investments at high speed.

- ✔ Use borrowings (known as *gearing* in the UK and *leverage* in the United States) in an aggressive fashion to improve returns.

Note that *hedging* is a term that has been used in commodity trading for over a century. It denotes a technique where producers and users of a commodity, such as silver or sugar, protect themselves against sudden price shocks. It has to do with risk reduction. Likewise, some hedge funds set out to cut back on risks, but many were established to take higher than average risks in the hope of really big rewards. A few are huge, with billions of dollars in assets. (The whole hedge fund world works in US dollars wherever they are based.) But most hedge funds are small compared with other collectives. Many either limit themselves by financial size or by the number of investors. This enables managers to operate freely and without the trading constraints that moving a billion or two in stock markets invariably brings.

Hedge funds came to prominence first in the 1990s and then again in the early years of the present century as top fund managers quit unit and investment trust firms to make more money for themselves by setting up their own hedge funds. Hedge fund managers take performance fees. If they do well, their contract gives them a hefty slice of the gains. If they flop, they earn comparatively very little even if it's still a lot compared with your salary slip.

Around the deep part of the share price collapse in the early years of the twenty-first century, hedge funds received a further boost in publicity because fund managers were able to make money out of falling markets. This was in contrast to even the most successful managers of other equity collectives who, at best, could only minimise losses and hope to lose less than their rivals.

Hedge funds are not for first-time investors. They're often secretive, and many of them operate out of tax havens where corporate governance rules are lax. Always check that you're happy with the management firm and where it's based before considering moving a penny in their direction.

Strategies to Choose From

Every hedge fund exists either to maximise returns or to offer a safe haven while trying to return more than an investor would get from leaving his or her money in cash deposits at the bank. Overall, around half of all hedge funds are run on a long–short strategy (see the section 'Opportunistic strategies' for the details). Beyond that, eight other well-defined strategies are available for managers to pursue. The strategies come under three main headings: relative value, event driven, and opportunistic.

Relative value strategies

This tactic is at the lower-risk end of the hedge fund spectrum because it doesn't depend on whether or not the market is enthusiastic for oil companies or banks or food producers or automotive engineers, just on the relative values of two closely connected stock market investments such as two banks or two oil companies. This is because the factors affecting one company in a sector are similar to those affecting a competitor company, especially over the short term.

With relative value strategies, the hedge fund tries to profit from price gaps between the same or similar investments in different markets For instance, some shares are quoted and traded on more than one stock market. Minor differences between the two might exist, often only available for a minute or so, as local prices react to something happening in another country, or because the local stock market is more enthusiastic (or less keen) on shares themselves that day. Currency differences can also be exploited. These differences are often minute, but multiply them by the millions of pounds, euros, or dollars a hedge fund can throw at the difference and then do this several times and you can make a little bit more. Remember that in investment, the gap between the best and the worst often comes down to either a few lucky trades that make big bucks, or being able to score a tiny extra percentage over competitors most of the time.

Three main types of relative value fund are available:

- ✔ **Convertible arbitrage.** Some shares have convertible bonds as well as conventional shares. Exploiting price differences can be profitable.

- ✔ **Fixed-income arbitrage.** This one is for the rocket scientists who try to make money by buying and selling bonds with the same credit risk (so they stick to UK gilts or US treasuries) but with different maturity dates or different headline interest rates.

- ✔ **Equity market neutral.** Traditional collective fund managers try to find shares that will go up, but equity neutral managers aren't concerned with the direction of markets or shares. Instead, they look for differences between shares and derivatives, so they may sell a bank share but buy a bank-based derivative. Another route is to sell overvalued shares and buy undervalued shares.

Event-driven strategies

This tactic focuses on shares in companies that are involved in takeovers, acquisitions, and other forms of corporate restructuring. Big rewards await those who get this strategy right, and huge losses occur if all goes wrong.

Here are the main types of event-driven strategies:

- ✔ **Merger arbitrage.** This type concentrates on companies that are either acquiring or being acquired through takeovers. The shares often have a life of their own, independent of general market forces. Hedge fund managers using this tactic hope to make money out of the fears of other investors that the deal will be scuppered either by other shareholders or government regulators.

- ✔ **Distressed securities.** Here, managers try to make money from equities and bonds on the verge of collapse. Some hedge fund managers end up with significant stakes in the company concerned, so they can influence any rescue attempt.

Opportunistic strategies

These are the riskiest hedge fund strategies, promising high returns. The hedge fund managers bet on stock market directions – up, down, or sideways. But they can also invest in other areas, such as commodities, bonds, and currencies.

Here are the main types of opportunistic strategies:

- ✔ **Long–short.** This is the big one, accounting for about half of all hedge fund activity. The idea is that expert managers (often with a track record elsewhere) aim for positive returns from a small portfolio of shares in companies they know well by either selling them (going short) if they think the price will fall or buying them (going long) as they see fit. Some go for more complicated tactics such as buying what they consider to be the best share in a sector and selling the weakest. So they sell the worst (in their opinion) oil company, for example, and buy the best.

  Short selling usually involves shares that were never owned by the fund. Techniques to exploit price falls are more complicated than those used to gain from rising prices.

- ✔ **Macro.** With this tactic, the managers take bets on big worldwide movements in all sorts of markets but especially those where their activities are hidden by huge amounts of trading by others. They hope to second-guess market moves.

- ✔ **Short selling.** This type specialises in techniques to make money out of falling equity and bond values. It's a very high-risk tactic. If the investment moves the other way, the losses can be massive. Purchasers of shares who hope the price will rise can only lose their stake if the asset falls to zero. Now suppose that you sell a share with a £1 price, hoping to buy it back later at 50p and take out 50p a share profit, but you get it wrong. That share could soar to £2, £5, or who knows how high. So short sellers face limitless losses. And when markets are rising steeply, short selling funds have to stay on the sidelines.

- ✔ **Emerging markets.** This type is really for the ultra-courageous. These are the riskiest hedge funds because they invest in less well-developed markets where information is sketchy, legal and administrative systems are often unstable, local politics are volatile, and the companies themselves are often run by managers who either lack experience or are corrupt. Most investors run a mile from this type. But hedge fund managers see it as an opportunity, trying to profit from the very problems that scare off others.

A Fund of Hedge Funds: The Easy Way In

The easiest (and for many investors the only) way into hedge funds is via a Financial Services Authority-recognised fund of hedge funds. Managers of these funds buy into anything from 5 to 40 other funds, trying to spread the risk by diversifying managers and management styles.

The advantages for investors are:

- ✔ Access to areas that are normally restricted to the ultra-wealthy
- ✔ Professional management, including constant monitoring
- ✔ A greater information flow than from often secretive funds
- ✔ Access to a variety of fund types

Many funds of funds come from major UK management groups, such as Henderson or Baring, so investors have a good idea whom they're dealing with. Managers from these companies tend to sidestep hedge funds that don't comply with high disclosure standards.

No strategy and no manager will always beat the odds. A manager who's successful in one market situation may fail in another. And a manager who's a big hit when heading a large team run by a major investment house may fail dismally as a hedge manager without the props of a team and huge fund management house employer. You have little comeback against a manager who fails to deliver. You have zero comeback if you buy into an offshore hedge fund that then goes bust.

Private investors with £7,200 (from 6 April 2008) can invest in a fund of hedge funds through an Individual Savings Account (ISA). That's not quite the same as going directly to a hedge fund manager, but your money will be in a variety of hedge funds.

Taking Hedging Some Stages Further

The big advantage of hedge funds is that they can make money when share prices fall as well as when they rise. But, if the truth be told, many investors are scared of hedge funds or think they are only for those with hundreds of thousands, if not millions, spare. So mainstream investment companies, such as unit trust management firms, have come up with some new ideas based on hedge fund thinking, but not carrying that label, and accessible to investors with relatively small sums. Many start at £5,000 and some will take as little as £1,000.

Only look at these fund ideas if you're experienced and able to withstand periods of losses. They are not intended for the first-time investor. Always check on how the managers intend to reward themselves. Some have been known to prioritise their own remuneration before that of their investors, so be careful.

Total return funds: Choose your risks and take your rewards

Total return funds aim to give you long-term gains using a flexible investment strategy that has little, if any, reference to traditional fund ideas such as geographic or industrial sectors. Instead, fund managers buy into a very large range of asset types that spread their risk. Total return funds can only profit from rising asset prices – they don't *go short* (market jargon for making money when values of stocks and shares fall).

So you don't buy into the US stock market or into property shares as you might with a standard unit trust. In total return funds, you buy into managers who promise to deliver the return you'd get on a cash deposit in the bank and then target a defined percentage on top of that. The higher that percentage, the greater the potential rewards but also the larger the possible risks. A fund advertising itself as cash plus 5 to 7 per cent would be higher up the risk ladder than a fund offering 2 to 3 per cent over the cash return. The first would appeal to adventurous investors; the second to more cautious savers.

Total return fund managers charge relatively low fees but increase them if they're successful in meeting or beating their target.

130–30 funds: An answer to the one-way bet

Traditional funds only make gains when values rise. One of the claimed advantages of hedge funds over traditional funds is their ability to make money when share and other asset prices are falling. But over most longer and many shorter periods, share prices do go up. The long-term trend has so far always profited those who buy shares rather than those who try to gain from their falls.

Many investors, large and small, are queasy about giving a hedge fund manager total freedom. So managers have now come up with the 130–30 fund. The idea is that the greater part of the fund – the 130 – buys into shares that the fund managers hope will rise, called the *long portfolio*. But the fund also has the flexibility to put the 30 into a *short portfolio* – assets that managers expect to fall.

Thanks to a slice of clever mathematics and some borrowing, each £100 you invest buys assets worth £130 long (going up, the managers hope) and £30 short (picking losers that will go down, they hope.) That equals £160 working for £100 – great if the fund managers get it right, but losses get magnified if your 130–30 manager isn't as clever as the publicity machine says.

The 130–30 is a structure, and not a recipe for instant success. Do they work? The jury's very much still out because they've not been around for long enough either to have been through a large variety of market situations or for investors to be able to sort out the good managers from the bad. And because those running these funds have to be expert in selecting both winners and losers, then they have to be well above the average standard. In addition, the costs on many 130–30 funds are high. They still have to prove themselves.

Absolute return funds: Ratcheting up the risks

Absolute return funds are hedge funds in all but name. Their managers operate a flexible strategy: They can borrow, *sell short* (sell stocks they don't have), and go into futures, options, and almost anything else they can think of to enhance their returns. Some adopt a strategy known as *market neutral*, where most of the fund aims to match the stock market, leaving a small proportion over for a handful of investments which the managers expect to rise substantially in price.

Other managers' strategies are *market directional*. These managers take decisions on market movements and try to magnify them, but they also use futures and options to try to dampen the impact of markets going the wrong way.

Absolute return funds should beat total return and 130–30 funds in a sustained falling market.

Some Do's and Don'ts: A Hedge Fund Checklist

Because very few investors other than the ultra-rich have ever bought into a hedge fund, and because hedge funds are rarely mentioned in the press, precious little help and advice is immediately on hand for the average investor. So you have to tread very carefully. Here are the basic do's and don'ts:

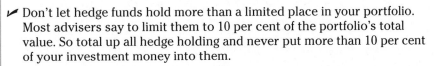

✔ Do ensure that a fund of funds manager reveals his or her standards for selecting and monitoring hedge fund managers.

✔ Don't let hedge funds hold more than a limited place in your portfolio. Most advisers say to limit them to 10 per cent of the portfolio's total value. So total up all hedge holding and never put more than 10 per cent of your investment money into them.

✔ Do check that the adviser or broker understands hedge funds and is up to date with information on them. Some brokers offer free education packages to private investors.

✔ Do always be sure that you know about fees and charges. They can be significant and erode stated gains.

✔ Do take individual advice from an expert broker to confirm that the investment is suitable.

✔ Don't invest if you're in doubt about a hedge fund or a hedge fund of funds. Hedge funds and your cash make a highly volatile mix, so if you're in doubt, just don't do it.

Chapter 18

Investing at Random

*T*his chapter is on a subject most investors have been conditioned to believe is pure fiction. It's not. It's about how you can perform as well as the average fund manager or stockbroker using no technology more complicated than a pin. My research using my own children as guinea pigs shows this. (Don't worry. My kids were old enough to handle a pin, and no animals were harmed in the videoing.) So take a deep breath and prepare to believe.

Pinning Your Hopes on Chance

One of my all-time favourite investment books is *A Random Walk Down Wall Street* (WW Norton, 1973) by US writer Burton Malkiel. The book was first published in the early Seventies and since then, it has been updated at least eight times and has been constantly in print.

Much of the book is high-flown investment theory. Malkiel is a top economics professor, after all. But in one part of the book, he describes the most devastating puncturing of the postures of all those highly paid experts whose views are featured almost nightly on TV news bulletins.

Back in June 1967, some bored journalists on US investment magazine *Forbes* were sitting around in their New York office waiting for the printers to complete some corrections. While waiting, they were discussing that they were fascinated by the way top fund managers produced results that ranged from marvellous to miserable each year and the way that a manager who did well one or two years in a row rarely made that three or four. In fact, over five years, only a tiny handful managed to perform consistently well.

One of their Wall Street contacts had once joked to them that a blindfolded monkey stabbing a share price page with a pin could do as well as some of the chumps working for big fund groups. So they decided to test the theory, which is now known as the Random Walk. The rest is history.

Let the darts land where they may

Those *Forbes* journalists weren't brave enough to raid the Bronx Zoo for the necessary apes. So they hit on the next best thing. They pinned up the shares price page of the *New York Times* on the wall and threw darts at it them-selves. They put an imaginary $1,000 on each of the stocks they hit.

They did this 28 times and invested their pretend $28,000. Later on, they wished it was real money. By 1984, their money had grown, with dividends re-invested, to no less than $131,697.61. They had easily outplayed the stock market index; more importantly, their result was only beaten by a tiny hand-ful of professional fund managers. One manager they beat was the top per-former of 1968 whose fund subsequently went down so far that it had to be shut down. The manager of this fund decided to give up stocks and shares to open a New York singles bar – not much consolation to the investors whose fortunes he had shrunk.

Yes, my children became fund managers

Forbes magazine gave up its dartboard portfolio in 1984 because only one in seven of the original companies had survived takeovers and mergers intact. But many others have since taken up the concept, including me!

In the 1990s, I regularly featured a New Year portfolio with a pin (selected by my children, Zoe and Oliver, from the share price pages in the *Financial Times*). It started as an antidote to those New Year share prediction articles, which promised to foretell the future but probably only wrote up shares already held by the writers' sources.

Most years, the portfolio selected by my offspring outperformed the average UK fund manager; one year, it was in the top 5 per cent and did better than all the professional newspaper tipster columns. Okay, on two occasions out of the ten times we did this, it fell below the average but not disastrously. The results were third quartile rather than bottom of the fourth division.

Why did I stop? The newspaper I used to write for shut down its business pages. (Nothing to do with my contribution, well, unless it was my scepticism that led to a dearth of fund manager adverts.)

Looking at the Worth of Fund Managers

Some of my best friends are fund managers. So it's worth saying that the fund management companies that employ them perform a number of useful tasks:

- ✔ They carry out all the purchase and sales dealing with stockbrokers, taking advantage of economies of scale.

- ✔ They deal with all the paperwork associated with dividends.

- ✔ They take care of taxation within the portfolio.

- ✔ They offer access to a diversified portfolio for a small sum of money.

- ✔ In some cases, they make asset allocation choices, such as moving from shares to bonds.

- ✔ They provide you with the comfort factor of being able to blame some-one else if your investments head nowhere.

Okay. Those are the positives. The difficulty is that the employers of these managers are in competition for our savings and the annual fees that will feed their often-luxurious lifestyles. Even my best-friend fund managers would admit that the average ability to pick shares is, well, average. A few manage to beat the market for some years. With each year that passes, however, the number of those with a good record goes down.

That's why I suggest that you always look at past performance tables that show discrete 12-month periods to test consistency (see Chapter 13). It's easy to have a lucky hit three or four years ago that stays in traditional tables.

Fund management is big business. Fund managers have to be optimistic about their speciality. What they say is then repeated by financial advisers who receive monthly performance bulletins. The advisers can use the bulletins as crib sheets when dealing with clients, who think they're getting unbiased advice that the adviser has researched. Some of those crib sheets are then relayed to the press as the financial adviser's own considered opinions.

Sure, some collectives will outperform the averages and let advisers proclaim why hiring a fund manager is important. But what's the accuracy rate of those whose job is to predict the managers who are likely to be successful? Just about the same as hitting the winners with a pin.

Looking at Why Random Choice Works

Random choice – or the random walk or the portfolio with a pin – works because investment markets are unpredictable. For example, some people (like me) doubted the staying power of the technology funds launched in 1999 and early 2000, but such people were derided by the experts. Thing is, trends always reverse at some time. Over the past decade or so alone, we've seen the rise and fall and often the rise again of Latin America, South East Asia, big companies, small companies, the United States, Russia, oil stocks, gold, banks, breweries, property, and tobacco companies. And that's just to name a few! Who predicted these with accuracy? Certainly not more than a handful of the fund managers who are happy to give their views to the press.

So if you can't forecast the future with any accuracy, why not give up and use your time productively on a healthy walk or a visit to your local gourmet pub?

Creating a random walk portfolio and then doing nothing, like the journalists described in the section 'Pinning Your Hopes on Chance', has the further advantage of low costs. In fact, after the shares are bought, that's it cost-wise. There are no more fees. In addition, your random portfolio isn't subject to close scrutiny every one or three months from experts who make their money telling big investors which fund manager to select and which to ditch.

Random choice is really a form of index tracking fund but without the index. As a do-it-yourself fund manager, you're in the realm of buy and hold, and you're away from the constant, and costly, active management collective managers offer to justify their huge fees.

Random choice has another advantage over the index fund. Trackers have to buy the shares in the right proportions. So during the dotcom boom, for example, the computer had to buy a chock load of high-tech stocks. You would've had at least one-third of your money riding on telecoms or computer stocks in a Footsie fund because this index, in particular, is hugely weighted toward a few big sectors. In fact, at the time of this writing, the index was dominated by banks, phone companies, and international mining concerns. But there's no way of knowing whether today's big sector will remain huge tomorrow or sink back into some sort of oblivion amongst the also-rans.

On the other hand, if you were throwing a pin at the share price page during the height of the dotcom boom, the pin may have turned up a tobacco stock or two, or any of the other sectors, such as retailing or food or alcohol, which fell less steeply in the subsequent *bear market* (the term used when share prices are falling, and the opposite to *bull market*. No-one really knows why either animal is used). Despite falling sales in Europe, tobacco companies have been among the best to hold shares in (if you can stand the health implications) for equity investors. No one made that forecast.

You need two people for optimal pin selections. The first person should be blindfolded and wield the pin. The second person should write down the choices and move the share price page around between stabs to prevent too many ending up in one place. If you're not keen on pins, try listing all the stocks in the Footsie index on separate pieces of paper, putting them in a hat, and picking at random. That works just as well!

Some collective funds have hundreds of stocks. But masses of academic research shows that once you have around 20 shares in a portfolio, the costs involved with buying, selling, and monitoring more than that outweigh the advantages in greater risk spread.

'What do 1 do with the dividends?'

Buy and hold has a far greater chance of success over time than chancing your luck on a fund manager. But one useful fund manager function is to sort out all the paperwork and re-invest money from dividends and takeovers. Now that you're your own manager, you must do it yourself.

Some companies, including most investment trusts and a number of major quoted companies, have dividend re-investment schemes where payouts are automatically directed to buying fresh shares in the company. If they don't have these schemes, try banking the dividends in a special account; then wait until you have enough money to buy another share and wield the pin again. You can also use this account to squirrel away regular small amounts you've saved from your salary – again looking for eventual stock market investment.

'But what about takeovers and other corporate actions?'

The random portfolio is a long-term strategy. You can't expect it to prove itself from Day 1. It needs time. But over a long period, the stocks in your portfolio may be subject to change.

Yes, there'll be takeovers, in which case you may have to make the choice of accepting cash for your shares or receiving stock in the company making the bid. Opting for cash means you have to get your trusty pin out again and re-invest the money. Because the past 50 years have shown that shareholders in companies taken over do better than those in firms who launch bids, this is a good idea.

But the truly, utterly lazy random portfolio managers take the new shares. Doing so is easier because there are no decisions to make and no acquisition costs or stamp duty to pay, and there's no need to account for a possible Capital Gains Tax bill.

If you take the shares, know that you'll still have to send back a form if a choice is available. Otherwise, your shares will be compulsorily acquired under Companies Act rules, and you'll get cash or some other default option.

Companies may also launch *rights issues*, which raise cash from existing investors in return for new shares that are issued at a discount, a lower price than the current quote. As a random portfolio manager, you can ignore these appeals. In doing so, you may end up with some more cash. Rights issue shares that aren't taken up by the closing date are sold in the stock market at the best price the company's brokers can obtain. This money is then divided up among shareholders who failed to take up their rights issue stock in proportion to their holding level.

Knowing the Limits of a Random Choice Portfolio

The pin is a pretty good investment-choice tool, but it's not all powerful. It's not a guarantee against losses. No collective manager can insulate against a falling stock market, and neither can the random choice method investor.

You need a long time span

You need time and patience for a random choice approach to work. Remember that doing nothing for ten years is worth a lot. In rough terms, investing £10,000 into a market that doubles would give you about £19,700 after a decade of doing nothing. The £300 loss is down to purchase costs and stamp duty. In comparison, with an active fund manager taking 1.5 per cent (plus VAT in many instances) annual fees plus internal costs of dealing in and out of shares, you'd be lucky to have £17,000.

Paid-for managers would have to be really on the ball to overcome that cost handicap. A minority of them manage to do so. A few do even better. The problem is that you don't know which funds will succeed and which will fail, but the failures will always outnumber the winners over time.

Note that if a market stood still for ten years, your buy and hold portfolio would be worth about £9,700 after costs. The same investment with a high-cost collective manager would go down to just over £8,500. (All these figures ignore dividends, by the way. Dividends really boost your fortune if you re-invest them. Remember that active fund managers grab about half or more of your dividend to pay for their champagne lifestyle.)

You need to select your assets

The toughest take in any investment decision is to select your asset classes. You have to decide what proportion of your money you want to go where. The pin can't do this task for you. Sorry.

You need to allocate your savings between the big-picture items:

- ✔ Equities
- ✔ Bonds
- ✔ Property
- ✔ Cash

And although you can choose to ignore foreign holdings, bond and equity purchasers may have to fine-tune between UK and overseas, which may involve foreign currencies.

Watch out for so-called alternatives such as wine, paintings, stamps, coins, gold bricks, and commodities. These are not mainstream asset classes, but you could be exposed to people trying to get you to consider investing in them. They will usually claim they can make big money. Disbelieve them. If the deal is so good, just why do they want to share it with you?

 A compromise route for equities is to split your share cash and invest half via whatever the pin lands on and half into a low-cost global growth investment trust. The lowest costs come from Alliance, whose total costs come in at well under 0.4 per cent a year of your total investment with them.

Understanding Modern Portfolio Theory

Volumes upon volumes are devoted to Modern Portfolio Theory, which I call MPT for short. MPT is how rocket scientist academics back up the random choice, or pin portfolio, concept with a whole lot of clever stuff. Some of the theory is really, really difficult to understand, but you don't need a doctorate or even a spreadsheet to get the basics.

First, know that MPT isn't actually modern any more. It was first invented by Harry Markowitz in an economics dissertation for his doctorate degree at Chicago University in 1952. Markowitz incidentally went on to win a Nobel Prize in 1990, so his thinking wasn't a one-day wonder.

MPT starts off with the assumption that investors aren't wild speculators or saloon bar gamblers. They want returns, but want to avoid risk as far as they can, although they know all life has some risks. (After all, leaving cash under the mattress risks fire, vermin, and theft, and it earns nothing.) And regarding their return, most investors are content to aim somewhere near the average.

Traditional investors focus on analysing each component share or bond in a portfolio. They prefer Bank A to Bank B because they like the former's chief executive, or they prefer Oil Company C to Oil Company D because the latter is involved in exploration in an expensive (and unlikely to produce) area.

MPT goes beyond the individual risk and looks at the overall risks in the portfolio. The idea is to see how portfolio components react or correlate with each other. For example, a hot weather spell is good for breweries. People drink more beer when it's warm. A hot weather spell is bad for gas sales because central heating is turned off. So brewery shares rise, and gas producer stocks fall. High oil prices are good for fuel companies but bad for airlines, which need to stock up with their products. Here again, there is a low correlation. So a portfolio is better diversified against the unexpected by having one brewery, one gas company, one fuel firm, and one airline than by having four banks or four of anything else.

Now for the really clever bit. Instead of looking at the risks in individual stocks, you measure how they all react with each other and calculate the overall risks inherent in your portfolio. MPT says that you can then get a higher return from the whole thing compared to the risk of each component stock. Using something called the *efficient frontier*, you can build a portfolio that maximises the return while minimising the risk.

So instead of looking at companies like a traditional fund manager from a business point of view, including factors such as management, profits, and prospects, you look at how a share moves up and down in relationship to the market as a whole.

MPT needs time to work. It's like an insurance company. In a bad weather spell that may only last a day, an insurance company will lose money to flood and tornado claims. The company also knows that wooden homes are a greater fire hazard than those built of brick. So it has lots of risks. But although each policy may represent a huge loss, the insurance company knows that if it gets its maths and customer mix right, then it will make some money for its owners over time.

Insurance losses are more predictable than financial markets, so because you can't know the future, you can take a random choice.

MPT can help reduce the risks inherent in share choices. These are known as specific or non-market risks. But it can't help you select an asset choice or a market. Nor can it protect you against the systemic risk that happens when all or nearly all shares are on a falling path.

MPT assumes that investors want to minimise risks and not take wild punts. It doesn't work well among the penny dreadfuls or tipsheet favourites, where small investor hope and greed overcome reason and moderation.

Part IV
Property and Alternatives

In this part . . .

The biggest investment most people ever make is in property – their own. The running costs of the roof over your head plus the expense of paying off the mortgage each month eat up a large part of most people's earnings. As a result, many people only start serious investment after their mortgage is paid off. In a low-inflation environment, it makes sense to get shot of the home loan as quickly as possible.

But this part looks at going one stage further than just buying a property to live in. Property as an investment has been a neglected asset in the UK. But with many financial markets taking on an uncertain air, putting money into what you can see can be a worthwhile, lower-risk route for your savings. So this part goes through the pros and cons of getting into bricks and mortar as an investment. Buy to let residential property is an increasingly popular way of investing for the future. And investing in commercial property, such as office blocks and shopping centres, is also an option.

In addition to covering property investments, this part looks at alternative investments. I'm not talking about old-fashioned alternatives, like wine or vintage cars. I'm talking about a new style of alternatives, like spread bets, hedge funds, and traded options. Alternatives are becoming more and more publicised, so you need to know about them, but consider yourself duly warned up front: They're an avenue in which you can literally lose not just your shirt but everything else you own.

Chapter 19

Investing in Bricks and Mortar

· ·

In This Chapter

▶ Looking at the benefits and drawbacks of buying a property to rent

▶ Examining how to finance the property

▶ Choosing where to invest and matching the right tenant to the property's location

▶ Looking at avenues for attracting tenants in general

▶ Working through the tax return

▶ Starting out in commercial property

· ·

*B*uy to let has been the fastest growing investment class in the UK over recent years. From virtually nonexistent in the mid-1990s, it has grown, along with prices for houses and flats, to more than rival many collective investment schemes. And if you believe some of the media, buy to let is the most talked about subject at dinner parties, other than the prices of people's own property. After all, who wants to discuss their sagging shares when they can boast of their burgeoning buy to let portfolios?

This chapter gives you the need-to-know basics about investing in a buy to let property – the pros and cons as well as the mortgage, location, tenant, and tax issues. In addition, this chapter introduces you to the idea of investing in commercial property, in case you want to go that route.

The Pros and Cons of Buying Property to Rent

Buying to let involves buying a second (or third or fourth or sometimes even more) property in addition to the one you live in yourself. You rent this extra home to a tenant, and if all goes well, you earn rent once a month and see your initial capital investment rise as well. You gain an income and increase your wealth at the same time.

What is correlation?

Correlation is the new buzz word amongst investment professionals, and means whether one sort of asset, such as shares or property or commodities, goes up or down in tandem with another. You need to know this if you want to spread your money successfully to avoid putting it all in one basket. You need to aim at low correlation.

For instance, shares in one sector, such as banks or house-building companies, would have a very high correlation because they mostly all go up or down together, even if over a long period the better shares out-perform the less good shares. Likewise, assets such as shares and bonds have a high correlation because both do well out of falling interest rates and suffer when they rise. So if you buy one, you really buy the other – not much diversifying there, then.

But sometimes the correlation is low. One example is between residential property – that's people's homes – and commercial property (offices, shops, and factories). Rising (or falling) house prices have little or no connection to what is happening in commercial property markets. Another asset that is becoming popular, because it has little link to shares or bonds, is the commodity sector where investors try to second guess the price of everything from copper to oil to wheat. Rising prices here are often bad for companies if they can't pass them on to consumers. So when wheat prices rise, food manufacturers and retailers can be hit. That's low correlation in action.

The popularity of buy to let has grown because:

- ✔ Investors are fed up with shares that don't deliver.
- ✔ Investors want an investment with a solid feel.
- ✔ Investors are looking for an investment they can get involved in.
- ✔ Investors don't want to be tied to expensive fund managers who fail to perform.
- ✔ The whole idea appeals to many people who want to operate their own spare-time business.
- ✔ Mobile people need somewhere to live but don't want to buy a property that they may have to quit at short notice.
- ✔ Property prices in some areas have soared out of reach of first-time buyers. Because they must live somewhere, they rent.
- ✔ Interest rates for borrowers have become attractive, especially because lenders now see this activity as mainstream and no longer charge a huge interest rate premium for buy to let loans.
- ✔ Estate agents have set up units to deal with rented property.
- ✔ It's far easier now to borrow in order to purchase a property to rent even if you still owe money on your original residence.

Buy to let is not guaranteed. You may find yourself without a tenant, and you may lose money on the property because prices can fall as well as rise.

Some other potential drawbacks exist as well:

- ✔ You can't get your money out in a hurry. Selling a property may take a year or longer, especially if house price rises stall or go into reverse.

- ✔ You need to be hands on, even if you employ an agent to deal with tenants.

- ✔ Getting a portfolio of properties is very expensive. Most buy to letters just have one property, so there's no diversification.

- ✔ You can unbalance a financial strategy by putting too many of your investment eggs into one buy to let basket.

A move into buy to let is far bigger than any move into equities, bonds, or cash. You can't change your mind in a few months' time. You may also have to do all the work yourself, including checking and cleaning the property between tenants.

Before considering affordability or whether buy to let is the right type of investment for your needs, use the negative points of buy to let as a checklist to see whether the idea even appeals to you.

The Affordability Issue

Very few buy to let investors can afford to pay cash for their property purchase even though in some, admittedly not too desirable, locations, flats and houses can still cost under £20,000. And even if you could afford to pay cash, you should never tie up so much of your capital in a property that it leaves you without an emergency fund or the ability to buy into other investment assets if you think the time is right. So most buy to let investors borrow the money.

The price you see or even agree to is not the property's real price. You have to pay for stamp duty (in most cases on properties starting from £60,000, although for certain rundown areas on properties starting at £150,000), legal costs, possibly a mortgage arrangement fee, a survey, and if you're letting a furnished property, an allowance for everything from curtains and chairs to cookers and cutlery. These extra expenses typically soak up £5,000 and represent money you can't recoup. You may also find that borrowing to fund these extra start-up costs is difficult.

Before you can think about borrowing, you need to start with how much you can put down as a deposit and how much will be soaked up by other costs. And until you know what price range you can afford, you can't go out to look at potential investment properties.

The Buy to Let Mortgage

Lenders will want to look at the colour of your deposit. There are no 100 per cent buy to let loans (and if there were, the interest rates would be prohibitive).

How much can you borrow?

Banks and building societies calculate a figure called *Loan To Value (LTV)*, which is the largest proportion of the property price that they'll lend you – the rest comes from you as a deposit. The LTV generally varies from 70 per cent to 85 per cent. Because you fund the balance, you need cash of between 15 per cent to 30 per cent of the property value.

If you have £20,000 to put up as a deposit, the least generous lender with a 70 per cent LTV would add £46,666, so you could buy a property costing £66,666. (In case you are worried about the maths, I've rounded the pounds in this paragraph. Accurately speaking, 30 per cent of £66,666 is £19,999.80.) The lender with the highest LTV (85 per cent) would convert your £20,000 into a loan of £113,333, so you could look at properties costing £133,333, or twice as much as the meanest lender's offering.

A higher LTV gets you a bigger property bang for your deposit bucks. But larger deposits often mean lower interest rates.

How much will you actually get?

Your deposit and the LTV set a maximum. But you may not get that amount.

When you apply for a loan to buy a roof over your own head, the lender looks at the property itself to check its condition, the proportion of its value that you want to borrow, and most importantly your ability to repay the debt from your earnings. A typical formula is 3.5 to 4 times the main earner's salary (or only earner if that person has no partner) plus one time the second earner's or 2.5 to 3 times their joint earnings.

Because many buy to letters already have a mortgage banging hard against the limits of their earnings, buy to let lenders use a totally different way of judging how much they offer you because they see this as a business proposition property.

Instead of looking at how much you earn, buy to let lenders judge how much the property will earn for you. Most banks and building societies are now involved in this market, although some specialise in buy to let loans. *Moneyfacts* magazine is a good first source of information on who is lending and their basic terms.

The simplest formula is where you tell the lender how much rent you expect each month. Suppose that the amount is £500 per month, or £6,000 per year. The lender then calculates how big a loan that monthly or annual amount would back.

Suppose that interest rates stood at 6 per cent. Then your £6,000 per year would, on pure mathematics, pay back enough each month to back a £100,000 loan – irrespective of your personal income. But few lenders are stupid enough to go for that amount, especially after the 2007 credit crunch, which was caused – in part – by over-generous lending. Giving you all you might want assumes too much. Interest rates were falling for the best part of a decade, but then started to go up again, although they remain on the low side by the standards of the past 30 years. And there is no guarantee what will happen over the 10- to 25-year life span of a typical buy to let mortgage.

On top of that are nasty things called *voids*, which are months where you have no tenant and hence no income, or where your tenant has disappeared while owing more than the tenancy deposit. And to cap it all, there are other, unexpected, costs of ownership, such as repairs and maintenance.

Lenders insist that the rent more than covers the mortgage so you don't run on empty if something goes wrong. Typically, the rent will have to be anything from 1.3 times to 1.6 times the monthly outlay, a number called the *cover*. You can, however, find lenders who drop this requirement to a lower figure.

But while high mortgage cover sounds mean, it's really not. High mortgage cover protects you (as well as the lender) and gives you a cushion against the unexpected. Do you want to end up in *negative equity* where you owe the lender more than your property is worth? In that situation, the lender could come after you, even demanding that you sell your own home to finance your debt.

Buying to let is a business proposition. So there will be risks along the way.

Items to consider about the mortgage

Before you contact a mortgage company or mortgage broker for a buy to let loan, take a look at the following points. They'll save you time and stop dodgy mortgage firms trying to pull the wool over your eyes.

- ✔ **Fixed versus variable.** A fixed rate is where every payment for a set period is identical. Variable rates go up and down with interest costs in the economy at large. The fixed rate gives you security of payment for a period but sometimes at the cost of inflexibility and slightly higher interest rates. You can often set a fixed rate to match a tenancy agreement. Doing so is a good idea because raising a rent for a sitting tenant can be difficult.

- ✔ **Fees.** Some mortgages are fee-free, so you have nothing to pay initially. But this setup may be offset by higher costs later on. Otherwise, expect to pay from £500 to £1,500 as a fixed fee or between 0.5 per cent and 1 per cent of the loan. Fees are often set according to the rate you pay. A higher percentage means a lower fee, and vice versa.

- ✔ **Minimum amount.** Few lenders lend on properties worth less than £30,000 (if you can still find one!). If you want a portfolio of low-price dwellings, you must find a specialist lender, likely to be more expensive, or fund your purchases either from cash or by re-mortgaging your home.

- ✔ **Maximum loans** Many lenders are happy to lend on more than one property provided that you can come up with a deposit and finance the loan through the rent. Generally, lenders put a ceiling on the number of properties so that you can't have more than five or ten, and some lenders also limit the total lending on your portfolio at anything from £250,000 to £2.5 million.

Buy to let is considered to be a commercial activity. Buy to let loans aren't covered by either present or proposed Financial Services Authority rules, which offer safeguards against misleading sales techniques to mortgage customers who are buying their own home.

The Property Yield: A Comparison Tool

Buy to let is not a magic way to make money. You need to compare its attractions against other asset classes, such as cash, bonds, or shares.

Think twice about the 'free' property seminar

Newspapers, radio stations, and your junk mail (both e-mail and post) can be full of adverts for 'free' property seminars which claim they can make you a property millionaire overnight (or at least in just two to three years). Now, my idea of a millionaire is someone who can spend £1 million if they want to. Their idea of a millionaire is someone who owes the bank £1 million in property loans.

The initial two- to three-hour seminar is free, but expect a heavy sell and not much in the way of learning about property. Most seminars feature a method where you apparently buy at a discount and then take another mortgage when the price rises and spend the excess. You can repeat the process over and over again.

The seminar organisers claim to be property experts. Some may be, but most are better at selling the next stage – the weekend property investment course. You'll be told this will cost £4,999 but if you sign up there and then you'll only pay £1,999 – and you can bring a partner or friend for free. You might also be told you'll get free DVDs worth £999! The courses do have some educational elements. You will learn

something. But you'll learn even more with a book such as *Property Investing All-in-One For Dummies*, which will also leave you with an awful lot of change from £1,999!

But the spend doesn't stop there. Seminar firms try to get you to join Diamond or Gold clubs for a further £5,000 or so, sometimes double that, a year. They claim this gives you first pick of newly available flats. You can get that for nothing by registering your details with estate agents who specialise in newly built flats.

The seminar firms often have their own deals with property developers. And you could end up with a large number of new-build two-bedroom flats. Some city centres now have so many of these that they can't be let at all – let alone at a profit.

And while the value of your flat may go up on paper, finding a buyer is more difficult. Who wants to buy a second-hand flat when they can find the same thing new from a developer at a discount?

Treat the seminars like all get rich quick schemes – they only work for the organisers.

The easiest way is to look at the *gross yield*, what you get in rent before you spend on financing a loan or calculating the lost interest on cash you've tied up in the property.

For an example, take a £100,000 property rented at £500 per month. That's a £6,000 total for the year, so the yield should be 6 per cent.

But hold on. You may be spending on property management, and you always run the risk of voids. It's far better to estimate the rent on ten months per year. Now in this example, the annual rent falls to £5,000 and so the yield drops to 5 per cent.

The yield on property goes up and down with the property value after you've bought. If a property price doubles, your yield halves. And if the value goes down by half, your yield doubles. So far, this arrangement is like a bond. But property has one big difference. When prices rise, you may be able to increase the rent over time. And if the value falls, you may have to cut your rental expectations back to ensure that you find a tenant. High property prices make renting more attractive or, often, the only way to find a home for cash-strapped people.

Serious buy to letters go in for several properties. If you can't afford the deposits all at once, buy one property, hope it goes up in value, re-mortgage it to free up the capital for a new deposit, and keep repeating this exercise. But don't forget that the more properties you have, the greater your exposure to losses if prices fall or interest rates rise.

Location, Location, Location

Why is a two-bedroom flat in Belgravia some 20 times more expensive than a similarly sized flat in Barnsley, Bolton, or Blackburn? The answer is in the property dealer's mantra of location, location, location. People pay not just for what they get but for where they get it.

Much may depend on what type of tenants you'll feel happiest with. You can provide fairly basic accommodation to students, up-market premises to top managers from abroad on short-term UK contracts, or somewhere in between.

There's no substitute for walking around an area, sizing up the amenities, looking at estate agents, and viewing properties. You can sometimes get a discount by buying *off plan*, buying from a developer who's selling units in a new or refurbished property before the building is completed (and sometimes before it's even started).

Buying off plan can be buying blind. Don't do so just because there's an advertised incentive.

Matching tenants to the property's location

Here's how to match your preferred group with the right property type:

✔ **Students.** They want low-cost premises near their college or university. You may be competing with subsidised halls of residence. Expect a fair amount of cosmetic damage, supply low-cost furniture (preferably from second-hand shops), and factor in long vacations, in which case you may have no tenants. You may also have costs involved in installing fire and other safety regulations, both to satisfy the educational body and the local council. You also need to be aware of the Houses in Multiple Occupation rules which impose extra safety standards where you let a property to five or more people. Plans to reduce this number to as few as two who are 'unrelated' are being considered.

✔ **Employed young people.** These are the ideal target for many landlords. Look at areas where parking is easy and that have good employment opportunities. This group prefers to be near city centres and not stuck on a distant estate.

✔ **Families with young children.** Go for properties with gardens near schools. Public transport and access to shops can be important.

✔ **Professional high earners.** They want upscale properties and will pay for them. Many of these people will come to you through company deals, such as a firm renting your property for a long period and then installing members of its staff who need a roof.

Buying a house rather than a flat may involve costs in keeping gardens tidy, especially in void periods. You won't be popular with neighbours if you let gardens run wild. In some cases, local authorities can oblige you to keep the place in good order.

Considering properties in poor condition

Investment properties are cheap, but the term is generally a euphemism for houses and flats in poor condition. They can be profitable, however, provided that you pay for a full survey and then factor in the costs of bringing the property to a habitable condition. The period of repairs will bring in no rent but will involve outlays.

Here are a few additional, important points to keep in mind:

✔ You may have difficulty getting a mortgage until the repairs are carried out.

✔ Some investment properties are in rundown areas where you'll find it hard to attract tenants, as well as miss out on future property price rises.

✔ Some unscrupulous firms have been advertising a scam with *managed investment properties*. Here's how the scam works: You buy a number of low-cost dwellings for £100,000 or £150,000. The properties may be worth £15,000 each on the open market, but you end up paying £30,000 a time. The extra goes, according to these firms, to bringing the properties up to a minimum standard, including central heating and new wiring, so they can be let to housing associations. Sounds good, doesn't it? The scam is that there are no housing associations prepared to buy and the firms themselves carry out no repairs, leaving you with rubbish properties. Meanwhile the firms disappear with much of your cash.

How to Attract Tenants

Your buy to let is worthless without tenants. You also must be sure that the tenants are the type of people you want. The easiest way to find them is to hand the whole job over to a firm of estate agents who'll manage your property, find tenants, interview them, and take security deposits. The firm does these tasks in return for, typically, 15 per cent of the gross rent each month. Some agents specialise in finding companies that will engage in a long-term contract.

The estate agent's cut can be the difference between profit and loss. Successful buy to let investors need more than financial skills. You're managing a business, so if you hand management duties over to a third party, you need an agent you can trust on a long-term basis.

If you don't want to hire an estate agent to find tenants for you, consider using the suggestions in this section.

Advertise for them

Take a close look at the for-rent pages in your local newspaper. Doing so will give you some idea of how similar properties are priced. You can always go out and look at those properties or send a suitable friend if the flat or house is likely to appeal to a specific age group. You can then come up with a competitive and attractive advert.

Some people are put off if you only give a mobile phone number. Tenants are as entitled to know who they're dealing with as landlords.

Contact local employers

Big local firms and educational establishments are always looking for suitable properties for new staff to rent. Some of the companies may want to enter a long-term contract in which the company does all the work, including repairs, in return for a fixed-rent agreement.

Use word of mouth

Often, people ask proprietors of local corner shops and news agents whether they know of places to rent. This is a cost-free advertising opportunity. Libraries and some supermarkets also have free noticeboards.

Use the Internet

A number of sites list property for rent. But you should probably use this avenue as a backup, not a first method of attracting people.

If you list your property for rent on the Internet, draw up an application form for potential tenants to provide their name, current address, and work details. This form could be part of the online offering. Alternatively, get prospective tenants to e-mail you and then you can send them a form. Always probe to see whether the potential tenants have any financial problems. They should have a bank account (or pay a large up-front deposit in cash). In addition, always ask for references but always check them out thoroughly. Don't take them at face value because forging references on a computer is easy.

Buying Overseas

Ever thought about buying an investment property in Albania, Bulgaria, Croatia, or even the Cape Verde islands? Enterprising property developers cite these, and other locations, as the 'next big place'. But just because they say that, don't throw caution to the wind. After all, their job is to promote what they intend to build.

You can even take 'free' inspection trips where you end up seeing a field and set of drawings, and are then persuaded to put a deposit down.

The difficulty is that while your developer is building, so too are many others. The result is over-supply and under-demand. Developers don't care because they have your money and you've signed a contract.

If you want to know what happens when building gets out of control, take a look at property prices from 2005 onwards in former hot spots such as Spain and Florida.

This brings us back to location and demand. Central London, central Paris, or central Manhattan property is always going to be expensive because there isn't much of it, and loads of people want to have a central city home. In places that have miles and miles of empty fields and not much in the way of planning controls, you have to take a reality test, look at the location and demand, and the future supply before buying property there as an investment.

Of course, if you want a second home in any of these places, then you're not buying as an investment.

The Tax Issue

As far as HM Revenue & Customs is concerned, buy to let is a business and not an investment. You have to pay income tax on your profits from rentals, but you can deduct interest and the cost of adverts, repairs, insurance, and council tax. What's left is added to your other income.

You're allowed to make a loss. And in some circumstances, losses can be carried forward against future profits.

You need to keep records. And you must send a balance sheet to HMRC if your gross receipts exceed £15,000 in any tax year.

Many people employ an accountant (the fees can be offset against tax). But always agree on terms first.

If or when you sell, you'll be liable to Capital Gains Tax on any profit, although you can deduct your annual Capital Gains Tax allowance if you've not used it elsewhere. In some circumstances, you can deduct losses. (Yes, there will be setbacks at some time, so don't get too complacent or optimistic.)

You have to voluntarily tell HMRC that you're engaged in buy to let. The tax people won't accept excuses such as 'I was waiting for a tax form' or 'I didn't know I had to declare this'.

Commercial Property Investments

Commercial property, such as offices, factories, warehouses, and retail premises, has been a lower-risk investment with a good return. But most of the investment has been indirect, through pension funds and with-profits policies.

Commercial property ownership is generally structured so that you need a minimum £50m to £100m to be considered a player – and even more to get a really diversified portfolio. However, some commercial property investment opportunities exist for those whose fortunes lack most of the zeroes of the standard sums in this investment area, usually via a specialist collective vehicle.

What's good about commercial property?

In a nutshell, here are the benefits of investing in commercial property:

✔ Rental yields are up with higher-risk corporate bonds but with less likelihood of financial problems.

✔ Rents tend to increase; some properties have automatic increases every five years.

✔ Demand for top-class property remains high. Property buyers like the term 'primary' which can be used for a location or the quality of the building, although the two often go together as you tend to put up the best buildings on the most attractive sites.

✔ Overseas investors like the solidity of UK property.

✔ Property values tend to at least keep up with inflation.

What's bad about commercial property?

In a nutshell, here are the drawbacks of investing in commercial property:

✔ It's illiquid, so buying and selling can take ages.

✔ Returns are very susceptible to interest rates. A substantial increase can wreck the best forecasts.

✔ So-called secondary properties, the rubbish that top-class tenants avoid, can be difficult to let. If you want to imagine 'secondary property', think of rundown shopping parades, decrepit factories, or office blocks that no big organisation would want to be based in.

✔ Types of property can go out of fashion. Buildings can become obsolescent or subject to new, and expensive, environmental regulations.

How to invest in commercial property

You may already have some exposure to commercial property through insurance-based with-profits or managed funds. Many packaged UK investments are also likely to have a percentage of property company shares in the portfolio. But if you want more, ways are available to get them other than going out and buying yourself an office block or retail development.

Property company shares

A number of property-owning companies are listed on the London Stock Exchange. Buying and selling their shares works the same as with any other quoted equity.

Some property-owning companies have enormous portfolios, but others focus on one type of property, such as office blocks or out-of-town retail parks. Bigger firms tend to concentrate on prime property, which they rent to top household-name firms. But a number of firms go for secondary properties, hoping to make more money out of cheap buildings that they rent to less-attractive tenants. Secondary property is generally more volatile.

Investors look at two factors beyond the portfolio constituents:

- ✔ **Dividend yield.** This is usually higher than the market average, with the highest returns coming from property firms that go for secondary properties. The normal investment rules apply. If the dividend yield is high, then the capital gains are likely to be lower for the same level of risk.

- ✔ **Discount.** This is the gap between the value of the property firm's underlying portfolio less borrowings and its stock market capitalisation. The stock market value should generally be lower than the worth of the buildings owned.

Most property companies are now officially Real Estate Investment Trusts (REITs). These offer the firms a fairer tax setup than they had before. REITs were introduced in January 2007, after which the commercial property shares market went into a tailspin. That was probably because the value of these firms had gone up a lot beforehand in the expectation that REITs would work a miracle. They didn't, because all REITs do is to help a bit with the tax.

This situation is like the old stock market saying 'buy on the rumour and sell on the fact'. Everyone bought while REITs were seen as a good idea for the future, pushing up prices. But the reality wasn't as exciting as the prospect so investors took a second look at property shares, decided the price rise was overdone, and then sold, sending share values down again.

Property unit trusts

These are standard unit trusts offered by a small number of investment groups to those wanting a specialist fund. They are a mix of direct investments in property, property shares, and cash. The minimum investment is usually £500 or £1,000. You can generally have your money back without notice when you want to sell, but one of the problems of dealing in property is that selling takes some time if a trust needs cash for paying out customers who want to exit. One way around this is to keep a fair stash of cash in the fund, but when that runs out, trusts deter withdrawal sales by adjusting the price downwards. The small print of their rule book says that they can do this, and many did in late 2007.

Property bonds

Property bonds take a minimum £1,000 to £5,000. They're insurance based but with only enough life cover to convince HMRC of their status. So this life cover is as little as possible, usually just a nominal 1 per cent of their value. There's also a bid-offer spread of around 5 to 6 per cent. Much of it goes to the seller in commission, so don't forget to demand a rebate.

These bonds usually invest in properties rather than shares or cash. In some cases, investors may have to wait up to six months for a withdrawal because the fund must sell properties if too many people want their money back.

Property bonds have nothing to do with _holiday property bonds_, a form of timeshare where you can use holiday accommodation in proportion to your holding. Holiday property bonds aren't intended as a serious investment.

Enterprise Property Zones

Enterprise Property Zones (or EPZs) are areas where the government is anxious to attract new commercial buildings, so it offers forms of tax relief to do the attracting.

Investors with a minimum £5,000 to £10,000 can buy into these projects and gain tax relief on their investment. Investors who borrow to raise the cash can also set off interest payments against tax.

The rental income is paid without any tax deduction, but it must be declared.

The tax relief that comes with EPZ investment sounds like a good idea. But there's no guarantee that the property will be profitable, and investors usually sign up for 25 years. That's a very long time, especially because no clear or easy exit exists. You could be left with a property lemon. This option is for serious investors with serious money and is best approached by taking serious advice from a professional property person!

Chapter 20

Delving into Exotic Investments

*I*f you have a nervous disposition, you may want to skip this chapter. It's all about how you can literally lose not just your shirt but everything else you own. It covers the one investment opportunity in this book from which you can end up with *minus nothing*, because not only can your investment money go down to zero, but you also can end up owing cash over and above those losses. Very financially painful!

That sounds unbelievably awful, and it can be. So why should you grit your teeth and read this chapter? Because these types of investment, which many people now call *alternatives*, are becoming more publicised. They include contracts for difference, spread bets, traded options, and covered warrants, and because of their more prominent publicity nowadays, you need to know about them if only to say no to their apparent charms.

Don't confuse these types of investment with fashioned alternative investments, such as art, wine, or vintage cars. These are the new style of alternatives – investments based on stock, commodity, and currency markets where you go nowhere near buying the shares, metals, or foreign exchange contracts on which they're based. Note, too, that some of these deals are called *derivatives* because they're derived from real financial securities.

What fans and critics say about alternatives

Fans of alternative investments say that they're cheaper and more flexible than conventional investments. These enthusiasts claim that alternative investments are the future, often pointing to overseas countries where their use is more widespread.

Detractors say that alternative investments offer rapid, high-risk routes to financial wipeout; that you should treat them no differently than a bet on an outsider in the 3.30 at Epsom; and that although they give the veneer of investment sophistication, the only winners are the bookies, specialist dealers, and others who sell these schemes.

All the financial schemes in this chapter are for experienced investors who can afford to make some losses. I reckon you should always stick to what you know. It's better to be safe than sorry, whatever the adverts for these products make out!

Getting into Gear for a Faster Ride

The big difference between the investments in this chapter and elsewhere in this book is *gearing*, an arrangement in which a set sum of investment money potentially works harder for you but involves greater risk.

To understand gearing, look at the difference between someone on foot and a cyclist. A pedestrian may cover 5 kilometres in an hour. But pedalling a bike, the same person may ride 10, 15, 20, or more kilometres in an hour. The difference is due to the fact that the cyclist has gears that transform the leg movement into greater distance once their physical effort goes through the mechanism to the back wheel. And the higher the gear used, the farther the person will go. The energy expended may be the same as when walking or even less if the cyclist freewheels.

Logically, it'd be better if everyone cycled. However, bikes have disadvantages and higher risks. It's easier to fall off a bike than to fall down as a walker. The gears are great when the going is good on the flat or downhill, but life can get tough on steep, uphill climbs. You get hit worse by bad weather. And cycling has costs.

With financial gearing, you buy an alternative or derivative of a share, a share index, or bond for a fraction of its price. If the value of the underlying security goes the way you want, your investment moves up very rapidly in percentage terms. Get it wrong, and you can face total wipeout (or worse).

To help you understand the concept, consider a simple example of a winning alternative investment scenario:

- ✔ **Conventional investment:** You have £1,000, and you buy 1,000 shares in a company called ABC plc at 100p each. The shares go to 110p. You sell and earn 10 per cent on your money, giving a £100 profit. Ignoring stamp duty, dealing costs, and the spread between bid and offer prices, you now have £1,100, a 10 per cent gain.

- ✔ **Alternative investment:** Instead of buying the shares, you go for a derivative where you only put down 10 per cent of the purchase price. You now have the equivalent of £10,000 worth of shares in ABC plc for £1,000. The shares go from 100p to 110p. But instead of having 1,000 shares, which have gained 10p, you now have 10,000, so your profit is £1,000. Again ignoring costs, your £1,000 has turned into £2,000, a 100 per cent gain.

Now look at how you can lose:

- ✔ **Conventional investment:** Your £1,000 buys 1,000 shares in ABC plc at 100p each. The shares fall to 90p. You sell. You have lost £100 but still have £900 left. Not good news but not a total disaster, either. You could've instead held on, hoping for an eventual uplift and taken the dividends as well.

- ✔ **Alternative investment:** Your £1,000 buys 10,000 shares in ABC plc at 100p each. The shares fall to 90p. You've now lost 10,000 times 10p, or £1,000, so your investment is worthless. Most alternatives don't pay dividends, and they have time limits, so you can't hold on for the longer term looking for a rebound.

  Now suppose that the shares fall to 80p. With all alternative products, you lose your money. But with some alternative products, such as spread betting, it gets worse. You not only give up your £1,000 (equal to the first 10p of the loss on each share), but you also owe the spread bet company £1,000 for the second 10p loss per share. If ABC plc suddenly goes bust and the shares are worthless, you have to pay the whole £10,000!

Hedging Your Bets

If gearing is one side of a coin, where you increase your risk and, hopefully, your reward, then hedging is the other side of the coin. *Hedging* is just like insurance: You protect what you have by paying a premium to someone else. If all goes well, you continue to enjoy the gains from your investment. But if the worst comes to the worst, the person who accepted your payment has to make good the losses. With hedging, you dampen down or eliminate your risk in return for losing part of any potential gain.

Suppose that your 10,000 shares in ABC plc are worth £10,000, and you'll need that money in three months' time to buy a car. The easiest route would be to sell now and put the £10,000 into the bank. But you think that ABC shares will soar upward over that time, although, naturally, you can't be sure and you don't want to jeopardise your car purchase.

The solution is to hedge. A variety of ways are available to do so, but in essence they come down to two methods. One way is to exchange the hoped-for gain for a premium from another investor by agreeing that you'll sell the shares for 110p each in three months' time. You'll gain 10 per cent on the present price (which is more than the interest you'd earn in the bank), and the purchaser gets them for 110p each instead of the 130p or so that they may cost in three months' time. In this scenario, you lock in your present value and make a profit.

Another way is to pay someone a premium such as 10p a share in return for a promise that the person will buy the shares from you in three months' time at 100p. You get your 100p less 10p no matter how far the shares fall. But you structure this deal in such a way that you get the full price if the shares rise – less the 10p premium you've already paid.

Trading Traded Options

Here's the good news about options: Unlike with some of the fancy stock market structures in this chapter, with options you can't lose more than you invest. And you can make a lot of money in a short time. The bad news? Many (probably most) option trades expire worthless. But then what do you expect from a geared investment?

What is an option?

An *option* is a promise, backed by the stock market, that you can buy or sell a set number of shares (nearly always in parcels of 1,000 shares) in a company at a fixed price between the start day and the expiry date. You can generally choose between a number of expiry dates and a number of strike prices. A *strike price* is the value the shares have to hit before your option has any value. Remember that while this promise comes from the market, it does, of course, need another investor (or investors) to be on the other side of the deal. The company whose shares are involved will know nothing of all this.

Options are available on all sorts of investments, including bonds, shares, and currencies. Equity options are the best known and the most likely to be chosen by private investors.

Worldwide, you can choose from thousands of options. In the UK, there are traded options on nearly all the shares in the FTSE 100 index, as well as on the index itself.

You have the right but aren't obliged to buy the shares no matter what happens, and that's what makes options more user friendly than many other derivative investments. If you don't like what's going on in your option, you can abandon it (and your option money). But if everything's going well, you can lock in your gains. You don't have to wait until the option date comes up.

Options can be traded at any time before expiry. They are worthless on expiry, so the nearer you get to that date, the less valuable they become – a process called *time value*, where you pay for hope. The amount you pay for the option is called the *premium*, and it goes up with time value.

What are call prices and put prices?

Each option series for an underlying share has two sets of prices:

- ✔ **Call prices.** These prices are for investors who think the shares will go up. They give the right but not the obligation for an investor to buy the underlying shares.

- ✔ **Put prices.** These prices are for investors who think the shares will go down. They give the right but not the obligation for an investor to sell at a pre-agreed price.

A call option example

Say that phone group BT has options that expire on a fixed date each month. You can buy up to one month ahead or for longer periods. A snapshot on one day with a stock market price of 194p per share shows that you can choose a 180p or 200p strike price. The 180p strike price is 'in the money' for call option purchasers because the underlying shares are more valuable. The 200p strike price is 'out of the money' and has no immediate value because it's higher than the current stock market price.

If you want to buy the call option at 180p expiring in one month's time, it costs 17.25p per share. So if the share price between now and then tops 197.25p, you have a profit.

If you think the price will go up even further, you will do better buying the 200p strike price series. Here, a one-month call option costs 5.5p. If BT tops 205.5p over the next month, you win. If not, your loss can't be greater than 5.5p a share.

Investors who want to take a chance on BT over longer periods pay more for their options – around 2p for an extra month.

A put option example

If you hold the shares and want to put a floor under the price, then take out a put option. Doing so gives you the right but not the obligation to sell so you receive a set price. With the BT example, guaranteeing a right to sell in around a month at 200p costs 11p a share.

Have a look at some possibilities:

- The BT price falls to 150p. You win! You collect 200p for each share less the 11p premium. So you get 189p.

- The BT price stays unchanged at 194p. You lose. You get 200p for each share less the 11p premium. So you end up with 189p.

- The BT price soars to 250p. Your right to sell is worthless. You lose 11p per share, but some investors think this worthwhile to buy insurance-style protection. The share price might have gone the other way.

Always study how traded option premiums move for a wide number of underlying shares before dipping your toe in this particular water. Options that have expiry dates each month rather than every three months are more heavily traded and tend to have lower dealing charges. Many strategies exist, but all involve either gearing up your investment or hedging your risk.

Strategies involving selling shares you don't own can bring limitless losses.

What is option volatility?

Winning on traded options requires having a good feel for the direction of a particular share. Will it go up or down? But you also need to know about *volatility*, the amount the shares jump around. High-volatility shares have unstable prices. The more volatile a share is, the greater the chance of the option making money but the higher the cost of the option. It's like motor insurance. The 20-year-old with the Ferrari pays a lot more for cover than the 60-year-old with a Ford Fiesta because the younger person is more likely to claim.

You never own the shares or other securities with traded options and other forms of derivative trading. So you have no shareholder rights. You don't get dividends either.

Taking a Gamble with Spread Betting

Died in the wool gamblers used to bet on which of two moths would hit the light bulb first and frazzle. But long gone are the days of just betting on winners in horse or dog races or football matches or moths. Nowadays, there are bets on the total number of runs scored in a cricket match or points total at rugby. Both of these bets are irrespective of which side scored them. You can take a punt on when the first goal will be scored in a football match or the number of players sent off for foul play in a month. You can take bets on house price moves. And you can bet on shares, bonds, currencies, stock market indexes, and other financial matters.

If there are numbers, there can be a spread bet. Whether the numbers are total points scored in a rugby match or a share price, all spread betting works in the same basic way:

1. **The bookmakers try to second-guess the most likely result.**

   Perhaps it's a total of 50 points in a rugby match or a probable price of 50p for a share in a week's time.

2. **The bookmakers create a spread either side.**

   In this case, it could be 47–53, which is called the *quote*.

3. **The punters must decide to be either long or short of the spread.**

   If they go *long*, they think that the match will be more high-scoring or the share price will be higher than the bookmakers' quotes. If they go *short*, they're thinking of a low-scoring game or a poor share price.

4. **The punters bet so much per point or penny.**

   There might be a £10 minimum.

5. **When the match is over or the share bet reaches its expiry date, the punters look at the result.**

In this example, assume £10 a point bet:

- ✔ Say that the result is 60. Those who were long win. They multiply their stake by the points over 53 to calculate their gain. So they collect £70. Those who were short lose. The bookmaker starts counting at 47, so they have to pay £130.

- ✔ Say that the result is 40. Those who shorted the bet receive £70, and those who went long lose £130.

- ✔ Say that the result is 50. All bets are lost, and all participants owe the bookmaker £30.

Spread betters on financial instruments can lose limitless amounts. They may have to put up margin money each day to cover losses if they want the bet to continue to the expiry date. But punters can take profits or cut losses whenever they want. They can also re-set limits one way or the other. Spread betting is leveraged, so there can be big gains and big losses without putting up money to buy the underlying investment.

Worried that the value of your home will drop or that your dream property will soar in price well out of reach? By taking out a spread bet on the Halifax House Price Index, you can protect yourself. If you worry that property values will soar, take a spread bet on the index rising. And if you think that prices are about to plummet, take a bet on the index falling. Of course, the Halifax index is an average across the country and won't exactly replicate what's happening to the prices that concern you. And know that if you get it wrong, it could cost you more than your shirt!

Limiting Your Betting Losses with Binary Betting

The warning words *potentially unlimited losses* accompany almost everything written about spread betting and are often enough to make even those who like a flutter run a country mile.

Binary bets are different. They let you take a gamble on financial markets knowing that you can lose no more than your stake. The other side of this coin is that you also know exactly how much you could win.

With a binary bet, you're either right or wrong. You could, for instance, bet that the stock market will be higher (or lower) at midday – or any time and any share as well as the Footsie index. You're quoted 33–36. If you think it is going up, then you bet a stake (£1, for example) at 36, costing £36. If you're right you gain £64, based on 100 less 36. Whether your prediction is right by a small or a large amount doesn't matter. If you're wrong, you lose £36. If you think it is going down, your stake is £67, based on 100 less 33. Those who are correct pick up £33, whereas losers give up £67. A quote of under 50 means that the bookmaker thinks the market will fall; over 50 implies that the market is likely to rise.

Getting Contracts for Difference – for a Different Kind of Deal

Contracts for difference, or *CFDs* as they're known to stock market insiders, are a low-cost route for frequent share buyers who want a deal with, well, a difference. Instead of buying a share and holding it, the CFD investor comes to a deal with a CFD provider (usually a specialist broker) that at the end of the contract, one side or the other will pay the difference between the opening price of the contract and the closing price. Some 20 per cent of all UK equity deals are now through CFDs.

You can trade CFDs on most large UK companies, share price indexes, and many foreign companies. You can take a position in a price fall as well as hope for a rising price. And because all you're paying is the difference, you get the advantage of leverage.

At the start of the contract, you may only have to put up a small proportion of the contract value. This amount is often around 10 to 20 per cent, depending on how volatile the share is. So expect a lower percentage for a dull utility share and a higher amount for a technology stock. But because your losses could eventually exceed this margin money, brokers often insist that you deposit a minimum £10,000 before trading.

How CFDs work

Suppose that you decide shares in ABC plc look cheap at 100p and expect them to rise over the next week. You want £10,000 worth. Instead of paying dealing charges of around 1.5 per cent, plus stamp duty, plus the cost of the underlying stock, which would add up to £10,200, you go to a CFD broker. Here, you put up 10 per cent (ABC is a big company that's not volatile), and you 'borrow' the other £9,000 from the CFD provider in return for interest at a pre-set but variable level.

For a week, this arrangement might cost £10. You'll probably pay 0.25 per cent commission on the whole £10,000 in costs (£25). There's no stamp duty.

A week later, ABC shares can be sold for 120p, putting the value of your holding up to £12,000. You receive a £2,000 profit less £30 selling commission (that's 0.25 per cent of £12,000). Subtracting this amount plus your interest and buying costs gives a total profit of £1,935. (Note, though, that if ABC shares had gone down to 80p, your bill would've been £2,000 plus all the £65 costs.)

You can also profit if you correctly guess that a share price or an index will fall in value. This scenario is called *short trading*. Suppose that you think ABC plc is going to fall in value. If you're right, you gain. If you're wrong, you lose. It's simply the preceding example turned on its head!

The benefits and drawbacks of CFDs

Here are some plus points and drawbacks of CFDs:

- You can go long (expect the price to rise) or short (expect it to fall).
- You have a wide range of shares and indexes to choose from.
- Commissions are low.
- You leverage your stake – bigger profits but bigger losses.
- There is no stamp duty.
- You are gambling so you can forget Capital Gains Tax or offsetting losses against capital gains elsewhere.
- You can hold CFDs for very short periods.
- They are bad value for long-term investors.
- You receive dividend payments where applicable.
- Investors who go short must pay the dividend to the broker.
- Not all brokers allow you to place a *stop loss*, a device that automatically closes a losing position to prevent even more of your cash from bleeding away.
- A few brokers allow free trading.
- If you buy CFDs, the Financial Services Authority will consider you to be a professional and experienced investor, even if you aren't. So you can say goodbye to a large slice of your consumer protection.

Don't ignore the commission and other costs, even if they sound small. CFDs are intended for short-term trading. But frequent traders face huge costs. If you have a £10,000 deposit and trade on 10 times leverage (that's playing with £100,000), each buy and sell round trip will cost you 0.5 per cent of the amount you're playing with at most brokers. That's £500. If you trade just once a week for a year at this level, you end up paying your broker an amazing £26,000 plus interest (say £6,000). You've got to be really good to make money after all of this.

Understanding Warrants

Warrants have been around for years, at least in their traditional form. They often came with investment trust launches as a free gift for the original investors (this sort is rare now because investment trust launches are few and far between). The traditional warrant gives the right but not the obligation to buy a set number of shares in the underlying trust (sometimes in other sorts of quoted concerns) for a fixed sum during a set period each year for a number of years.

A typical launch deal might be to offer one warrant for every five shares bought at the original 100p. A £1,000 investor would get 200 warrants. These warrants then give the option to buy the underlying shares for 100p no matter what the price each September for seven years. After seven years, the warrants expire worthless.

But warrant investors in this particular trust aren't limited to trading in September. While the warrants have value, they can be bought or sold at any time on the stock market. They're a long-term gamble on the price rising.

How about an example? Say that the warrant you received as part of an investment trust flotation allows you to buy the actual shares for 100p in any July for the next five years. The underlying shares are worth 200p at the moment, but you want out. So another investor buys the warrant for 110p. The 10p extra is compensation for the hope value. Four years later, the shares stand at 400p. The warrant holder converts into shares. The bill is 100p, plus the 110p for the warrant, plus the interest cost of holding the warrant (there are no dividends), but the final reward is 400p. Not bad! But note that if the trust shares had slumped to 50p and stayed there, the 100p-a-time warrant money would've been wasted. Disaster!

Note that *covered warrants* are the latest in the menagerie of high-risk, high-reward geared derivative products, which allow you to bet equally on falling as well as rising prices. The good news is that a warrant investor (whether of traditional or the new covered versions, which can be created on any major company or share price index) can't lose more than his or her original investment no matter how bad the forecast turns out to be.

Note, too, that warrant producers have also come up with *certificates*, which are just as artificial and let investors go short as well as long. But unlike the other exotic creations in this chapter, they aren't geared so you can't gain or lose more than you would with conventional shares. What you buy is what you get.

So what's the point?

- ✔ Low cost
- ✔ No stamp duty
- ✔ Can be created for a sector, such as banks or pharmaceuticals
- ✔ No annual management fees

Growing an Interest in Commodities

Commodities are all the raw materials that we use both to make things and for our food. Besides oil, commodities include metals such as silver, copper, and aluminium, and *softs*, which are generally foodstuffs, that include wheat, sugar, coffee, and orange juice.

Prices fluctuate according to the very basic laws of supply and demand. When a commodity is in short supply, perhaps because industry wants more copper or the sugar crop was hit by a tornado, the price goes up. And when supply increases, maybe because a huge new silver mine goes into production or the year sees a bumper wheat harvest, the price goes down.

In 2007, wheat shortages in the shops have led to more expensive baguettes for the French, pricier pasta in Italy, and dearer porridge for Scotland. People have blamed these shortages on everything from bad harvests to the Chinese wanting a change in diet from rice. Even the fact that more people are eating meat has been blamed, because cattle feed for meat production uses up much more grain than producing the same amount of food for vegetarians would require.

Commodity traders try to second-guess the future trend of prices, usually three months to a year ahead. If they get their sums right, they can make money whether prices are due to rise or fall. If they get their sums wrong, they can lose enormous sums. If you've ever seen the 1983 film *Trading Places*, where a snobbish investor and a wily street con artist find their positions reversed, you'll know just how frightening commodity markets can be.

Some people think commodity trading will be the route to gaining a fortune over the next few years. They think this will be a new asset class that could be as important as property or bonds.

But remember that as raw material prices go up, miners and farmers are encouraged to increase production, which brings down prices again. Conversely, if prices fall, producers cut back especially on anything that is expensive to mine or farm. Eventually, this reduction cuts the amount of that commodity on the market, prices stabilise, and then, perhaps, rise.

Understanding commodities is a good move if these prices do become more important. You can't really expect to trade yourself, however. Commodity trading is almost all for professionals as you can literally lose your shirt in this area.

However, you can find some ways in for non-professionals where your potential losses are limited to your investment instead of being open-ended. One way in is to find a unit trust that invests in companies involved in producing raw materials, such as mining firms and food manufacturers, or shares that benefit from greater activity on farms such as tractor manufacturers. Or you could find one of the new breed of exchange-traded funds which specialise in metals or soft commodities, or even farm machinery.

If you're prepared for a really up-and-down ride, some of the spread betting firms will let you take a punt on commodity prices (see the section 'Taking a Gamble with Spread Betting' for more info). But always practise first. Most spread betting sites have a 'dry run' facility where you can try it out without needing to lay out money. Of course, if you win on a dry run, you don't collect anything!

Part V
The Part of Tens

'Ah — here comes Mr Greystoke,
our Green Fund manager.'

In this part . . .

The Part of Tens contains two vital chapters. I start with how to deal with others – the middle people who so often stand between you and your investment choices. Whether they call themselves brokers, advisers, or consultants, they can make or break an investment strategy as well as your savings. You don't have to listen to them. But it's difficult to avoid them. So I offer ten tips for finding a good adviser.

In this part's second chapter, I take a look at an even more difficult factor in your investment life. And that's you. Before you invest even one penny, you need to read and apply ten helpful suggestions relating specifically to you.

Chapter 21

Ten Tips for Finding a Good Adviser

In This Chapter

▶ Finding a good adviser

▶ Working out value for money from waste of money

▶ Checking out adviser expertise

▶ Looking for a long-term relationship

What's the point of having a financial adviser? For a growing number of investors, there's absolutely no point. Such investors have read this book, understand how investments work, know the limitations of forecasting, might like the idea of beating the so-called experts with the strategy of buying what they're selling and selling what they're buying, and can carry out all their transactions online at the lowest possible cost.

But most of us do like a hand to hold sometimes or a bit of help with something new. Or we simply like to seek validation or otherwise for a course of action we've worked out for ourselves. Masses of people out there are willing to do these things and earn some money as a result.

Investment advisers are divided into the good, the bad, and the downright ugly (just like professionals in any other field). This chapter provides ten tips for sifting out the useless and the harmful.

Know the Difference between Tied and Independent Advisers

Financial advisers who deal with the public, as opposed to professional investors such as insurance companies and unit trusts, must show you their status under the Financial Services Act. The essential difference between these two types of professionals involves the terms *tied* and *independent*, a distinction that came into force in 1988.

Essentially, a *tied adviser* works for one investment or insurance company and can't comment on the workings or investment products from any other. An *independent financial adviser (IFA)* can discuss any investment from any firm that they want. But that doesn't mean IFAs know everything about everything. Some pretend to do so, but others wisely restrict themselves to advising on what they're really good at.

Most banks and building societies employ a tied sales force, which only promotes the often-narrow range of products on sale from that institution. These tied agency firms may carry the same name as the bank or building society – Abbey or Nationwide, for example, or another brand name. So Lloyds TSB sells Scottish Widows and Barclays deals in Legal & General. Some life companies, such as Zurich or Co-op Insurance Services, also sell all or most of their products through tied agents.

Not all tied agency firms carry the same name as the investment group whose products they sell.

But nowadays the waters are being muddied. Under new rules, a small number of banks and other firms are multi-tying, meaning that they are selling products from a number of sources but are still far from independent. Treat these firms as tied.

Always ask tied agents what advantages they can offer to make up for the lack of variety. They'd have to promise a really good deal to get my vote.

IFAs can't claim all the moral high ground here, however. Some big firms take a radio play list approach to investment. The top people in the firm seek out a restricted number of investment deals and push them mercilessly. Sometimes, play list investment firms have done deals with IFAs.

Still, their independent status does allow them to go beyond the play list if you push them. So refuse to take their first ideas as their final ideas. Some independents effectively use a restricted number, however.

Look at Adviser Listings and Ask Questions

Why look at listings when so many advisers are screaming for your attention from the media and Internet? Because there's nothing like a local person whose office you can visit and check out. Start with your local phone directory. Look under *financial advisers*.

Work backward through the financial adviser listing, starting with Z and ending with A. People at the end of listings often get ignored. But avoid anyone who doesn't give a full address. Remember to check the Financial Services Authority Web site at www.fsa.gov.uk if you're in any doubt.

Financial advisers are no different from anyone else you employ to help you. You should receive an initial free consultation. Use this time to work out whether potential advisers are organised or haphazard, and whether they listen to what you want or try to impose their views on you.

Treat an adviser like a partner. Most advisers expect you to know nothing, so if you do your homework first, you'll have a good chance of getting what you want rather than their default option.

Most financial advisers like to quiz you about your life, your ambitions, your pension, and, most importantly for them, how much money you may have to invest. Turn the tables on them. At the first meeting, ask as many questions about them as they ask of you. Here are some questions to ask:

- ✔ **What's your preferred customer profile?** This is a good early question because some advisers specialise in high-value clients or the elderly or taxation-linked investments.

- ✔ **How long have you been in business under your present firm's name?** Avoid someone who has changed jobs too often. Check the FSA register (www.fsa.gov.uk/register) if you have doubts.

- ✔ **How many clients do you have?** A registered individual can't really deal with more than a few hundred clients. Any more than that risks a one-size-fits-all approach.

- ✔ **Do you have a regular client newsletter?** If so, ask for back copies from the past three to five years to reflect a variety of investment scenarios.

- ✔ **What sort of financial problems or areas of investment do you not want to get involved with?** This is like the first question but from a different viewpoint. It's useful toward the end of the initial conversation. Advisers who say they really can't help in your circumstances should get a plaudit for honesty.

- ✔ **If I sign up, will I get face-to-face advice when I want it or have to phone a call centre?** Many advisers are now cost-cutting by reducing all but their biggest clients to a 'press one for pensions, press two for investment funds' approach.

- ✔ **What about regular financial checkups?** Ask how often the adviser provides them and whether you must pay extra for them.

- ✔ **Are you a member of an independent financial adviser network?** If so, ask whether the network just takes care of regulatory and other paperwork or whether it dictates a list of investments. The former is preferable.

Don't forget that you should always make a final check on an adviser via the Financial Services Authority Web site. The site shows not just whether an adviser is registered under the regulatory regime but also whether the adviser has been disciplined.

Work Only with Advisers Who'll Negotiate Their Fees

Imagine this: A widow deposits £100,000 into her savings account after selling her home and moving somewhere smaller. The bank or building society sees this deposit and offers her a chance to improve her income. Half an hour later, she has been sold whatever the bank is pushing that month for those in her situation. The adviser may have earned as much as 7 per cent in commission. That's £7,000 for 30 minutes of easy work. Great money! And no investment risks!

Tied agents and those working for big firms rarely negotiate even if you ask. If you're happy handing out so much of your money for so little work, fine, as long as you're aware of what you're doing.

The alternative is to avoid the non-negotiators and either ask for a commission-sharing scheme or pay for services by time, at a pre-agreed hourly rate, and get a 100 per cent rebate of all commission.

Expect to pay a minimum £100 per hour, so always ask for an estimate of how long the job will take.

A list of fee-based advisers is available from the Money Management Register on 0870 013 1925.

Examine the Adviser's Good and Bad Points

This tip is short and to the point: We all talk up our good points and play down the bad. Ask for examples of both. Take them away, study them, and then make up your mind.

Know the Difference between Junk Mail and Real Advice

Many of the national advice firms pay a top person to natter all day on the phone to financial journalists. Doing so makes sense for them because paying for editorial mentions brings in business far more effectively than paying for adverts.

Others sponsor educational booklets with publications such as newspapers or magazines. These booklets generally offer unbiased advice of a generic nature on matters ranging from investing for income to inheritance tax.

These activities are fine, but they often lead to mailing lists, which advisers exploit to send out regular material, detailing investments that they strongly recommend. Under a controversial but gaping loophole in the Financial Services Act, such direct mailings (even when personalised with name and address) don't constitute advice but count as an advertisement on par with a poster or a magazine advert. So, if there has been no advice, even when words such as 'I strongly recommend' appear, then logically, there's no come-back from customers when they've received bad advice or been mis-sold.

The situation is quite mad. But that's the law at present. So check whether any communication you get is individual advice or not. Treat communication that's not as junk mail. Recycle it, help save the planet, and save your money.

Know the Adviser's Training Qualifications

All advisers, whether tied or independent, have to pass FPC3 – Financial Planning Certificate level 3 – before they can advise on anything unsupervised. FPC3 covers protection, savings, and investment products; financial regulation; and identifying and satisfying client needs.

FPC3 is the equal of GCSE, a starter-level exam that's not very difficult. But here's a loophole in the rules (isn't there always a loophole?): Those who've only passed the even easier FPC1 and FPC2 can look after clients provided that they're supervised. The degree of supervision can vary from hands-on to just checking that the junior hands have done nothing too outrageous.

Refuse to pay top-dollar rates for apprentice investment advisers!

Ask if the adviser has the Advanced FPC. This is the A Level exam and includes taxation and trusts, investment portfolio management, and holistic financial planning.

The Associateship of the Society of Financial Planners is a degree-level qualification that builds on the advanced course. And if advisers do even more courses, they end up with a Fellowship.

The Institute of Financial Planning also runs courses for advisers leading to similar qualifications.

Define and Limit the Adviser's Role

Don't be afraid to delineate where you want any advice to stop. You may want to leave the basics of investment allocation up to your adviser and just take on the more interesting part, where you feel your own efforts and time will make a real difference. Or you may want to play it the other way around, asking for help with the tougher tasks.

You can't expect an adviser to take responsibility for areas where you insist on taking a do-it-yourself approach.

Determine Whether the Adviser Is Adding Real Value

Is your broker really adding value or just reading to you what's available on the Internet for free from packaged product makers – or copying that info word for word and sending it out as the advice firm's view?

Brokers obviously need a reference because no one can be expected to learn and remember all the facets of a portfolio. But the interpretation added is what makes the difference.

A good test is to see how critical the broker or adviser is of heavily advertised products. An adviser who says 'I don't know' is at least being honest and not trying to sell something doubtful.

Know Whether the Adviser Always Plays It Safe

In the past, no adviser was ever sacked for recommending IBM. But that scenario may no longer be true because Big Blue (the stock market nickname for IBM) is no longer the be-all and end-all of computers.

Advisers who stick to the safe options are fine, but they should make it clear what they're doing. You may want to up the risk profile, and you may want something more unusual. Sometimes, today's small investment company is tomorrow's superstar. If you hope to find these shares, you've got to act now, because tomorrow will be too late.

Know Whether the Adviser Will Be There Tomorrow

It sounds daft, but you really do need to know that your adviser will be there tomorrow, and as many days as possible after that. Some firms turn their staff over every year or two.

If you find advisers on your wavelength, cherish them and follow them to new firms when they move.

One-person businesses are supposed to set up arrangements to provide cover in the event of illness or other reasons that your adviser can't be present. Bigger firms should have their own setups.

Chapter 22

Ten Helpful Hints for You

In This Chapter

▶ Achieving your goals

▶ Protecting the essentials

▶ Working out your timescale

▶ Going to sleep happily

*W*hen it comes to investing, you won't be 100 per cent right in what you do even if you read and inwardly digest every word of this book, or even dozens more. But if you figure out nothing else about investment, the key lesson to remember (and here you can score maximum marks) is that it's your money, your needs (and the needs of those who depend on you), and your life that count.

Losing all your hard-earned savings is far easier than increasing them. So don't invest a penny until you've read this chapter.

Define Where You Want to Be

Really basic questions here: What do you want from your money? Who do you want to benefit? And can you afford to lose? Investing is not a game like rugby or bridge where you hope to get a greater score than opponents.

Always know what you want and where you're going. Don't be afraid to say that your aspirations are modest. And don't be nervous to admit that you enjoy taking a risk if you do and when you can afford to. But don't forget to put a limit on your more speculative investments.

Protect What You Have

You'll feel worse if you lose what you have than if you miss out on an invest-ment opportunity. That safety-first option can also apply to your life and salary. Insuring the first is generally inexpensive. Buying protection against losing your earning capacity is more expensive but can be worth it if you're the only breadwinner in the family.

Always check on the cover you already have from other plans and from employment before taking on more.

Pay Off the Home Loan

Most people have mortgages. Getting rid of the home loan as fast as possible is the best risk-free use you can make of spare cash because you'll save a for-tune on interest payments. So do it. Ensure that paying down the home loan is at the top of your list of tasks.

Equally important, never re-mortgage to a larger loan to pay for an invest-ment venture.

Accept Losses

Not all your investments will work. Full stop. Some of them will fail to gain as much as the best or even the average. Others will lose money absolutely.

As an investor, you have to be tough. You have to accept that there will be days, weeks, months, or even years when the signs are negative and the price screens are red with losses. Don't forget that a loss is only a loss (and a profit only a profit) when you close out the position by selling.

Don't get too worried about newspaper headlines showing one-day percent-age losses. The market typically goes down in big lumps and rises in bite-sized amounts. Quality is what counts. If your investment has real potential, stick with it. Otherwise, cut it out.

What's really tough is the first time you accept that you have backed a real turkey and the only exit is the fast one. But it's like cutting out dead wood. You'll come out of it knowing more, feeling stronger, and looking happier. Promise.

Take Your Time

Time and patience have been the great healers of investment difficulties. Or at least they have been for the past century, and there's no reason for a change. So time is on your side. Panic is pointless, but you can profit when others rush to sell indiscriminately. If you can keep your head when all those around you are losing theirs, you should end up well ahead.

This works the other way around, too. Don't get sucked into a buying vortex unless you're very disciplined, with a clear and firm exit route.

Do the Groundwork

Are you willing to do the hard work involved with investments? This groundwork includes selecting, monitoring, and making tax returns even if you opt for an easy portfolio building method such as picking with a pin and then holding on. There's no gain without some pain.

If you don't want to make any effort, you can hand all your money over to a professional investment company (some will provide your tax return details as well), but there can be no guarantees that you'll get what you pay for.

Get a Handle on the Odds

There's nothing wrong with taking bigger-than-average risks that others may consider little better than playing roulette or backing horses, provided that you're clear about what you're doing and you can afford the losses.

Don't forget that big risks really do mean slim chances of winning. Try to get a handle on the odds. The big mistake previous investors in precipice or high-income bonds made, other than taking notice of commission-chasing advisers, was that they didn't get a handle on the odds. They didn't compare the most they could gain with the most they could lose. (Okay, the advisers didn't exactly publicise the downsides, so only those who really understood could do the calculations, and they wouldn't have been stupid enough to buy.)

The maximum upside in these dodgy bonds was around 12 per cent of their money over three years compared with a really risk-free investment in the local building society or in UK government bonds. The downside was losing all their capital. This was hardly a balanced or fair deal. If there's a chance you can lose all your money, there should be an equal possibility of doubling or tripling it.

Know When to Sell

Knowing when to sell is really tough. So set yourself some rules. What about selling when an investment makes a certain percentage gain or loss? Or giving it a fixed period of time? Or determining a need, such as a home improvement, family occasion, or retirement, where you'll require cash and then selling when that need's time comes no matter what?

An investment must be consistently very clever to produce more than the interest rate on a personal loan.

Read the Small Print

Cigarette packets must now have at least 30 per cent of their surface covered in health warnings. Yet there are no rules for the prominent display of wealth warnings on investments. But even if they're buried away, phrases such as 'investments can go down as well as up' mean something. Sellers and product providers will cite them as a defence if things go wrong. If you don't believe how much those who push rubbish packaged products depend on almost invisible get-out clauses, look at recent scandals with endowment mortgages, precipice bonds, and split-level investment trusts.

Take time to read *all* the material. (Check that you have the total material and not just selected bits that some sellers try to send out.) Then ask what the worst possible scenario is. Get it in writing. If the reality is even worse, you may have cause for compensation.

Wake Up without Worries

Your investment strategy and portfolio should allow you to go to sleep happily and to wake up without worries.

The last 25 years have seen two of the most amazing stock market manias ever. They culminated in the Japanese Nikkei index falling by around three-quarters since its late 1989 peak and the bursting of the high-tech bubble in 2000, which led to some stocks losing 99 per cent or more of their value.

Sensible investing is about not losing out to insanity. If it looks too good to be true, it probably is.

Index

• *C* •

• F •

• *G* •

• *H* •

Notes

Notes

FOR DUMMIES®

Do Anything. Just Add Dummies

UK editions

SELF HELP

978-0-470-51291-3

978-0-470-03135-3

978-0-470-51501-3

BUSINESS

978-0-7645-7018-6

978-0-7645-7056-8

978-0-7645-7026-1

PERSONAL FINANCE

978-0-7645-7023-0

978-0-470-51510-5

978-0-470-05815-2

Answering Tough Interview
Questions For Dummies
(978-0-470-01903-0)

Being the Best Man
For Dummies
(978-0-470-02657-1)

British History
For Dummies
(978-0-470-03536-8)

Buying a Home on a Budget
For Dummies
(978-0-7645-7035-3)

Buying a Property in Spain
For Dummies
(978-0-470-51235-77)

Buying & Selling a Home For
Dummies
(978-0-7645-7027-8)

Buying a Property in Eastern
Europe For Dummies
(978-0-7645-7047-6)

Cognitive Behavioural Therapy
For Dummies
(978-0-470-01838-5)

Cricket For Dummies
(978-0-470-03454-5)

CVs For Dummies
(978-0-7645-7017-9)

Detox For Dummies
(978-0-470-01908-5)

Diabetes For Dummies
(978-0-470-05810-7)

Divorce For Dummies
(978-0-7645-7030-8)

DJing For Dummies
(978-0-470-03275-6)

eBay.co.uk For Dummies
(978-0-7645-7059-9)

Economics For Dummies
(978-0-470-05795-7)

English Grammar For Dummies
(978-0-470-05752-0)

Gardening For Dummies
(978-0-470-01843-9)

Genealogy Online
For Dummies
(978-0-7645-7061-2)

Green Living For Dummies
(978-0-470-06038-4)

Hypnotherapy For Dummies
(978-0-470-01930-6)

Neuro-linguistic Programming
For Dummies
(978-0-7645-7028-5)

Parenting For Dummies
(978-0-470-02714-1)

Pregnancy For Dummies
(978-0-7645-7042-1)

Renting out your Property
For Dummies
(978-0-470-02921-3)

Retiring Wealthy For Dummies
(978-0-470-02632-8)

Self Build and Renovation
For Dummies
(978-0-470-02586-4)

Selling For Dummies
(978-0-470-51259-3)

Sorting Out Your Finances
For Dummies
(978-0-7645-7039-1)

Starting a Business on
eBay.co.uk For Dummies
(978-0-470-02666-3)

Starting and Running an Online
Business For Dummies
(978-0-470-05768-1)

The Romans For Dummies
(978-0-470-03077-6)

UK Law and Your Rights
For Dummies
(978-0-470-02796-7)

Writing a Novel & Getting
Published For Dummies
(978-0-470-05910-4)

Available wherever books are sold. For more information or to order direct go to www.wiley.com or call 0800 243407 (Non UK call +44 1243 843296)

FOR DUMMIES®

Do Anything. Just Add Dummies

HOBBIES

Poker For Dummies
978-0-7645-5232-8

Knitting For Dummies
978-0-7645-5395-0

Drawing For Dummies
978-0-7645-5476-6

Also available:

Art For Dummies
(978-0-7645-5104-8)

Aromatherapy For Dummies
(978-0-7645-5171-0)

Bridge For Dummies
(978-0-471-92426-5)

Card Games For Dummies
(978-0-7645-9910-1)

Chess For Dummies
(978-0-7645-8404-6)

Improving Your Memory
For Dummies
(978-0-7645-5435-3)

Massage For Dummies
(978-0-7645-5172-7)

Meditation For Dummies
(978-0-471-77774-8)

Photography For Dummies
(978-0-7645-4116-2)

Quilting For Dummies
(978-0-7645-9799-2)

EDUCATION

Psychology For Dummies
978-0-7645-5434-6

The Koran For Dummies
978-0-7645-5581-7

Anatomy & Physiology For Dummies
978-0-7645-5422-3

Also available:

Algebra For Dummies
(978-0-7645-5325-7)

Astronomy For Dummies
(978-0-7645-8465-7)

Buddhism For Dummies
(978-0-7645-5359-2)

Calculus For Dummies
(978-0-7645-2498-1)

Cooking Basics For Dummies
(978-0-7645-7206-7)

Forensics For Dummies
(978-0-7645-5580-0)

Islam For Dummies
(978-0-7645-5503-9)

Philosophy For Dummies
(978-0-7645-5153-6)

Religion For Dummies
(978-0-7645-5264-9)

Trigonometry For Dummies
(978-0-7645-6903-6)

PETS

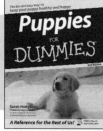

Puppies For Dummies
978-0-470-03717-1

Dog Training For Dummies
978-0-7645-8418-3

Cats For Dummies
978-0-7645-5275-5

Also available:

Aquariums For Dummies
(978-0-7645-5156-7)

Birds For Dummies
(978-0-7645-5139-0)

Dogs For Dummies
(978-0-7645-5274-8)

Ferrets For Dummies
(978-0-7645-5259-5)

Golden Retrievers
For Dummies
(978-0-7645-5267-0)

Horses For Dummies
(978-0-7645-9797-8)

Jack Russell Terriers
For Dummies
(978-0-7645-5268-7)

Labrador Retrievers
For Dummies
(978-0-7645-5281-6)

Puppies Raising & Training
Diary For Dummies
(978-0-7645-0876-9)

Available wherever books are sold. For more information or to order direct go to www.wiley.com or call 0800 243407 (Non UK call +44 1243 843296)

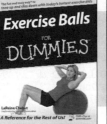
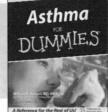